1,000
TESTED MONEY–MAKING MARKETS
FOR WRITERS

*the text of this book is printed
on 100% recycled paper*

1,000 TESTED MONEY-MAKING MARKETS FOR WRITERS

Walter G. Oleksy

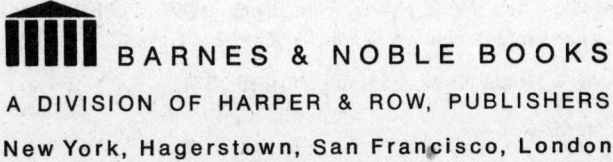

BARNES & NOBLE BOOKS
A DIVISION OF HARPER & ROW, PUBLISHERS
New York, Hagerstown, San Francisco, London

A hardcover edition of this book is published by Parker Publishing Co., Inc. It is here reprinted by arrangement.

1,000 TESTED MONEY-MAKING MARKETS FOR WRITERS. Copyright © 1973 by Parker Publishing Company, Inc. All rights reserved. Printed in the United States of America. No part of this book may be used or reproduced in any manner without written permission except in the case of brief quotations embodied in critical articles and reviews. For information address Parker Publishing Co., Inc., West Nyack, New York 10994. Published simultaneously in Canada by Fitzhenry & Whiteside Limited, Toronto.

First BARNES & NOBLE BOOKS edition published 1974.

ISBN: 0-06-463411-6

80 81 82   10 9 8 7 6

HOW TO SELL MORE OF YOUR WRITING TO MORE MARKETS

You can earn thousands of dollars a year in extra income, or earn a substantial income as a full-time freelance writer—*if* you can write, and *if* you know what to write and where to sell it.

Friends and associates often ask how they can make more money by writing. Some are teachers, others are in business, some work on newspapers and magazines or for public relations or advertising agencies. Still others are lawyers, housewives, and retired people. All have an ability to write and have earned some income or have made a living at least partially by writing.

If you have asked the same question—how can *I* make more money by writing?—this book will give you at least 1,000 practical answers. You *can* make extra money by writing! How much money you can earn will depend largely on how much you write and where you market your writing.

This book presupposes you *can* write, though you need not be a Hemingway. It is not a handbook on *how* to write, though it does contain much information on how to write for specific markets.

Rather, this book is intended for those who *can* write, either for a living or for freelance sales. It is intended to help you to sell *more*. It is one complete source book for ideas on where to sell articles, and contains at least 1,000 proven best markets. Some are major markets, some are less well-known, some are high-paying markets, others more modest-paying. All add up to many extra sales.

As it is a fact of writing that the more you write, the better you will write, so also it is a fact of selling that the more you write, the more you will sell.

—Walter Oleksy

CONTENTS

How to Sell More of Your Writing to More Markets 5

1. How to Sell to More Local Markets. 17
    FOUR ROUTES TO WRITING   17
    TIPS ON SELLING   19
    HOW TO QUERY AN EDITOR   20
        Newspapers, Sunday Supplements, Features   23
        City, State, and Regional Magazines   27
        Television, F M Markets   33
        Local Public Relations, Advertising Agencies   34
        Community Service Organizations   34
        Local Business Markets   35
        City, County, State Public Relations Markets   36
        School, University Markets; Stringing   36
        Special Local Markets   37

2. How to Sell to General Markets 38
    HOW MUCH RESEARCH   39
        General Interest National Magazines   40
        Specialized National Magazines   41
        Syndicates   45

CONTENTS

3. **How to Sell to Trade Journal Markets** 48
    WISE TO SPECIALIZE 49
    SPEECH-WRITING AND CONSULTANT WORK 50
        House Magazines and Trade Journals 52

4. **How to Sell to Special Interest Markets** 59
        Health Markets 59
        Health and Medical Markets 60
        Ecology-Conservation 61
        Photography, Music, Art, and Theatre Markets 63
        Education Markets 65
        Agriculture Markets 67

5. **How to Sell to Travel and Outdoor Markets** 70
    MULTIPLE ASSIGNMENTS 70
    NEW SLANTS ON TRAVEL WRITING 72
    REWRITE AND RESUBMIT 72
        Travel Magazines and General Travel Markets 74
        Motor Club, Auto Markets 76
        In-Flight Magazine Markets 77
        Outdoor Markets 78
        Sports and Recreation Markets 83
        Car and Motorcycle Markets 86
        Boating Markets 88

6. **How to Sell to Men's Markets** 90
    SEX OR NO SEX? 91
        Men's Magazine Markets 92
        Other Men's Markets 96

7. **How to Sell to Women's Markets** 98
        Women's Magazines 100
        True Confession and Romance Magazines 108
        Confession and Romance Magazines 109

8. **How to Sell to Detective, Mystery, and Science Fiction Markets** 113
    SCIENCE FICTION AND FANTASY 115
        —Science Fiction and Fantasy Magazines 116

CONTENTS

9. How to Sell to Juvenile and Teen-Age Markets 118

    THE PUBLISHER'S "LIST"   119
    THE MONEY SIDE   120
    HOW TO GET STARTED   121
        Juvenile Magazines   122
        Teen-Age and Young Adult Markets   129
        Book Markets for Children, Teen, and
        Adult Fiction and Nonfiction   136
        Childrens Book Publishers   136
        Paperback Publishers   144

10. How to Sell to Black Publications 146

    WHAT EDITORS DO NOT WANT   146
    OTHER MARKETS   147
        Black Magazines   148

**11. How to Sell to Fraternal, Religious, and
     Foreign Markets** 151

        Fraternal Markets   151
    FRATERNAL NEEDS VARY   153
    ARTICLES BRING ACTION   154
        Fraternal and Service Organizations   155
        Religious Magazines   156
        Foreign Markets   161
        British Markets   162
        Canadian Markets   163

12. How to Sell to Science and Technical Markets 164

        Scientific and Technical Markets   165

**13. How to Sell to Literary Journals, Poetry, and
     Greeting Card Markets** 168

    WHAT DO EDITORS WANT?   169
        Literary Magazines   170
        Greeting Card Markets   175

14. How to Sell Humor and Filler 179

        Humor and Fillers for Special Markets   181

15. How to Sell to Book Markets 183

    BOOKS THAT SELL   184
    SHOULD YOU GET AN AGENT?   184
    ON THE SUBJECT OF MONEY   186
    WITHOUT AN AGENT   188
    HOW TO SELL YOUR BOOK   188
    HOW A BOOK IS BORN   190
        Book Publishers   191

Index 211

1,000
TESTED MONEY–MAKING MARKETS
FOR WRITERS

1

HOW TO SELL TO MORE LOCAL MARKETS

Local markets can be some of the best for freelance writers and photographers. They may not pay as well as the major markets, but they have decided advantages in being right in your own town or city. And if you collect enough of them, you can realize that dream of most writers; you can work right at home.

Too many writers, especially those who do not earn high incomes from writing, set their sights too high, submitting to *McCall's* when their article or short story is rejected by *Mademoiselle,* and sending it to *Redbook* when *McCall's* rejects it. This sad roundelay of freelance writing is time-consuming, discouraging, expensive, and usually ends in a dozen rejects and no sale. If the writer would localize his story and aim for a more realistic market, he could earn a tidy few hundred dollars and many repeat sales.

Setting one's sights high is not necessarily bad. It would be foolish not to try to get the most money for your work. But if you honestly don't think your article or story has the polish or the broad national appeal necessary for a major market sale, turn it into a definite local sale. And the local woods are full of sales, if you'll search through them carefully and optimistically.

Four very successful writers who sell regularly to a wide variety of local markets are Norbert Blei, Gerry Souter, Jeanne Smith, and Charlotte Stone, all of whom write for publications and businesses in the midwest.

FOUR ROUTES TO WRITING

Norbert Blei teaches school for a living, but writes articles and short stories for a number of publications. His subjects range from his personal experiences trying rural living, in peaceful Door County, Wisconsin, to how a suburban Chicago German pastry chef makes his mouth-watering specialties.

Blei specializes in the human interest side of life, finding subjects in both likely and unlikely places. His ability to describe people and places, and how average people feel about what makes them happy and unhappy, has proven to be a rewarding talent. Writers who concentrate on local markets, whether they be Sunday newspaper magazine supplements or internal and external company publications, would do well to specialize, as Blei does, on human interest subjects that appeal to a wide readership.

Souter, who also is an accomplished photographer and cartoonist, specializes in humor and satire. His many sales to Sunday magazines reflect a good sense of humor along with the basic skills of reporting and writing. And he also adds to his income by illustrating his own articles, either with photos or art work.

In these "up-tight" days, writers with a talent for humor can find many ready markets for their articles or short stories. Of course, humor and satire are two of the most difficult forms of writing. Editors say they are crying for humor, and if a writer can produce in this field, he will find a waiting market.

Jeanne Smith is a housewife and mother of two children who has turned her domestic experiences into constant sales, especially to local Sunday women's feature pages. Everything from the family budget to the "tooth fairy" is grist for her writing mill, and her work appears weekly in *Lifestyle,* the Sunday women's section of *The Chicago Tribune.*

Mrs. Smith, a former general assignment reporter for *The Tribune,* was determined not to let motherhood end her writing career. Many housewives, with and without professional writing experience, can turn their everyday domestic experiences into sales to local markets. Finding the time is usually the difference between selling and not selling.

Charlotte Stone also is a housewife who writes. She specializes in travel articles that offer a "round-up" approach to a subject. She will take a subject like fall festivals and gather research from festivals held all over the country. Generally, she writes to the chamber of commerce in the town or city where the festival is held. They send her brochures or letters, and often photographs, which she uses to compile a cross-country feature article on festivals from coast to coast. Travel magazines, especially for motor clubs or airlines, are especially interested in this type of feature.

Mrs. Stone also gets out of the house, usually on weekends, and she and her husband take one-and-two-day drives into towns or parks or historic places that often turn into article sales.

Few of us, whether we are writers or not, can travel more than the usual two weeks we get off for a vacation each year. But this need not keep us from writing about travel or from finding interesting subjects of all types. They're there, many of them, right under our noses, if we learn to look for them.

Most writers, whether they make a full-time living from their writing or merely write an occasional article to supplement their income, find the majority of their subjects and sales right in their own town or city.

What can you expect to be paid for an article to a Sunday magazine or feature section? The going rate is from 5 to 10 cents a word, and editors seem to prefer articles of from 1,500 to 2,000 words, so a writer can earn from $75 to $200, and sometimes more, for this type of sale. Magazines usually pay 10 cents a word.

TIPS ON SELLING

Before listing and discussing local markets, a few tips on freelance writing in general, and how to please an editor and sell an article. In brief, here are the most important:

Write. Try never to call an editor! Magazine editors are extremely busy, harassed people, assigning stories, editing and rewriting, working with artists and layout designers, assigning photography, planning, and attending meetings. They don't need out-of-the-blue phone calls or in-person visits from writers. Always query by letter, briefly suggesting an article. Never suggest more than six stories in a letter. And try to come up with a new angle!

Read the publication you want to sell to. Know what kind of material the editor buys, and know what he has run in the last year or two. Don't waste his time suggesting stories he already has done, especially if he just did it last month.

If the editor doesn't know your work, send some samples of your writing (Xeroxes will do). If you write for an appointment and the editor has time to meet you, bring samples you can leave with him (no editor wants to read your work while you stand anxiously by), and limit your visit to half an hour, if possible. He may seem like he is enjoying the visit and can afford an hour, but he will think more of you if you make your visit brief.

Don't follow up your visit with a phone call asking if he has read your material and has made a decision to assign you an article. He will contact you, probably by mail, when he has time. If you make a pest of yourself, or try a hard-sell approach, he'll just forget you when he's making assignments.

Don't send amateurish photography, even if that is all you have. You'll only waste the editor's time by sending him anything but your best slides or photos.

Some editors prefer completed manuscripts to query letters, especially if they are not familiar with the writer's work. If you send a manuscript, be sure to send a return addressed, stamped envelope, and send only one manuscript per package.

HOW TO QUERY AN EDITOR

Most editors prefer query letters for nonfiction material, whether for a book or an article. A query letter should be short and to-the-point, perhaps led off with an attention-getter that may serve as the lead for your article, and include some indication of your knowledge of the subject and your professional background. If you are a new writer or new to the editor, it helps to send along a few Xeroxes of your published work.

A typical query letter, one which helped me sell a feature article to the *Chicago Tribune Sunday Magazine,* and addressed to its editor, read as follows:

Dear Editor:
Home winemaking is not only a smart hobby, it's one that helps save in the family pocketbook, where it counts these days. Many people are discovering, or rediscovering, the art of making wine at home, like grandmother used to. Maybe a part of it is just that—a return to the old ways of doing it yourself.

Making wine at home, you can also control the sweetness yourself, and it's a great joy to uncork a bottle of your own wine and serve it to guests who didn't think you had it in you. Besides which, wine is known to be good for you, both nutritionally and emotionally. Many doctors say wine is better than pills as a tranquilizer.

I have more than a dozen years' experience as a magazine feature writer and editor (detailed resume attached), and could write you an article of any length and approach on home winemaking. I make it myself and also have interviewed some people who have made wine at home for years. (It's legal—you're allowed by law to make up to 200 gallons of wine at home each year.)

I can describe the resurgence of home winemaking, tell the reader how to make wine with grapes or fruit, and also with the new concentrates (which even people who make wine from grapes say is as good or better).

If you're interested, I'd be happy to write the article along any lines you suggest. I am also a photographer and can shoot black and white and/or color slides for you. I have 35mm Nikon equipment and my photography is of magazine quality.

Such a letter gives the editor a good idea of what the article will be about, that the writer knows his subject, that he has written articles before, and that he is a qualified photographer. If the idea appeals to the editor for his publication, he is likely to either assign the article to the writer outright or, as some editors of larger publications do, ask the writer to submit the article "on speculation." In this case, the writer has to do all the research and writing, and submit the article on the chance that the editor will buy it. It is up to the writer to decide whether he should invest that much effort into a possible sale. Generally, it is a good idea to follow through and submit the article. If the editor expressed interest in the subject, and you are a capable writer, it is likely that you will sell the article.

A book query should be written much along the same lines, but in addition should include the book's title, length of the book, a brief description of what the book is to be about, a detailed outline and synopsis of the book, and one or more sample chapters.

Of course, always send a stamped, self-addressed, return envelope with anything you send a publisher or editor, whether it is a query letter, an article or short story, or a whole novel.

As to how to mail out an article or book, the least expensive way is to send the material "fourth class book rate—manuscript." If you send a letter along, you must add "letter enclosed" and stick a first-class stamp on the envelope or package.

Never staple pages together. Use paper clips to keep them together or leave them loose. Editors seem to hate staples.

Books are best mailed in the box in which typing paper is sold. Place the pages loose in the box, without clips or rubber bands.

In sending slides, put them in plastic sheets rather than in Kodak boxes. Sheets displaying twenty slides are easier to view than handling each slide.

Remember that editors are looking for new angles. Don't submit ideas or articles that say what has been said before all too often. Always look for a new slant to anything you're writing.

If you follow the above guidelines, you will sell to editors and work your way onto that select list all editors rely on to fill their assignments ... the list of writers an editor knows can produce.

The market list that follows is highly selective and intended to suggest the great variety and number of local markets open to freelance writers and photographers.

No writer can afford to overlook the extra income there is in photography. If a writer can learn to handle a camera, whether it be a 35mm, 2¼ x 2¼, or Speed Graphic, he will soon find he will at least double his freelance income.

With the following markets as a guide, the writer should take inventory of the similar markets in his area and make it his business to contact them, preferably by mail, to set up appointments to discuss freelance possibilities.

When you do get to meet the editor or other client, be sure to bring along samples of your writing and photography, as well as some ideas for assignments. Study your local markets so you can come armed with ideas the client will buy. *Asking* him what he needs isn't good enough; you must *tell* him what he needs, and then convince him he not only needs it, but *you* are the person to do it, whether it be a feature article for a Sunday supplement or a brochure for a new hospital opening in your community.

The local freelance hills are lucrative ones, for the writer who will do a little digging.

Newspapers, Sunday Supplements, Features

One day, early in my freelancing career, I got four rejects in the same mail. I had gotten them one and two at a time, but four nearly crushed me. I was still too young and inexperienced to know how many rejects you may have to suffer through before you make a sale.

I must have had some reserve courage that day because, rather than flee the house for some artificial encouragement, I sat down at my typewriter and wrote a travel article. I hadn't been to Germany in almost a year, when I was in the army, but I remembered what it was like there at Christmas, and thought maybe the local travel editor might use a piece on it since the holiday season was approaching. I sold it for $15 and the day it ran in the *Chicago Tribune* Sunday travel section, I was convinced: it pays to try local markets.

I have since sold lead feature articles and photography to the *Chicago Tribune Sunday Magazine,* their book section, travel section, women's feature pages, and even became a staff member for six years.

Local newspapers and Sunday supplements can be some of your best local freelance markets. Payment may range from $10 to $250, but if the money isn't high, the exposure can earn you higher sales. Others see your byline, read your articles, and become acquainted with your name and the type of writing you do. When they need a writer, they may well call on you.

The thing to remember is, newspapers print more than just news. To balance the news, mostly bad, editors run features to brighten their pages and cheer up their readers. Many of these are staff-written, but many others are written by freelancers. Check your local newspaper (and papers in nearby towns and cities) to see if they need a specific column (from bridge to gardening to sports car coverage to income tax tips). Or they may need a stringer in your area (someone to write about local news). Or they may buy special feature articles for their various sections.

Acquaint yourself thoroughly with your local newspaper and its departments. Find out where they're weak; what they need that they don't have. Then write a sample column or two, or query the editor with one or more article ideas. The first sale may not be as hard as you think. And once you've made your first sale, they will be more responsive to future ideas and articles.

Some of the major local newspapers and Sunday supplement markets follow. *Editor and Publisher Yearbook,* 850 Third Ave., N.Y.C., N.Y., 10022, and N.W. Ayer & Son's *Directory of Newspapers and Periodicals,* both available in most libraries, are good sources for learning what departments are on newspapers and in magazines throughout the country, along with editors' names, publication addresses, and other helpful information.

Akron Sunday Beacon, Sunday supplement of *Akron Beacon Journal,* 44 E. Exchange St., Akron, Ohio, 44309. Uses articles of general and local interest, to 2,500 words, with illustrations. Payment varies, on publication.

Atlanta Journal-Constitution Sunday Magazine, Box 4689, Atlanta, Ga., 30302. Editor George Hatcher pays 5 cents a word and up, on publication, for articles of local interest to 1,500 words. Query first.

California Today, weekly magazine distributed with *San Jose Mecury-News* Sunday edition, 750 Ridder Park Dr., San Jose, Calif., 95131. Editor Ted Bredt buys shorts and articles on "the good life" in California, particularly the north and west parts of the state. Subjects range from outdoors, leisure, home, sports, to history and humor. Pays 5 cents a word and up, on acceptance.

The Canadian, 401 Bay St., No. 1100, Toronto, 1, Ontario, Canada. Weekly supplement. Editor Denis Harvey pays from $200 to $600 for articles to 3,000 words about Canada and Canadians.

Chicago Sun-Times Showcase, entertainment and book section of *Chicago Sun-Times,* 401 N. Wabash Ave., Chicago, Ill., 60611. Editor Herman Kogan pays up to 10 cents a word, on acceptance, for articles to 1,500 words, about the arts, letters, profiles, interviews of people engaged in music, drama, literature, etc. Book reviews are on assignment.

Chicago Today Magazine, 441 N. Michigan Ave., Chicago, Ill., 60611. Editor Scott Schmidt pays from $100 to $150 for articles, on publication, 2,000 to 3,000 words, of interest primarily to young people in the city. Query first.

Chicago Tribune Sunday Magazine, 435 N. Michigan Ave., Chicago, Ill., 60611. Editor John Fink pays up to $300, on acceptance, for articles from 2,000 to 3,000 words. Wide variety of subjects, from current events and people to history and humor. Query first.

Christian Science Monitor, One Norway St., Boston, Mass.,

02115. Pays various rates for freelance material on travel, family features, education, homemaking, etc.

Cincinnati Pictorial Enquirer, 617 Vine St., Cincinnati, Ohio, 45202. Editor Joseph Eble pays 3 cents a word, on publication, for articles of local interest, from 600 to 800 words. Pays $5 per photo. Query first.

Columbus Dispatch Sunday Magazine, Columbus, Ohio, 43216. Editor Clyde C. Long pays 2 cents a word and up, after publication, for articles to 1,800 words, of local or Ohio interest.

Contemporary, Sunday supplement of the *Denver Post,* Denver, Colo., 80201. Editor Joan White buys features from 500 to 1,500 words on the Rocky Mountain area including Colorado, Wyoming, and New Mexico. Pays $20 and up, $5 for photos, on acceptance.

Dallas Times Herald Sunday Magazine, Pacific and Griffin Sts., Dallas, Tex., 75202. Editor Paul Rosenfield buys articles of interest to readers in Texas and the Southwest, from 500 to 1,000 words. Payment varies, on publication.

Des Moines Sunday Register Picture, Sunday supplement of the *Des Moines Register and Tribune,* 715 Locust St., Des Moines, Iowa, 50304. Payment varies, on publication, for articles and photos of interest to Iowans. Maximum length 1,000 words. Pays $5 for black-and-white photos, $25 for color transparencies used.

Detroit News Sunday Magazine, 615 LaFayette Blvd., Detroit, Mich., 48231. Editor Jack Martin buys articles to 2,500 words on Michigan and also national subjects. Likes short humor to 800 words. Payment varies, on publication. Query first.

Dixie-Roto, Sunday supplement of *The Times-Picayune,* 3800 Howard Ave., New Orleans, La., 70140. Editor Philip Sperier pays $50 on acceptance for articles to 2,500 words, with Louisiana and Mississippi slant. Pays $5 for black-and-white photos, $25 for color.

Empire, Sunday magazine of *The Denver Post,* P.O. Box 1709, Denver, Colo., 80201. Editor Bill Hosokawa pays 4 cents a word, on acceptance, for articles 500 to 3,000 words on people, events, history of area. Pays good rates for photos. Query first.

Family Magazine, published by *The Army Times,* 475 School St., S.W., Washington, D.C., 20024. Editor Ruth Chandler buys articles from 1,000 to 1,500 words, for army men and their families. Payment varies, on publication.

The Floridian, St. Petersburg Times, Box 1121, St. Petersburg, Fla., 33731. Pays $70 to $150, on acceptance, for general interest articles and features on Florida. Query first.

Grit, Williamsport, Pa., 17701. Editor James Sheen buys articles of interest to residents of small towns. Payment varies, on acceptance.

Houston-Chronicle Texas Magazine, 512-25 Travis St., Houston, Tex., 77002. Editor Jack Loftis pays good rates for photo features on Texas.

Island Monthly Reader, Box 610, Siasconset, Mass., 02514. Editor Michael Davis pays $50 for fiction and articles about Nantucket, Martha's Vineyard, and the Mid-Cape.

Louisville Courier-Journal & Times Magazine, Louisville, Ky., 40202. Editor Geoffrey Vincent uses articles to 2,000 words of local and national interest, but especially Kentucky and Southern Indiana. Uses black-and-white and color photos. Payment is good, on publication.

Midwest Magazine, Sunday Supplement of *Chicago Sun-Times,* Chicago, Ill., 60611. Payment ranges from $35 to $200 for articles from 1,000 to 1,500 words, primarily of interest to Chicago area readers. Query first.

Panorama, Chicago Daily News, 401 N. Wabash Ave., Chicago, Ill., 60611. Editor Richard Christiansen pays 2 cents a word and up, on publication, for articles from 500 to 1,500 words on the lively arts, literature, and humor, nostalgia.

Panorama, Sunday supplement of the Morgantown, W. Va., *Dominion-Post,* Green Bldg., Morgantown, W. Va., 26505. Editor Arthur Buck uses articles to 2,000 words on literary subjects.

Philadelphia Inquirer Today Magazine, Broad and Callowhill Sts., Philadelphia, Pa., 19101. Editor George Beezer uses articles of local interest, from 500 to 3,500 words. Payment varies, on publication. Query.

Potomac, Sunday supplement of *The Washington Post,* 1515 L St., N.W., Washington, D.C., 20005. Editor Joe N. Anderson pays from $75 to $550 for articles of local and national interest. No word limit.

Rhode Islander, published weekly by the *Providence Journal and Evening Bulletin,* 75 Fountain St., Providence, R.I., 02902. Editor Ted Holmberg pays $35 to $250, on publication, for articles from 1,500 to 4,000 words of interest to Rhode Islanders.

Seattle Times Sunday Magazine, Box 70, Seattle, Wash., 98111. Editor Richard Johnston pays $35 to $50, on publication, for articles about the Pacific Northwest, both current and historic, from 800 to 1,200 words. Query first.

Southland Sunday Magazine, Long Beach *Independent Press-Telegram,* 6th and Pine Sts., Long Beach, Calif., 90801. Editor Robert Martin pays 5 cents a word, on publication, for articles about southern California, from 500 to 2,000 words.

The Star Weekly, 401 Bay St., 11th floor, Toronto 1, Ont.,

Canada. Editor Mrs. Jeanette Moore pays 10 cents a word and up, on acceptance, for articles to 2,000 words of interest to Canadians. Subjects range from profiles and outdoors to entertainment.

Toledo Blade Sunday Magazine, Toledo, Ohio, 43604. Editor Mrs. Mary Jane Spencer pays up to $40 for articles for and about Toledo. Also buys fiction. Pays $5 each for photos. Query.

Tropic, Sunday supplement of *The Miami Herald,* 1 Herald Plaza, Miami, Fla., 33101. Editor John Parkyn pays up to $250, on publication, for articles of general interest to readers of South Florida. Lengths from 1,500 to 3,000 words. Especially likes personality profiles. Query.

Washington, Magazine of the *Sunday Star,* 225 Virginia Ave., S.E., Washington, D.C., 20003. Editor Peter Maiken uses mostly freelancers who have worked for him before, but also considers new writers who query him. Payment is 5 cents a word and up, on acceptance, for articles to 2,500 words of interest to Washington readers.

West, Los Angeles Times, Times Mirror Sq., Los Angeles, Calif., 90053. Editor Marshall Lumsden pays about $500 for articles from 2,500 to 4,000 words of interest to readers in the western states. Pays $100 per page for black-and-white photos, $200 a page for color. Query.

Zest, The Houston Chronicle, 512-20 Travis St., Houston, Tex., 77002. Editor Don Warren pays $10 to $20 for short articles and humor of interest to Houston readers.

City, State, and Regional Magazines

One of the newest phenomenons of publishing, and delights to freelance writers and photographers, is the growth of the city and regional magazine.

With the continued growth of the cities, and the resultant problems, publishers have come to realize that in-depth, magazine-length articles are necessary to cover a subject, whether it be about local pollution problems or what the Singles Set is up to now. Newspapers simply do not have the space to devote to such articles, except on day-to-day coverage. The city and regional magazines that have resulted, financed by independent publishers or business men and Chambers of Commerce, have been and will continue to be a boon to freelancers.

As editor of *ChicagoLand,* a monthly feature magazine for the Chicago area, I learned first-hand how important a city magazine can be, both to the public and to freelance writers. The only trouble is, some of these magazines don't survive. Being privately financed, often by one or two adventurous backers, they require a great deal of capital.

ChicagoLand, unfortunately, did not survive, after about seven years of innovative publishing. The writers and photographers who contributed their work to the magazine quite often were not paid as well as they should have been. But the exposure the magazine gave them helped them to land other freelance assignments that have since brought them comfortable incomes.

So while city and regional magazines may not be the best-paying local markets, they can give you some of the best space and layouts available to show off your work. And, happily, other city magazines are more soldily financed and pay top rates to freelancers. They are also good markets for columns and other monthly assignments.

Study your local city or regional magazine the way you would any top market. See in what area they are weak, and suggest you fill that hole, whether it be reporting on monthly showings at the art galleries or writing an expose on the mayor. City magazines will take on almost anything and anyone, bless them!

City magazines need a lot of help from a lot of local talent if they are to survive. If you are an editorial misfit in your community, not comfortable writing for the journalistic establishment, get in touch with the editor of the local city magazine. He can put you to work in a hurry!

One day on *ChicagoLand,* overworked and over deadline, a young man just out of Yale poked his head into the office and asked if there were any jobs open on the staff. I tried to hide my glee and invited him to step inside my office and talk about it. He admitted he only had experience on his college literary magazine, but wanted to learn the magazine business. I then admitted I could offer him a lot of work, but very little money. But I would teach him the magazine business. He said he also needed money, so he got a bread-and-butter job running copy for one of the Chicago television station news rooms, and worked for me on his off-hours. He, and a managing editor who didn't know when to sleep, helped me put out a magazine each month that defied all the rules of journalism: we operated on half a shoestring, we worked almost around the clock, we stepped on everyone's toes, and we put out a whale of a magazine. What killed us? Probably all of those things! But it was fun dying, and what a way to go!

Here are some of the leading city magazines, as well as state and regional magazines. If some of them are no longer publishing, or new ones have taken their place, keep in mind their lifespan is as fickle as the summer wind. Refreshing, though perhaps brief.

Alabama Review, University of Alabama Press, Drawer 2877, University, Ala., 35486. Editor Malcolm McMillan uses articles of historic and scholarly interest to readers in Alabama and the South.

Alaska, Box 4-EEE, Anchorage, Alaska, 99503. Editor Bob Henning pays up to $100 for articles and fiction about life in Alaska, past and present. Photos should accompany manuscript. Pays $25 for color cover, $5 to $15 for others, on publication.

Arizona, 120 E. Van Buren St., Phoenix, Ariz., 85004. Editor Bud DeWald pays from $25 to $175 for articles 500 to 2,500 words related to Arizona.

Arizona Highways, 2039 W. Lewis, Phoenix, Ariz., 85009. (See listing in Chapter 5.)

Atlanta, Atlanta Chamber of Commerce, 1104 Commerce Bldg., Atlanta, Ga., 30303. Editor Norman Shavin pays $100 to $350 for articles 1,300 to 3,000 words of interest to readers in Atlanta and other Southern states. Wide variety of subjects. Query.

Austin, Austin Chamber of Commerce, Box 1967, Austin, Texas, 78767. Editor George Seagert pays good rates for articles and fiction about Austin, 800 to 1,000 words. Query.

Baltimore Magazine, Baltimore Association of Commerce, 22 Light St., Baltimore, Md., 21202. Editor William Stump pays up to $150 for articles to 2,500 words on all aspects of life in Baltimore. Query.

Birmingham, Birmingham Chamber of Commerce, 1914 Sixth Ave., North, Birmingham, Ala., 34211. Pays good rates, on publication, for articles 1,500 to 3,000 words, especially history, current problems, personalities. Photos are assigned. Query.

Boston Magazine, 125 High St., Boston, Mass., 02110. Editor Helen Irwin pays from $25 to $400, on publication, for articles to 3,000 words. Subjects range from history to social problems, personalities, entertainment. Query.

Bostonian Magazine, 3 Arlington St., Boston, 02116. Editor

Robert Mamis pays up to $200 for articles from 2,000 to 3,000 words of interest to Bostonians, from sports to politics. Query.

Buffalo, Buffalo Area Chamber of Commerce, 238 Main St., Buffalo, N.Y., 14202. Editor Earle Hannel pays $50 for articles or photo essays on Buffalo area subjects. Pays $10 to $25 per photo run with article.

Chicago, Suite 1120, 110 S. Dearborn St., Chicago, Ill., 60603. Editor Richard Frisbie pays good rates for articles 1,000 to 2,500 words of interest to Chicago area readers. Subjects range from the arts to politics and current urban problems.

Cincinnati, 309 Vine St., Greater Cincinnati Chamber of Commerce, Cincinnati, Ohio, 45202. Editor Richard Gordon pays 8 cents a word, on publication, for articles 800 to 1,800 words of interest to residents of Cincinnati and the area.

Colorado Magazine, 7190 W. 14th Ave., Denver, Colo., 80215. Editor David Sumner pays 10 cents a word for articles from 2,500 to 3,000 words on adventure, people, history, current subjects about the Rocky Mountain West. Photos should accompany articles. Query.

Commonwealth, Virginia State Chamber of Commerce, 611 E. Franklin, Richmond, Va., 23219. Editor James Wamsley pays 4 and 5 cents a word for sophisticated articles about Virginia, from 1,500 to 3,000 words. Query.

Cue, 20 W. 43d St., New York, N.Y., 10036. Editor Stanley Newman pays $100 to $150, on acceptance, for articles to 1,500 words about New York life. Query.

Dallas, 1507 Pacific Ave., Dallas, Texas, 75201. Pays $150 and up, on acceptance, for articles to 4,000 words of interest to Dallas and area readers. All articles assigned; query first.

Florida Trend, P.O. Box 2350, 1306 W. Kennedy Blvd., Tampa, Fla., 33601. Pays 6 cents a word for articles to 3,000 words of interest to Florida business men. Query.

Focus-Midwest, Box 3086, St. Louis, Mo., 63130. Editor Charles Klotzer pays good rates, on publication, for quality articles, poetry, and art for Midwest readers. Especially interested in controversial subjects dealing with problems in major cities in Illinois and Missouri.

Fort Worth, Fort Worth Chamber of Commerce, 700 Throckmorton, Fort Worth, Texas, 76102. Editor Betty Ecker prefers to be queried first for articles on Fort Worth and West Texas.

Georgia Magazine, Box 1047, Decatur, Ga., 30031. Editor Ann E. Lewis pays up to $25, on publication, for articles to 2,000 words on Georgia. Subjects range from history to recreation.

Greater Indianapolis, Chamber of Commerce, 320 N. Meridian

St., Indianapolis, Ind., 46204. Editor Susan White pays $25 and up for articles about Indianapolis.

Lincoln Business and *Lincoln Review Preview,* Lincoln Chamber of Commerce, 200 Lincoln Bldg., Lincoln, Nebr., 68508. Editor Robert Snow pays $50 to $100, on publication, for articles to 2,500 words of interest to Lincoln readers.

Los Angeles Magazine, 271 N. Canon Dr., Beverly Hills, Calif., 90210. Editor David R. Brown pays 5 to 10 cents a word, on publication, for articles to 2,500 words of interest to affluent readers in Southern California. Also buys humor and photo essays. Query first.

Louisville, 300 W. Liberty St., Louisville, Ky., 40202. Editor Betty Lou Amster pays $35 and up, on acceptance, for articles 1,000 to 2,000 words concerned with business development in the Louisville metropolitan area. Query.

Milwaukee, 720 N. Jefferson St., Milwaukee, Wisc., 53202. Editor Frederick Schmidt pays 3 cents a word and up for articles of interest to Milwaukee area readers.

Nashville, 315 Union St., Nashville, Tenn., 37219. Editor Bill Armistead pays good rates, after publication, for articles about Nashville. Lengths from 1,500 to 3,000 words.

Nevada, Carson City, Nev., 89701. Pays up to 8 cents a word for articles 1,000 to 2,000 words on travel, history, life in Nevada.

Nevada Highways and Parks, State of Nevada Dept. of Highways, Carson City, Nev., 89701. Pays to 8 cents a word for articles 1,000 to 2,500 words with Nevada slant, from recreation to history. Pays $10 to $40 for photos (prefers 2½ x 2¼ and larger format).

New England Galaxy, Old Sturbridge Village, Sturbridge, Mass., 01566. Editor Catherine Fennelly pays $75 to $150 for articles to 3,000 words on New England, preferably historical. Also buys poetry.

New Englander, Walsh Publishing Co., 150 Causeway St., Boston, Mass., 02114. Editor Richard Livingstone pays good rates, on publication, for articles 500 to 2,000 words on New England businesses.

New Hampshire Profiles, 3 Sheafe St., Portsmouth, N.H., 03801. Editor Peter Randall pays good rates, on publication, for articles to 2,000 words for New Hampshire readers. Query.

New Mexico Magazine, 113 Washington Ave., Santa Fe., N.M., 87501. Editor Walter Briggs pays up to $400 for articles about New Mexico. Pays $10 to $35 for photos. Query.

New York, 207 E. 32d St., New York, N.Y., 10016. Editor Clay Felker pays up to $350 for articles to 2,500 words of interest to active, affluent, sophisticated readers in the New York area. Subjects range from politics to the arts. Do not send manuscripts; query first, to Jack Nessel, managing editor.

Oklahoma Today, Will Rogers Memorial Bldg., State Capitol, Oklahoma City, Okla., 83105. Editor Bill Burchardt pays 3 cents a word, on publication, for articles to 1,500 words on Oklahoma subjects. Query.

Philadelphia, 1500 Walnut St., Philadelphia, Pa., 19102. Editor Alan Halpern pays $50 to $500, on acceptance, for articles of interest to Philadelphia area readers. Query.

Roll Call: The Newspaper of Capitol Hill, 101 D St., S.E., Washington, D.C., 20003. Uses articles and fiction to 1,000 words of interest to those in the political life in Washington. Humor and satire especially wanted. Payment on acceptance.

San Antonio Magazine, Chamber of Commerce, P.O. Box 1628, San Antonio, Tex., 78206. Editor Roddy Stinson pays 3 cents a word, on acceptance, for articles about San Antonio and area.

San Francisco, 120 Green St., San Francisco, Calif., 94111. Editor Geoffrey Link pays up to $150 for articles about San Francisco, from current topics to history. Lengths run to 3,000 words. Query.

Spectrum, 407 Security Bank Bldg., Sioux City, Iowa, 51101. Pays up to $50 for articles to 2,000 words of interest to readers in Iowa, Nebraska, South Dakota area. Photos should accompany manuscript.

The State, Box 2169, Raleigh, N.C., 27602. Editor Bill Curight pays up to $35, on acceptance, for feature articles to 1,500 words on North Carolina.

Sunset Magazine, Menlo Park, Calif., 94025. Editor Proctor Mellquist uses freelance ideas for staff-written articles on Western living, food, travel, gardening, etc. Payment varies, on acceptance. Query.

Texas Parade, P.O. Box 12037, Capitol Station, Austin, Texas, 78711. Editor Kenneth Lively pays $25 per printed page for articles to 2,000 words on Texas subjects. Query.

Trenton, Trenton-Mercer County Chamber of Commerce, 104 N. Broad St., Trenton, N.J., 08608. Editor Donald Congram pays up to $100 for articles 500 to 1,500 words of interest to Trenton area readers. Pays $5 for photos. Query.

Tulsa, Tulsa Chamber of Commerce, 616 S. Boston Ave., Tulsa, Okla., 74119. Editor Larry Silvey pays from $25 to $75, on acceptance, for articles 800 to 1,600 words on Tulsa and area.

Valleys of History, Potomac Edison Co., Downsville Pike, Hagerstown, Md., 21740. Editor Donald Whipp pays $150 and up, on acceptance, for historical articles to 6,000 words about people, places, and events in Western Maryland, Northern Virginia, South-Central Pennsylvania, and Eastern West Virginia. Query.

HOW TO SELL TO MORE LOCAL MARKETS

Vermont Life, 61 Elm St., Montpelier, Vt., 05602. Pays 10 cents a word, on acceptance, for articles to 2,000 words on Vermont.

The Washingtonian, 1218 Connecticut Ave., N.W., Washington, D.C., 20036. Editor Laughlin Phillips pays up to 10 cents a word, on acceptance, for articles 1,000 to 4,000 words of interest to well-informed Washingtonians.

Westways, 2601 S. Figueroa St., Los Angeles, Calif., 90054. Editor Larry Meyer pays 10 cents a word, on acceptance, for articles 800 to 2,500 words on Western states, Canada, and Mexico. Wide variety of subjects from natural science and travel to history. Pays $50 and up for color photos, $25 per black-and-white photo. Query.

Wisconsin Tales and Trails, 6120 University Ave., Madison, Wisc., 53705. Editor Mrs. Jill Dean pays $40 to $125 for articles, on publication, about Wisconsin, both current and past. Lengths run 1,500 to 3,000 words. Pays $50 for color, $10 for black-and-white. Query.

Yankee, Dublin, N.H., 03444. Editor Judson D. Hale pays $25 to $400 for articles to 2,000 words of interest to New England readers. Prefers black-and-white photos to accompany manuscript.

Television, FM Markets

Local television and FM radio stations offer freelancers opportunities for additional sales. Some will buy freelance talk shows, interview programs, historic oddity fillers, etc., either using the author and his voice or just his material. Many stations also buy freelance documentary programs or dramatic shows, especially if they are of a public service nature.

Not all writers enjoy being closeted in a room with a typewriter. For those who enjoy contacting the public and whose appearance and voice are both pleasant to wide audiences, television and radio can be rewarding in many ways.

For those interested only in off-camera and off-microphone writing assignments, there are often freelance news and feature writing positions available on local television and FM radio stations. Writers with newspaper backgrounds can either work part-time or perhaps head up news departments.

Quality FM stations in major cities often publish their own magazines. Some of these are merely listings of music to be played during the month, while others also contain feature articles and photography and artwork of cultural interest.

If your top FM station does not have a guide, you could suggest one. But first be armed with a plan for its contents, perhaps submitting a few sample articles. And some figures on cost would help you sell your idea, especially if you know a local printer who will do the job at a discount, for the extra work. Writers who know printers and work well with them are smart writers who bank often.

For information on television and AM-FM radio stations in the United States, see *Broadcasting Yearbook,* available in many libraries. Or send for a copy, for $13.50, to Broadcasting Publishing Inc., Broadcasting-Telecasting Bldg., 1735 DeSales St., N.W., Washington, D.C., 20036.

Local Public Relations, Advertising Agencies

Public relations and advertising agencies, especially smaller ones, quite often assign freelance writers and photographers to help out on specific assignments. These may be brochures, magazines, magazine articles, public service campaigns, speeches, new business projects, slide presentations, television or radio commercials, etc.

One of the best ways to get in on these local markets is to write a query letter, have it printed up in sufficient quantity, and send it to all public relations and advertising agencies in your area. You'll be surprised how far your letter travels. One letter I sent out was passed on to a book and magazine publisher out of the state and brought some totally unexpected, and lucrative, freelance jobs.

Let the creative director know what types of subjects you specialize in, Xerox samples of your work if possible, and send off an "out of the blue" query letter. Your telephone directory will list all the potential clients. If your query letter is convincing enough, some of them will soon become real clients.

Community Service Organizations

Most cities and towns have chapters of the Elks, Rotary, Kiwanis International, and other service organizations. A great deal of their publications come from their national headquarters (see Chapter 11), but this does not rule them out as local markets. Quite often, local slants are needed for national projects, and these may be assigned to local freelancers.

Again, a query letter asking about possible freelance work will let the local Community Service Organizations know you are available.

In some cases, freelance work for these organizations may be without fee. The smart freelancer will not close his typewriter case to this market, even if no fee is offered. Doing a good job on an occasional non-paying assignment for a local Community Service Organization can win you future sales because of the contacts and good will you will encounter. Like a singer who sings a few songs at a charity benefit, the freelance writer can win many friends, and future clients, by occasionally offering his professional services gratis. But since "gratis" won't pay the grocery bills, it shouldn't be made a habit. If you're repeatedly asked to do free writing jobs, respectfully decline with the excuse that you have some pressing deadlines on other projects.

Local Business Markets

One of the most pleasant, and lucrative, local business markets I enjoyed recently was producing copy and photography for art gallery brochures. The client needed small monthly brochures to advertise exhibits of etchings by Rembrandt, some modern sculpture, and an ever-changing inventory of paintings. Working with a friend who is a printing salesman, we were able to write, photograph, edit, lay out, and print these brochures at a cost under what the director of the art gallery had been paying and still made a tidy profit.

Art galleries are just one source of freelance income from local business markets. Automobile dealers frequently hire freelance public relations men to write promotional copy about their dealership. Small manufacturers may hire a freelancer to produce a monthly internal house organ for their employees. Hospitals need public relations freelancers, and when a new hospital is built, it needs to be publicized.

Another excellent local business market is the suburban entrepreneur oasis, the shopping center. Suggest to the owners of shops that they produce a brochure or small monthly magazine containing collective advertising. If each buys a page, or half a page, it doesn't hurt their budget much at all. And since it is an economic fact that shopping centers that advertise together stay together, the local merchants should be convinced. But when you suggest the publication, come armed with a dummy layout and some features to give the brochure or magazine reader appeal.

Clothing shops usually send out advertising sheets announcing seasonal sales. Freelancers often write and photograph these.

The list of local business markets is limited only by the number of businesses in your community. A phone call lining up an interview, or a query letter asking about possible freelance assignments, can make you known to clients in this market area.

City, County, State Public Relations Markets

Who prints more publications than the government? The answer is, of course, no one. And not all the government publications are mailed out of Washington, D.C. A staggering amount of brochures, pamphlets, and even books are published annually by local government agencies in the city, county, and state.

Most local government agencies have full-time staff writers to handle the speeches and other writing they constantly produce. But when the load gets too heavy, freelancers are called in. And, as in the case of the above-mentioned markets, the freelancer who is known to the local government agencies will get the job.

School, University Markets; Stringing

Next to the government, schools print the largest number of magazines, brochures, catalogs, etc. If you live where there are a few private prep schools or colleges, or city-or-state-supported colleges or universities, you have an excellent potential freelance market.

You may find that you can obtain freelance or part-time employment with these academic establishments if you will only contact them. Learn what publications they put out, what staff they have, and ask if you might be of service to them. An occasional freelance assignment can get you a foot in the door and you may be asked to produce material for special projects or, best of all, you may be retained for more regular writing.

Schools and colleges are also sources of income for "stringers." Newspapers or wire services often hire local writers to feed them news and feature stories about people and activities on college and university campuses. A letter to your local newspaper or wire service editor will tell you whether there is any stringing work available.

Special Local Markets

If your community is about to celebrate a centennial or other important event, you can be certain there will be some choice freelance assignments handed out. If you and your work are known around your town or city, you have an excellent chance of landing some of them.

Annual events like Christmas pageants, festivals for spring or autumn, ethnic holidays, etc., all provide sources of work for local freelancers. The client may be the local Chamber of Commerce or perhaps a local merchant who is helping finance the event.

Another good local market is politics. It takes more than just a candidate to win an election; it takes a well-organized staff of experts to help by writing speeches, preparing leaflets, brochures, etc. As soon as you learn there will be an election, and the names of the candidates are rumored about, contact one of them for possible freelance work, in both writing and photography. Perhaps you can be the candidate's press representative or public relations man, or woman.

A friend has made a tidy business of offering a wide variety of editorial services to local markets. He writes, edits, lays out, photographs, and directs printing of every type of publication from monthly magazine to one-sheet handbill for a used car sale. He knows the local market inside and out. Without ever selling to a single major market, he makes a very comfortable living from his typewriter and camera, selling to markets right in his own back yard.

2

HOW TO SELL TO GENERAL MARKETS

Major national magazines are not dead or dying, they're simply undergoing a change of life. Happily for everyone, including freelance writers, this is good.

William Barry Furlong, a midwest writer who enjoys a six figure income, says the magazines that will survive and prosper are those that publish beyond what he calls "The New York Idea."

" 'The New York Idea,' " says Furlong, "is a type of story or a way of looking at people, events, and life in general that gets New Yorkers excited. It may leave them flat in Des Moines or Duluth, but for years the editors of the major national magazines didn't care, so long as it excited New York.

"But times have changed, and *Colliers, Liberty, Look,* and the old *Saturday Evening Post* died, to a large extent because they didn't change with them and look beyond 'The New York Idea.' "

In order for a national magazine to make it today, it must appeal to the widest audience and, as Furlong says, recognize that people outside New York also have opinions, emotions, attitudes, and interests.

This broadening of reader appeal is happy news for freelance writers. Competition remains just as keen for sales to these top markets, but now the sales won't all be to New York writers. The freelancer who can spot a trend before it becomes a national way of life can sell his article for top money. Today, more than ever, the market is wide open to sell to the major general markets.

Ideas are usually what distinguish one writer from another, and especially distinguish selling writers from non-selling writers. Where do you get your ideas? The answer is, everywhere.

A writer who intends to sell to the major markets must be

especially well-read. You don't have to spend days reading every magazine and newspaper you can get your hands on, but you should spend quite a few hours at least leafing through magazines and newspapers, to see what is being published. And you certainly do not have to buy the magazines and newspapers—look at them at your local library.

If you have a university library nearby, so much the better. Most universites subscribe to many American and foreign magazines and newspapers. These are a veritable gold mine of article ideas for writers. And they are also invaluable research tools.

When you come upon a subject you are especially interested in writing about, and are reasonably sure you can sell to a major market, check out the subject first in *Reader's Guide to Periodical Literature* to see what articles, if any, have been published on the subject in recent years. If the subject *has* been written up, but not extensively, or you are certain you have a new approach or recent development important enough to warrant a new article, begin gathering some research material.

HOW MUCH RESEARCH?

At this stage, you need not do a thorough job of research. Just gather enough information to do the job of getting an editor interested in your proposed article. Write it up in a brief query letter, send it off to the magazine you feel would be most likely suited to the article, and get to work on another idea.

An editor will usually reply within two weeks to your query letter. He may like your idea and ask to see the article, perhaps on speculation, or he will say his magazine has done the subject or it is not suited for his magazine. If you draw a reject, submit the idea immediately to the next most likely magazine. Perhaps the editor who rejected the idea was kind enough to comment on the subject, maybe giving you a tip on how to rework your idea before submitting it to another editor.

If you are encouraged to write the article on speculation, do it. Let's face it: you've hooked an editor. If you can produce what he wants, you have not only that lucrative sale, but a good chance at repeat sales. The time and energy you will put into writing your first article for him, even on speculation, is worth it.

It may be another two weeks or longer before you hear back from the editor after you have sent him your completed article. He may like it as is, or may ask for revisions. Whether he has definitely offered to buy the article or not, stick with it. You've not only got your editor on the hook, he's alive and fighting. You have only to work a little harder and you'll land him.

Once you make a sale to a major market, you'll know it was worth it. National magazines usually pay 10 cents a word and up, or fees reaching $1,000 and more. If you're lucky, *Reader's Digest* will pick it up for a reprint and give you an additional $750 or $1,000. And often, textbook publishers scan the magazines and digests for articles they can reprint, bringing you an extra $150 or so.

With that kind of money as incentive, it is only natural that the major general-interest markets attract the most writers. But do not let competition frighten you off, especially if you know you can write and have proven it by selling to local markets. Often, the only difference between selling to a local market and selling to a national market is the courage to try.

Elsewhere in this book you will find many other major national magazines besides those listed below. Be sure to check the subject of your article against the other chapters in this book, to find the best market for your work.

General Interest National Magazines

The Atlantic Monthly, 8 Arlington St., Boston, Mass., 02116. Editor Robert Manning pays about $100 per printed page for quality articles on a wide range of subjects including current events, politics, education, business, the social sciences, literature, the arts. Lengths run from 2,500 to 8,000 words. A good market for quality fiction, especially by new writers.

Coronet, 23 E. 26th St., New York, N.Y., 10010. Yvonne Dunleavy, editor, prefers mail queries for articles of general interest or picture essays.

Harper's Bazaar, 717 Fifth Ave., New York, N.Y., 10022. Editor Enid Harlow pays up to $300 for articles on the arts, travel, and ideas of advanced interest. Payment on acceptance.

Harper's Magazine, 2 Park Ave., New York, N.Y., 10016. Editor-in-Chief Robert Shnayerson will not accept unsolicited manuscripts, but welcomes queries about articles. Pays $300 and up for controversial articles from 2,000 to 7,000 words on all aspects of American life.

Life, Time and Life Bldg., Rockefeller Center, New York, N.Y., 10020. Mostly staff written and photographed, but if you think you have the picture of the year, try them.

The Nation, 333 Sixth Ave., New York, N.Y., 10014. Editor Carey McWilliams pays 2 cents a word, on publication, for articles to 2,500 words on current issues. Query.

The New Republic, 1244 19th St., N.W., Washington, D.C., 20036. A weekly journal of politics and the arts. Editor Gilbert Harrison pays 8 cents a word, on acceptance, for articles 500 to 2,000 words with a liberal viewpoint toward politics and world affairs.

The New Yorker, 25 W. 43d St., New York, N.Y., 10036. *The New Yorker's* appeal has broadened into one of national scope. Payment is very good for articles of varying lengths for the intelligent reader. Do not send manuscripts; query first.

New York Times Magazine, Times Square, New York, N.Y., 10036. Editor Danile Schwarz pays up to $750 for articles about 3,500 words in length on a wide variety of subjects with a timely news peg. Pays $35 per picture. Freelance manuscripts accepted.

Pageant, 205 E. 42d St., New York, N.Y., 10017. Do not send manuscript. Query only for articles of general interest including health, education, current social trends, humor. Pays about $300.

Reader's Digest, Pleasantville, N.Y., 10570. Publishes mostly condensations of articles from other publications, but also buys original material, especially personal experiences and human interest articles. Prefers query. Pays top rates. Study the magazine in order to submit to various departments.

Saturday Evening Post, 1100 Waterway Blvd., Indianapolis, Ind., 46202. Managing Editor Frederic Birmingham wants articles from 2,500 to 3,000 words in length for and about people, science, the arts, education, politics, etc. Query first with brief outline. No opinion or retrospective articles. Also query about photo essays. Also buys short stories and short-shorts. Prefers dramatic narrative style. Poetry accepted, especially modern. Payment is competitive with highest markets.

Saturday Review, 380 Madison Ave., New York, N.Y., 10017. Managing Editor Roland Gelatt pays top rates for articles and essays on current topics and the arts. Prefers query. Pays on publication.

Specialized National Magazines

You have only to look at the racks of a large magazine display to realize there is a magazine for practically every subject. Some of these specialized national magazines are top-paying markets, others are small. All are wide open for freelance sales.

Staffs of these magazines are usually small, requiring editors to buy most of their articles and columns and photography from freelancers. Most editors prefer articles which have a personal how-to or practical approach. The more helpful the article is to the reader, the better its chances of selling, and your chances of making repeat sales to an editor.

Study the specialized magazines carefully. Libraries stock back issues of most of them. Try to send the editor something he hasn't already run. And query him first, before you set out to write the article. If the editor is interested in your idea, he may have specific guidelines he wants you to follow, to assure the article is just what he wants. But it is also a good idea to submit samples of your published articles along with your query, to convince the editor you are qualified and knowledgeable to write the article. You should also suggest how you or the editor can illustrate the article.

Here are some of the best markets among specialized national magazines. Be sure to study the markets in other chapters that are listed under other specific categories.

American Heritage, 551 Fifth Ave., New York, N.Y., 10017. Editor Oliver Jensen pays from $500 to $750 for articles 3,000 to 5,000 words that have a fresh, lively approach to American history. Articles must be factual, not fictionalizations of historic events. Writers should check the library for back issues and the index to see what has been written. Accepts articles or queries.

American Scholar, 1811 Q St., N.W., Washington, D.C., 20009. Editor Hiram Haydn pays $150, on acceptance, for nontechnical articles on politics, current events, culture, religion, and science. Lengths run 3,000 to 4,500 words.

The American West, 599 College Ave., Palo Alto, Calif., 94306. Editor Donald Bower pays up to $250, on acceptance, for well-documented, illustrated articles on the American West, past, present, and future.

Carte Blanche, 3345 Wilshire Blvd., Suite 501, Los Angeles, Calif., 90005. Editor Frank Hiteshew pays good rates for articles on travel, entertainment, "the good life."

Confidential, 8060 Melrose Ave., Los Angeles, Calif., 99046. Editor Tracy Cabot pays good rates, on acceptance, for articles that are exposes on celebrities, political figures, or any well-known personality.

Also medical or specific consumer exposes. Articles must be documented. Query first.

The Continental Magazine, Publications Office, Ford Motor Co., The American Road, Dearborn, Mich., 48121. Editor Robert M. Hodesh pays 25 cents a word and up for articles to 1,300 words on gracious living for readers of above average income. Subjects include travel, food, art, gardening, etc. Query first.

The Freeman, Foundation for Economic Education, Irvington-on-Hudson, N.Y., 10533. Editor Paul Poirot pays 5 cents a word, on publication, for articles analyzing and explaining aspects of freedom, including the free market, private enterprise, and the philosophy of limited government. Study the magazine well before submitting articles or queries. Lengths run to 3,000 words.

Friends, 17390 West 8 Mile Rd., Southfield, Mich., 48075. Buys illustrated articles on travel, recreation, personalities, sports, trends of life in America, etc. Pays up to $150. Query.

Harvest Years, 104 E. 40th St., New York, N.Y., 10016. Editor Peter Dickinson pays 5 cents a word and up for articles 1,000 to 2,000 words in length dealing with subjects of interest to retired people or those about to retire. Topics include health, hobbies, travel, job opportunities, finances, etc. Pays $5 to $25 for photos. Payment on publication.

Horizon, 551 Fifth Ave., New York, N.Y., 10017. Editor Joseph Thorndike buys articles on the arts and history as they relate to contemporary living. Pays good rates, on acceptance.

Interplay, 342 Madison Ave., New York, N.Y., 10017. Editor Anthony Hartley pays up to 10 cents a word for lively articles to 3,000 words on politics, economics, culture, and social issues. Query first.

The Leatherneck, Box 1918, Washington, D.C., 20013 Editor Ronald Lyons pays up to $200, on acceptance, for articles of interest to Marines. Query first with outline.

Military Life, W.B. Bradbury Co., 5 E. 42d St., New York, N.Y., 10017. Editor Will Lieberson pays $75, on acceptance, for articles to 1,000 words with military slant, especially of interest to military families. Photos should accompany manuscripts.

Modern Maturity, 215 Long Beach Blvd., Long Beach, Calif., 90802. Editor Hubert Pryor pays from $50 to $500 for articles and fiction, on acceptance. Buys service articles on food, health, housing, employment for persons over age 55. Also uses inspirational articles, personality pieces, Americana. Pays $50 and up for color photos, $15 and up for black-and-white.

National Enquirer, 210 Sylvan Ave., Englewood Cliffs, N.J., 07632. Editor Mel Snyder pays $125 and up, on acceptance, for lively, in-depth articles of general interest. Especially buys human interest, personality profiles, self-help, medical "firsts," success stories.

National Insider, 2713 Pulaski Rd., Chicago, Ill., 60639. Editor Roger Rohn prefers to be queried on articles of human interest, crime, scandals, frauds, sensational subjects. Pays 2 cents a word and up.

National Motorist, 65 Battery St., San Francisco, Calif., 94111. Editor Jim Donaldson pays ten cents a word for articles of interest to California motorists. Travel, car care, history, outdoor activities, hobbies, are some of the subjects bought. Lengths run from 500 to 1,100 words. Buys color and black-and-white photos.

Pen Magazine, 444 Sherman St., Denver, Colo., 80203. Editor Jean Blair Ryan pays up to 3 cents a word for articles to 2,500 words for government employees and public servants. Sample copy sent on request.

The Progressive, 408 W. Gorham St., Madison, Wisc., 53703. Editor Morris Rubin pays up to $100, on acceptance, for articles to 3,500 words on politics, social, economic, and international problems.

Psychic, The Bolen Co., 680 Beach St., San Francisco, Calif. 94109. Pays $75 to $150 for articles on psychic phenomena. Articles should be for sophisticated reader. No fiction, personal experiences. Query.

Railroad Magazine, 205 E. 42d St., New York, N.Y., 10017. Editor Freeman Hubbard pays 5 cents a word for articles to 3,500 words on railroad subjects. Uses nostalgia and articles about the building and operation of all locomotives, especially steam. Query first.

Real Frontier, 108 S. Franklin Ave., Valley Stream, N.Y., 11580. Editor Hazel Krantz pays $30 per article, to 3,000 words, on little-known pioneers before 1900. Likes humorous or eccentric slant. Pays $10 per illustration. Also publishes *True Frontier* with same requirements.

Real West, Charlton Publications, Inc., Charlton Bldg., Derby, Conn., 06418. Buys articles 3,000 to 5,000 words on pioneering in the West during late 19th and early 20th centuries. Pays 2 cents a word, on acceptance.

Signature, 660 Madison Ave., New York, N.Y., 10021. Diners Club Magazine. Managing Editor Kenneth Gouldthorpe pays good rates, on acceptance, for articles and photo stories of interest to business-oriented readers, especially males. Uses sports, social issues, humor, personality in business, lively arts, etc. Query.

Small World, Volkswagen of America, Englewood Cliffs, N.J., 07632. Editor Jonathan Fisher pays $100 per printed page for articles 600 to 1,800 words about Volkswagens and VW owners.

Smithsonian Magazine, Arts and Industries Bldg., 900 Jefferson Dr., Washington D.C., 20560. Editor Edward K. Thompson pays good

HOW TO SELL TO GENERAL MARKETS

rates for articles on a variety of subjects including wildlife, environment, ancient art, and other topics of interest to members of the Smithsonian Institution. Query first.

Success Unlimited, Arcade Bldg., 6355 N. Broadway, Chicago, Ill., 60626. Executive Editor Og Mandino pays 5 cents a word for articles of inspirational and self-help nature stressing positive mental attitude. Also features on well-known people who overcame handicaps to find success. Query.

Vogue, 420 Lexington Ave., New York, N.Y., 10017. Editor Allene Talmey pays good rates, on acceptance, for articles to 2,000 words of interest to intelligent readers. Subjects include the arts, medicine, travel, music, etc. Query.

Syndicates

Syndicates are companies that buy articles, fiction, columns, and photography and artwork from freelancers, and sell it to newspapers throughout the world. Authors and artists are paid a percentage of the gross proceeds of the material, or in some cases, they are paid a flat fee for the material.

Well-known writers are most often preferred by the syndicates, but lesser-known writers can sell to this market if their writing is slick and their subject very timely. Syndicates usually only buy columns that have proven success locally or regionally in newspapers or magazines. Fiction is usually a reprint of a short story previously published.

Editors of syndicates prefer query letters to manuscripts. The following list includes only the major syndicates and publications. For a complete list, see *Editor and Publisher's Annual Directory of Syndicated Features,* available at the library or from *Editor and Publisher,* 850 Third Ave., New York, N.Y., 10022.

AP News Features, 50 Rockefeller Plaza, New York, N.Y., 10020. Editor Dan Perkes buys news, women's, and sports features. Query.

B P Singer Features, 3164 W. Tyler Ave., Anaheim, Calif., 92801. Editor Jane Sherrod buys fiction of all lengths that have previously been published, biography, and features of interest to women, books for foreign reprint, and color slides and comic strips. Pays outright fee or arranges percentage.

Bell-McClure Syndicate, 1501 Broadway, New York, N.Y.,

10036. Editor Elmer Roessner buys daily columns, cartoons, puzzles, etc. Offers contracts. Query.

Central Press Association, 1380 Dodge Ct., Cleveland, Ohio, 44114. Editor Courtland C. Smith pays $25 for feature stories of national interest. Also buys photos.

Chicago Tribune-New York News Syndicate, 220 E. 42d St., New York, N.Y., 10017. Editor Arthur Laro buys articles of national interest to run in seven installments of 1,200 words each. Rates are negotiated, payment on publication.

City Desk Features, 310 E. 75th St., New York, N.Y., 10021. Editor Sylvia Fenmore buys columns that are timely and of national interest. Lengths from 500 to 700 words.

Federated Feature Syndicate, 663 Fifth Ave., New York, N.Y., 10022 and 1250 N. Kingsley Dr., Hollywood, Calif., 90029. Query first, with ideas for features mainly in entertainment field. Bart Andrews, feature editor; Alan Grossman, photo editor.

General Features Corp., Los Angeles Times Syndicate, Times Mirror Square, Los Angeles, Calif., 90053. Chief Editor Edward Grade buys daily columns, comic strips. No fiction or one-shot articles.

Hollywood Informer Syndicate, Box 3049, Hollywood, Calif., 90028. Director John Austin pays on percentage basis for features to 1,500 words on movie and television celebrities.

Intercity News Service, 103 Park Ave., New York, N.Y., 10017. Editor John Kelly buys business, financial, and trade publication articles.

King Features Syndicate, 235 E. 45th St., New York, N.Y., 10017. General Manager Milton Kaplan buys columns and comic features as well as photos for picture pages. Payment varies.

The Ledger Syndicate, Overseas Press Club Bldg., 54 W. 40th St., New York, N.Y., 10018. Buys from published writers only. Uses series on topic subjects from 750 to 1,100 words per installment for 6 or 12 installments per series. Pays 50 percent of net.

McNaught Syndicate, 60 E. 42d St., New York, N.Y., 10017. Editor William A. Kennedy pays good rates, on acceptance, for humorous material and drawings.

National Newspaper Syndicate, National Newspaper Syndicate, Inc., of America, 20 N. Wacker Dr., Chicago, Ill., 60606. Editor Frank M. Kroll buys humor to be illustrated for syndicated cartoon panels. Length: 1 to 10 words. Write for fact sheet.

Newspaper Enterprise Association, 230 Park Ave., New York, N.Y., 10017. Murray Olderman, executive editor, uses features, news features, and background material. Mostly staffwritten.

North American Newspaper Alliance, 1501 Broadway, New York,

HOW TO SELL TO GENERAL MARKETS

N.Y., 10036. Editor Sid Goldberg pays $25 and up for news and feature stories of national interest.

Parade, 733 Third Ave., New York, N.Y., 10017. Associate Editor M. David Detweiler prefers query with outline on articles of timely nature of interest to the whole family, about personalities, new modes of living. Lively style with quotes. Lengths run 1,000 to 2,500 words.

Publishers-Hall Syndicate, 30 E. 42d St., New York, N.Y., 10017. Richard Sherry, editor, buys columns, comic strips, panel cartoons, and reprints fiction in serialization form.

Register and Tribune Syndicate, 488 Madison Ave., New York, N.Y., 10022. General Manager Lewis A. Little buys daily newspaper columns, comic strips, and running features for newspapers. Query first. Pays percentage.

Religious News Service, 43 W. 57th St., New York, N.Y., 10019. Managing Editor Lillian R. Block pays 2 cents a word for spot religious news and features. Pays $5 and up for photos on religious subjects. Payment on acceptance.

Spadea Syndicate, Milford, N.J., 08848. Editor J. McDonald prefers queries on books and newspaper syndication.

Toronto Star Syndicate, 80 King St., West, Toronto, Ont., Canada. Manager J.F. Cherrier buys nonfiction of interest to Canadian readers.

Transworld Feature Syndicate, 141 E. 44th St., New York, N.Y., 10017. Editor Harriet Fried prefers query for features for overseas markets.

United Feature Syndicate, 220 E. 42d St., New York, N.Y., 10017. Managing Editor James L. Freeman buys columns, comics, and occasional series of articles. Pays on a 50-50 basis.

Universal Trade Press Syndicate, 37-20 Ferry Hts., Fair Lawn, N.J., 07410. Director Leon Gruberg uses spot news and features for trade papers. Prefers query.

World Book Encyclopedia Science Service, 516 Travis St., Houston, Texas, 77002. Editor William J. Cromie pays top rates for science features to 2,500 words. Query with idea and qualifications.

3

HOW TO SELL TO TRADE JOURNAL MARKETS

Trade journals, industrial magazines, house organs, and company publications for both internal and external audiences may not have the glamour of the national magazines, but some of them pay almost as well for articles, and many of them look slicker than those put out by the leading publishers.

Len Hilts, a midwest writer, adds a minimum of $6,000 a year to his freelancing income from sales to trade journals. His advice on writing for this market is gleaned from hard years of experience both as an editor and freelancer of trade magazines.

"Most trade journals are desperately underbudgeted," says Hilts. "They pay from 1 to three cents a word, and want photos besides. For the whole package of up to 3,000 words and half a dozen black and white photos, you may be offered $100. Take it. But ask for $200 the next time. If you've done a good job and the editor learns he can depend on you, he'll pay you $200 and more, and you'll become his man in your part of the country.

"Trade journal editors live an even more hectic life than editors of most national magazines, if that's possible," Hilts continues. "They work with smaller budgets, smaller staffs, and larger numbers of vice presidents to please. Most of their lead stories are needed in only a matter of a few days. And usually it is to run under the byline of the president of the company. They need the story right away, and need it written so accurately that it can pass the chain of command for approvals without hardly a change.

"Writing for trade journals is a highly specialized business. You have to know how to be a good reporter, how to dig for research, how to interview, how to write, and how to meet early deadlines. You also have to know executives, and how to interview them on-the-run, because if you think you're busy, they're busier.

"To make money writing for trade journals, you should be able to do your story in from one to two days. If it takes longer, you simply won't make enough money to come out ahead.

"But if you know how to get the editor to spell out specifically what he wants in the article, and can keep your interviews to-the-point, you can do it all in a day or two. Tape-recording the interview is a must. And in many cases, you can shoot your own photos the same day. Then you can take your tapes home and write up your story in a day and come out ahead."

Hilts believes in looking for another story while he's covering one. It may be sold to the same editor or to another, in an unrelated field. But his method is to make a trip pay for itself in ideas for more stories.

"Most trade journal editors need writers in various parts of the country that they can count on to cover a story on short notice," Hilts says. "If you specialize in three or four industries, and editors of trade journals in those fields know you can produce for them, they'll call on you regularly."

WISE TO SPECIALIZE

With the wide variety of trade journals being published monthly and quarterly throughout the country, it is a good idea to specialize in perhaps half a dozen subjects. Contact these editors for samples of their publications if you can't get copies of them in the library. Read their journals thoroughly, then submit queries by mail or write for an interview.

Len Hilts says that despite his success as a writer, he is a poor writer of query letters. He prefers jotting his ideas down on 4 x 5 file cards. When he has an interview with an editor, he reads from his file cards, and the editor makes his decision. Luckily for Hilts, his in-person salesmanship works.

Most trade journals are intended to promote a company's line of products, explain its services, spread good will, or present the company's viewpoint on its own or community issues. But many contain articles strictly for entertainment, including travel, human-interest stories, humor, and some even publish short stories and poetry.

Many house magazines and trade journals have their own staff photographers who will illustrate your article. But for those who don't, a writer can often add several hundred dollars to his sale if he can take his own pictures, provided they are of high enough quality to please an editor.

William Barry Furlong, another very successful freelance writer, says he makes a considerable part of his annual six-figure income by writing for corporate executives. He will write speeches and magazine articles for presidents and other high officials of companies of all sizes, whether or not they have their own public relations staff.

"Many corporation executives prefer to go outside the company public relations office for writers who are more used to writing for national magazines and audiences impartial to or even biased against the company and its policies," Furlong reports. "This means the freelance writer, and if you become the 'ghost writer' of speeches and articles for one or more company officials, you can enjoy a steady flow of high-paying assignments.

SPEECH-WRITING AND CONSULTANT WORK

"I write speeches and act as a management and communications consultant for corporate executives. I am asked to sit in on high-level policy-making meetings and contribute ideas as to how the company's message can best be put to the public, whether in a speech by the president or in a local or national newspaper or magazine article. Of course I'm paid well for these 'think' sessions.

"After the company officials have agreed on what the message should contain, I begin my research, usually assisted by one or more persons in the company's public relations department, to help guide me through company policy.

"Good research is 90 percent of the job in writing for corporations. The other 10 percent is in good writing.

"In speech-writing, you should try to know how the speaker acts and talks. This comes from listening to him closely at preliminary meetings. The better you know your speaker, the better the speech you can write for him. It is the same in writing articles for a company. The better you know the company, the better the article you can write for it.

"The thing to keep in mind is, there are more and more jobs waiting for freelance writers and photographers in the field of company publications and speech writing.

"The new writer in this field should check out the businesses in his community, learn what they manufacture or sell, decide which products or services they are especially knowledgeable in, and then send a letter to the company's director of public relations. Ask if there is any need for the services of a freelance writer or photographer.

"You may get no assignment on the first inquiry, but when the company's needs arise, as they always do sooner or later, your letter will remind them of you, and you may be called in to discuss a particular project, either writing a speech or an article. If you handle the initial assignment to their satisfaction, you have won the first round toward getting yourself a lucrative freelance retainer job, handling most or all of their future freelance needs."

Those markets that follow are among the leaders in the field of company publications and corporations that use freelance articles and photography. For a complete list, consult the *Gebbie House Magazine Directory,* published by House Magazine Publishing Co., Sioux City, Iowa, 55102. A copy is available in most libraries.

By all means do not overlook your local companies. Often, editors and corporate executives prefer to work with local writers and photographers who can come in for meetings. If you live in a metropolitan area, check the classified pages of your telephone directory. Select the companies you might like to write for and send them a query letter.

Many companies prefer not to publish how much they will pay for articles and photographs, because payment generally varies according to assignment. You will have to be the judge of how much your time is worth. If the magazine editor or publications director offers you less than you think it is worth to do the job properly, try to negotiate him higher. If he won't budge a dollar, consider taking the assignment at his price anyway, keeping in mind that future assignments will probably come your way if you cooperate with their budget problems. Eventually, they will raise your rate.

House Magazines and Trade Journals

Action Time, 601 N. Fairbanks Ct., Chicago, Ill., 60611. Bimonthly, 24-page color magazine for the AC Spark Plug division of General Motors Corp., intended for employees, customers, and the general public. Buys industry news and also male-oriented articles such as sports, camping, sailing, adventure.

Agway Cooperator, Agway, Inc., Box 1333, Syracuse, N.Y., 13201. Editor Kenneth Hinshaw pays from $50 to $80, on acceptance, for articles on agriculture in the northeastern states, preferably by college and industry agriculturalists. Query.

Air Line Pilot, Air Line Pilots Assn., 1329 E. St., N.W., Washington, D.C., 20004. Editor Frank Martineau pays good rates, on publication, for aviation-oriented articles to 5,000 words, emphasizing the pilot's point of view. Also safety articles on aircraft, airports, and articles about stewards and stewardesses. Pays up to $25 for black and white photos, higher for color.

Allis-Chalmers Reporter, Construction Machinery Div., Allis-Chalmers Mfg. Co., 3000 S. 6th St., Springfield, Ill., articles 500 to 1,500 words on use of Allis-Chalmers construction equipment. Queries accepted from experienced technical writers only. Send samples of work. Also uses color and black and white photos.

The American Way, 420 Lexington Ave., New York, N.Y., 10017. Pays from $200 to $600, a month after acceptance, for articles 2,000 to 2,500 words of interest to employes of American Airlines and their customers. Query.

American Youth, 4-123 General Motors Bldg., Detroit, Mich., 48202. Editor R.M. Girling pays good rates for articles to 1,200 words of interest to young readers 16 to 18 years old, on motoring subjects and topics of general interest. Query.

ARCO Spark, Atlantic Richfield Co., 260 S. Broad St., Philadelphia, Pa., 19101. Pays 10 cents a word, on acceptance, for articles to 2,500 words, with photos, with tie-in on either the energy industry or Atlantic-Richfield specifically. Query.

Area Development, 114 E. 32d St., New York, N.Y., 10016. Editor Albert Jaeggin pays $32 per printed page for articles on industrial facility planning: finding new plant sites, expanding or relocating existing companies, community relations, financing, insurance, plant design, safety, water and air pollution controls, etc. Must be useful to manufacturing executives. Query.

Astrojet News, American Airlines, Inc., 633 Third Ave., New

York, N.Y., 10017. Editor Bill Hunter pays good rates, within 30 days of publication, for articles to interest American Airlines employees and travel agents. Subjects include features about cities on the American Airlines route and humorous or unusual incidents aboard their planes.

Auto and Flat Glass Journal, 6654 Chestnut St., Cincinnati, Ohio, 45227. Editor James Colborne pays 5 cents a word, on acceptance, for articles about 1,000 words which will interest professional auto glass replacement dealers. Especially interested in articles that help dealers to sell their products, such as sales campaigns and promotions. Also articles on how other glass men operate their business. Query.

Bausch & Lomb Focus, 619 St. Paul St., Rochester, N.Y., 14602. Editor Ralph Feister pays 3 cents a word for articles to 3,000 words about new methods in science teaching or interesting applications of scientific optical instruments. Pays $5 per photo. Send for free pamphlet S-301 for information for writers.

The Bolex Reporter, Paillard Inc., 1900 Lower Rd., Linden, N.J., 07036. Pays $50 per published page for short articles and photos on moviemaking, and travel articles with moviemaking details, preferably using Bolex cameras. Query.

Business West, P.O. Box 536, Oakland, Calif., 94604. Pays $50 for articles to 2,000 words that analyze the business and corporate development of West Coast companies. Sample copy sent for $1.

Canner/Packer, 300 W. Adams St., Chicago, Ill., 60606. Editor Thomas Serb pays 5 cents a word, on publication, for articles on the packaged food industry: labor, processing methods, growing areas, labor, etc. Pays $5 per photo. Query.

The Caravanner, 1900 Beverly Blvd., Los Angeles, Calif., 90057. Pays about $75 for articles to 2,000 words, with photos, on the pleasures and unusual uses of Airstream travel trailers. Articles should include photos with Airstream trailers, and are more about how people enjoy the use of their Airstream trailer than its technical qualities. Query.

Channels of Business Communication, Northwestern Bell Telephone Co., Rm. 910, 100 S. 19th St., Omaha, Nebr., 68102. Editor Gerald Metcalf pays $100 and up for articles 500 to 1,200 words on how businesses in the Northwestern states use communications to best advantage; also communications in a broad sense. Pays $10 and up for cartoons. Query.

College Store Executive, P.O. Box 788, Lynbrook, N.Y., 11563. Editor Pamela Kay Smith pays good rates, on acceptance, for articles 800 to 1,600 words of guidance in operating college stores. Uses black and white photos. Query.

The Compass, Mobile Sales and Supply Corp., 150 E. 42d St.,

New York, N.Y., 10017. Editor K.V.W. Lawrence pays up to $250 for articles with color photos on the sea and deep sea trade, especially of international interest. Query.

Computer Decisions, 850 Third Ave., New York, N.Y., 10022. Editor Robert Haavind pays from $30 to $50 per printed page for articles 800 to 4,000 words on general uses of computers. Also short computer games including program. Query.

The Continental Magazine, Room 950, Central Office Bldg., Ford Motor Co., Dearborn, Mich., 48121. Editorial Director Robert M. Hodesh pays up to $500 for articles to interest owners of the Lincoln Continental luxury car. Articles may be on travel, the arts, home decoration, gourmet dining, and other subjects for an audience of better than average income. Pays $50 each for color photos. All payment on acceptance. Query.

Cooking for Profit, 1202 S. Park St., Madison, Wisc., 53715. Editor Helen Sanstadt pays varying rates, after publication, for articles 1,000 to 1,500 words that help gas utility companies promote the use of gas-fired cooking equipment, air-conditioning, and water heating in the food service industry. Query.

The Counselor, NBS Bldg., 2d and Clearview Aves., Trevose, Pa., 19047. Managing Editor Ann Newman pays from $35 to $75 for articles 1,500 to 5,000 words about the speciality advertising industry. Prefers solid case history stories of specialty promotion programs and interviews with industry suppliers and distributors. Payment is on publication.

Cushman Dealer, Cushman Motors, 920 N. 21st St., Lincoln, Nebr., 68501. Pays 3½ cents a word, on acceptance, for articles on industrial and pleasure use of Cushman vehicles (golf cars, four-wheel-drive vehicles). Pays $5 per photo, with Cushman vehicle in picture. Query.

Design, 1100 Waterway Blvd., Indianapolis, Ind., 46202. An art magazine published for students, teachers, craftsmen, and professional artists. Associate Editor Miss E. Catherine Cummins pays on publication for articles primarily for the grade school art teacher on new techniques of teaching art. Also articles on the work of both new and established artists, and step-by-step method articles. Uses no drawings, only black and white photos. Emphasis is on a new look in art.

Design and Environment, 6400 Goldsboro Rd., Washington, D.C., 20034. Editor Miss Janet Vrochota pays varying rates, on publication, for articles from 500 to 2,000 words to interest engineers, architects, industrial designers, graphic designers, landscape architects, and city planners. Emphasis is to combine interests and problems of designers and environmentalists in achieving solutions. Query.

HOW TO SELL TO TRADE JOURNAL MARKETS 55

Dodge News Magazine, 5435 W. Fort St., Detroit, Mich., 48209. Editor William Hinds pays top rates, on publication, for articles to interest owners and prospective owners of Dodge cars. Subjects range from travel and sports to interesting personalities. Automotive articles are staff-written.

Dust Topics, Gelman Instrument Co., P.O. Box 1448, Ann Arbor, Mich., 48106. Pays $100 and up, on acceptance, for articles about use of Gelman products in air pollution control. Send for catalog of Gelman products and/or query C. Larry Stinedurf, Advertising Coordinator.

Floor and Wall Covering News, 155 E. 44th St., New York, N.Y., 10017. Weekly tabloid newspaper for the floor and wall covering industry. Editor Pincus Tell pays 4 cents a word, on acceptance, for articles about floor covering retailers who are doing exceptional merchandising and promotional jobs. Also new and unusual store location stories. Pays $6 per photo. Query.

Florist and Nursery Exchange, 434 S. Wabash Ave., Chicago, Ill., 60605. Editor Donald Scheer pays up to $25 per published page, after publication, for articles with black and white photos to interest florists and nursery owners. Lengths to 1,000 words.

The Flying A, Aeroquip Corp., 300 S. East Ave., Jackson, Mich., 49203. Pays $50 and up per published page for articles on the use of Aeroquip Corporation products. Pays $10 per photo. Editors are interested in working with professional photojournalists with experience in industrial writing and photography. Query.

Ford Truck Times, 420 Lexington Ave., New York, N.Y., 10017. Editor Henry Zaleski pays good rates, on publication, for how-to articles from 500 to 1,500 words, to interest Ford truck owners. Also sports, adventure, outdoor, general-interest, and business success stories related to use of a Ford truck. Uses color photos. Send for writer's fact sheet.

Founders Express, American Founders Life Insurance Co., Box 2068, Austin, Tex., 78767. Editor Mrs. Vonciel Shooter pays $10 and up for short articles to 250 words about life insurance selling. Prefers photos to accompany articles. Also buys sales motivation filler items.

The Furrow, John Deere, John Deere Rd., Moline, Ill., 61265. Editor Ralph Reynolds pays up to $200, on acceptance, for articles emphasizing agricultural-technical subjects, social and economic trends in small rural towns.

Going Places, American Express Co., 65 Broadway, New York, N.Y., 10006. Editor Sybil Edwards pays varying rates, on acceptance, for travel articles to 1,000 words.

The Grace Log, 7 Hanover Sq., New York, N.Y., 10005. External company publication of the W.R. Grace Co., producers of chemicals, packaging materials and other products and services. Pays up to $250 for illustrated articles about the company, its interests, and various locations. Also travel, public service, outdoor sports. Query.

Harvest, Campbell Soup Co., Campbell Pl., Camden, N.J., 08101. Pays on acceptance for articles with a company tie-in or of a general food industry nature. Uses black and white and color photos. Sample copy and requirement sheet sent on request. Query.

Industrial Ecology, 777 Third Ave., New York, N.Y., 10017. Editor Ben Miyares pays 10 cents a word, on publication, for factual reports to 2,500 words, on industry approaches to solving pollution problems, or interviews with environmental authorities. Also buys 300-word fables with an ecology message. Query.

Inland, quarterly external magazine of Inland Steel Co. Pays about $300, on acceptance, for articles of broad current interest to people in the Midwest; also history, reminiscence. Send query to Sheldon A. Mix, Managing Editor, 18 S. Home Ave., Park Ridge, Ill., 60068.

International Railway Journal, 30 Church St., New York, N.Y., 10007. Executive Editor Luther S. Miller pays $35 per page for articles to 1,500 words on railway equipment, especially that which is built in one country and used in another. Query.

The Iron Worker, Lynchburg Foundry Co., Lynchburg, Va., 24505. Editor B.J. Hillman pays varying rates, on acceptance, for articles on Virginia history, from 3,500 to 5,000 words. Query.

The Lookout, 15 State St., New York, N.Y., 10004. Editor Harold G. Peterson pays up to $40 for articles related to old or modern merchant marine, to 1,000 words. Also buys quality cover photos.

Marathon World, Marathon Oil Co., 539 S. Main St., Findlay, Ohio, 45840. Editor Joe Callanan pays from $150 to $500 for articles 1,500 to 3,000 words that are either about petroleum or general interest and travel, preferably about the Midwest. Query.

Minutes, Nationwide Insurance, 246 N. High St., Columbus, Ohio, 43216. Managing Editor Mrs. Martha Sliter Sheeran pays about $50 per printed page, on acceptance, for people-oriented articles on community problems, safety, family, humor. Likes good black and white photos to accompany manuscript.

The Office Economist, Art Metal Inc., Jamestown, N.Y., 14701. Editor Herbert Kiehn pays 3 cents a word, on acceptance, for articles to 1,000 words, about office management, for office managers.

Office Products Magazine, 288 Park Ave. W., Elmhurst, Ill., 60126. Pays $25 per printed page, on acceptance, for articles with photos, on dealers of office supplies including machines and office furnishings. Dealer's success story or story of unusual store or merchandising welcome. Pays $10 for cartoons.

Our World, Tupperware, Box 2353, Orlando, Fla., 32802. Magazine for Tupperware home party dealers. Editor Joe Lambert pays from $50 to $200 for articles with photos, on acceptance, to aid Tupperware dealers and managers. Mostly assigned interviews with dealers and managers. Send query and samples of writing and photography.

Points, 465 W. Milwaukee, Detroit, Mich., 48202. Pays from $125 to $400 for articles with photos on new or unusual family activities, hobbies, women's features, arts and crafts, sports, travel. Pays from $60 to $150 for color transparencies without article. Query.

Playthings, 51 Madison Ave., New York, N.Y., 10010. Editor Thomas Murn pays from $35 to $125, on publication, for articles to 2,000 words on toy retailer and wholesaler buying procedures, toy store layout of merchandise. Also buys 100 to 300-word shorts on sales promotions for $15, on publication.

Printing Salesman's Herald, Champion Papers, 245 Park Ave., New York, N.Y., 10017. Editor Lionel L. Fisher pays from $50 to $75, on acceptance, for articles on the buying and selling of printing, to help printing salesmen to sell more, and about humanitarian members of the profession.

Profitable Hobby Merchandising, Pleasantville, N.Y., 10570. Trade magazine for craft and hobby retailers, to help them attract new customers and improve their business. Editor Jack Wax pays 3 cents a word and $5 per black and white photo, on publication.

The Record, Fireman's Fund American Insurance Companies, 3333 California St., San Francisco, Calif., 94120. Editor William Lawler pays from $300 to $500 for a short story with a strong Christmas theme, about 3,000 words.

Seventy-Six Magazine, Union Oil Co. of California, Box 7600, Los Angeles, Calif., 90054. Articles Editor Lauritz Miller pays $150 and up, on acceptance, for articles with photos on employees of Union Oil. Query.

Shoe—The Coast Shoe Reporter, 256 Sutter St., San Francisco, Calif., 94108. Editor Sally Ann Bell pays 50 cents per column inch for articles, on publication, for retailers and buyers for shoe stores and shoe departments in the Western states. Uses color and black and white photos. Pays $25 for color cover.

Texaco Tempo, Texaco Canada Ltd., 1425 Mountain St., Montreal, 107, Quebec, Canada. Pays from $100 to $150 for articles 800 to 1,200 words related to Canadian oil industry.

Think, International Business Machines, Armonk, N.Y., 10504. Editor James B. O'Connell pays $500 and up for articles on management, science, education, and public affairs. Lengths from 2,000 to 4,000 words.

Trained Men, International Correspondence Schools, Scranton, Pa., 18515. Editor Catherine Harrington pays up to 3 cents a word for articles to interest management officials. Subjects include new management methods, systems, etc. Lengths from 1,200 to 3,000 words, with photos.

The Water Skier, American Water Ski Assn., Box 191, Winter Haven, Fla., 33880. Editor Thomas Hardman pays varying rates, on acceptance, for new slants on water skiing. Lengths to 2,500 words. Query.

4

HOW TO SELL TO SPECIAL INTEREST MARKETS

Specialization is often the secret to success for freelancers. Those who know one or more fields with authority can enjoy that most rewarding of incomes: a steady one.

Month-to-month, the writers who specialize sell regularly to editors who learn to rely on them. The pay may not be as big as from the major markets, but it is steady pay, often providing the "retainer" or "bread-and-butter" income from which writers can expand their markets and sales.

Take stock of your interests and skills. If you can write authoritatively on one or more subjects, perhaps you can sell to magazines and newspapers publishing in those fields. If you are only a good amateur, study the fields you know best, until you can write on them as an expert.

Write what you know about, whether it be short stories based on your childhood, or articles about antiquing. The special interest markets will provide you with steady checks.

Health Markets

Knowing your subject, doing a thorough job of research, and quoting from authorities are essentials in writing for the health market.

Most of the national magazines, Sunday supplements, and many house organs use articles on health, in addition to more than a dozen magazines which specialize in health subjects. But all require the articles to be well-researched and factually accurate. If you state a medical opinion, be sure to back it up with the name of a medical authority.

The trend in some of the leading health publications, such as *Today's Health,* is to popularize the subject of health for family readership. Editors are running some articles you would be very surprised to find in a health magazine.

Sheldon Mix, a versatile writer who sells regularly to *Today's Health,* recently sold them a reminiscence piece about the disappearance of the streetcar, a travel article about motoring around Lake Michigan, another travel article on visiting off-shore islands, a study of the problems of solid waste disposal, an article on old age, and another on walking as exercise. Only the last three were health-oriented, and even those were not typical health articles.

"The health field is wide open for new article ideas," says Mix. "*Today's Health* is growing more free in subject matter each issue. The editor runs sports, hobbies, humor, child-parent education, and even history with no health slant at all.

"It's always best to query this market first, whether you're writing on health or a general subject," Mix advises. "You'll find the editors will give prompt, helpful replies. And if you sell one or two articles to this market, the editors will begin to assign you articles in the areas of your special interests."

Health and Medical Markets

Accent on Living, P.O. Box 726, Bloomington, Ill., 61701. Editor Raymond Cheever pays up to $50, on publication, for articles dealing with the handicapped. Likes success stories, features on rehabilitation, and self-help devices. Also buys humor concerning physical disabilities, with a positive slant.

The Active Handicapped, 526 Aurora Ave., Metaire, La., 70005. Editor Richard McCaughan buys articles of interest to the handicapped, including biographies, helpful hints, and new devices. Pays about $25 for articles 600 words, on acceptance.

American Baby, 10 E. 52d St., New York, N.Y., 10022. Editor Judith Nolte pays good rates for articles to 1,200 words of interest to new or expectant mothers. Likes medical articles for lay readers written by authorities.

American Family Physician/GP, American Academy of General Practice, Volker Blvd. at Brookside, Kansas City, Mo., 64112. Editor Walker Kemp pays $50 and up, on publication, for articles from 1,600 to 3,200 words, on clinical medicine. Prefers photos or illustrations with manuscript.

American Journal of Nursing, 10 Columbus Circle, New York, N.Y., 10019. Editor Barbara Schutt pays $20 per printed page, on publication, for articles 1,500 to 2,000 words on nursing. Query.

Dental Economics, (formerly *Oral Hygiene),* 708 Church St., Evanston, Ill., 60201. Editor E. James Best pays on publication for articles of interest to dentists relating to dental-practice management. Lengths from 1,200 to 1,500 words.

Expecting, Parents' Magazine Enterprises, Inc., 52 Vanderbilt Ave., New York, N.Y., 10017. Pays from $50 to $125, on acceptance, for articles 700 to 2,000 words, of a medical nature for expectant mothers, written by nurses, doctors, or knowledgeable personal experiences of mothers.

Family Health, 1271 Avenue of the Americas, New York, N.Y., 10022. Pays on acceptance for articles about 3,000 words, and picture essays, on health, beauty, physical fitness, marriage, child care, etc. Prefers query and outline of article.

Fitness for Living, 33 E. Minor St., Emmaus, Pa., 18049. Editor John Haberern pays $50 to $120 for articles to 2,000 words on exercises and physical fitness of interest to the general public.

Health, 212 E. Ohio St., Chicago, Ill., 60611. Associate Editor Barbara Peterson pays 4 cents a word for articles 1,000 to 2,000 words on health and medicine for the general public. Pays $5 per photo.

RN, RN Publications, Oradell, N.J., 07649. Pays 10 cents a word, on acceptance, for articles 500 to 1,500 words, of interest to graduate, registered nurses. Query.

Strength and Health, 26-52 N. Ridge, York, Pa., 17405. Editor Bill Starr pays $50 and up, on publication, for articles 1,500 words and up, on weightlifting and physical fitness.

Today's Health, 535 N. Dearborn St., Chicago, Ill., 60610. Editor Byron T. Scott pays 10 cents a word and up for articles to 3,000 words on all aspects of health including nutrition, child development, community health problems, mental health. Does not accept unsolicited manuscripts; query first.

Ecology-Conservation

At least a dozen publications now specialize in articles on ecology and conservation, in addition to general magazines and Sunday supplements which now run articles on these subjects. They all add up to more sales for freelance writers and photographers who can develop new slants or solutions to some of the environmental problems facing people all over the world.

As in writing for the health market, those who specialize in conservation should know their subject thoroughly and be able to attribute their comments and opinions to qualified authorities.

American Forests, 919 17th St., N.W., Washington, D.C., 20006. Editor James B. Craig pays up to $150 for articles to 2,000 words on forests, soil, water, wildlife, outdoor recreation, and environment. Readers are well-educated and many are authorities.

Animal Kingdom, New York Zoological Park, Bronx, N.Y., 10460. Editor Edward Ricciuti pays from $75 to $250 on acceptance for articles about wildlife, zoos, aquariums, and conservation subjects related to natural history. Lengths run 2,000 to 3,000 words. Prefers photos with manuscripts; photo rates are negotiated.

Environmental Quality Magazine, 6464 Canoga Ave., Woodland Hills, Calif., 91364. Editor Richard Cramer prefers queries, on in-depth studies of environmental subjects, whether describing beauty of an area, or the threat of its destruction from misuse. Uses color and black and white photos. Payment is on publication.

Frontiers, a Magazine of Natural History, Academy of Natural Sciences, 19th and the Parkway, Phila., Pa., 19103. Editor Mrs. Beverly Mowbray pays $30 to $50 for articles 1,000 to 2,000 words on science and nature, written for high school students and adult laymen. Prefers articles accompanied by half a dozen black and white photos or drawings.

The Living Wilderness, 729 15th St., N.W., Washington, D.C., 20005. Editor Michael Nadel buys articles on wilderness experiences, ecology, and other subjects of interest to members of the Wilderness Society. Sample copy sent on request, for $1. Prefers query. Lengths run 1,500 to 2,000 words.

National Wildlife, 534 N. Broadway, Milwaukee, Wisc., 53202. Editor John Strohm pays $50 and up per printed page for articles on all phases of outdoor recreation, wildlife, conservation. Query.

Natural History, 79th and Central Parkway W., New York, N.Y., 10024. Editor Alfred Meyer pays from $100 to $400 for articles 2,000 to 5,000 words on all phases of science and natural history, with emphasis on biological sciences. No chemistry or physics. Prefers articles by professional scientists. Query.

Oceans, 1150 Anchorage Lane, Suite 316, San Diego, Calif., 92106. Editor Joseph E. Brown pays 8 cents a word, on publication, for articles 3,000 to 5,000 words on sea travel, adventure on water, boating and exploration, aquatic sports, and management of oceanic resources. Prefers queries with outlines. Pays from $25 to $100 for black and white and color transparencies, $150 for color cover.

Organic Gardening and Farming, Organic Park, Emmaus, Pa., 18049. Editor Robert Rodale pays $35 to $100, on publication, for articles about 1,000 words on organic or natural concepts of agriculture, such as the use of natural fertilizer, avoidance of chemicals, poisons, etc. Free copy of magazine on request.

Pacific Discovery, California Academy of Sciences, Golden Gate Park, San Francisco, Calif., 94118. Editor Bruce Finson pays 5 cents a word for articles 1,500 to 3,000 words on the natural history of plants and animals, conservation, ecology, astronomy, and relationship between man and nature, particularly on the Pacific region. Prefers queries. Pays $10 and up per photo.

Prevention, Organic Park, Emmaus, Pa., 18049. Editor H.J. Taub pays $150 for articles, on acceptance, dealing with the healthful advantages of natural, unchemicalized nutrition. Also interested in articles on environment. Lengths run from 1,500 to 3,000 words. Prefers manuscripts accompanied by photos.

Water Land and Life, Western Pennsylvania Conservancy, 204 5th Ave., Pittsburgh, Pa., 15222. Editor Bruce Tibbo buys in-depth articles on all aspects of environment: water, air, noise pollution, waste disposal, pesticides, etc. Prefers reportorial, factual style.

World Wildlife Illustrated, World Wildlife Publishing Co., 1 Lincoln Ave., Holden, Maine, 01520. Editor Michael Ursin buys articles on conservation, wildlife understanding and appreciation, and color and black and white photos. Query.

Wyoming Wildlife, Box 1589, Cheyenne, Wy., 82001. Editor George Sura buys articles on Wyoming outdoor life and conservation.

Photography, Music, Art, and Theatre Markets

Many local publications, including Sunday feature pages and magazine supplements, run articles on the fine and lively arts with localized slants. They are good markets, especially for the writer who wants to build a national reputation in order to sell to the major markets.

Once again, the writer must know his field, because he will be selling to editors who are experts and writing for readers who may be just as knowledgeable.

The following publications specialize in the arts. Many of their editors are already buying from a stable of writers they can depend on. The new writer to these markets can sell if his idea or slant is new, and if it has authority.

After Dark, The Magazine of Entertainment, 268 W. 47th St., New York, N.Y., 10036. Editor William Como pays from $15 to $35 for articles covering the whole entertainment spectrum: films, theatre, television, dance, popular music, etc. Likes features on unusual new theatres or theatrical ventures anywhere in the U.S. Also buys personality stories. Pays $5 to $25 for photos, on publication.

American Artist, 165 W. 46th St., New York, N.Y., 10036. Editor Sterling McIlhany pays up to $100, on publication, for articles 1,500 to 2,500 words on artists and their techniques. Prefers query with outline.

Arts Magazine, 23 E. 26th St., New York, N.Y., 10010. Buys articles 1,000 to 2,000 words on art and architecture. Pays good rates, on publication.

Auction, 200 W. 57th St., New York, N.Y., 10019. Editor Linda Rosenkrantz pays 5 cents a word and up, on publication, for articles 1,000 to 3,000 words on the business of art auctions, including paintings, sculpture, antiques, books, etc. Query.

Camera 35, U.S. Camera Publishing Corp., 132 W. 31st St., New York, N.Y., 10001. Editor James Hughes pays $50 per printed page, $100 per page for color photos, on publication, for instructional articles about 35mm photography. Articles run 800 to 3,000 words.

Craft Horizons, 16 E. 52d St., New York, N.Y., 10022. Editor Rose Slivka buys articles on all aspects of arts, crafts, design, in all mediums. Payment varies. Query.

Creative Crafts Magazine, 31 Arch St., Ramsey, N.J., 17446. Managing Editor Sybil C. Harp buys illustrated how-to articles with photos, on handicrafts. Prefers articles in which the author himself has worked on the craft, rather than interviewing an artist. Payment varies, on publication.

Dance Magazine, 268 W. 47th St., New York, N.Y., 10036. Editor William Como buys articles on dance personalities, new or unique dance productions.

Dance Perspectives, 29 E. 9th St., New York, N.Y., 10003. Editor Selma Jeanne Cohen pays $150, on acceptance, for in-depth articles 15,000 to 20,000 words on historical or critical aspects of dance.

Exhibit, Box 23505, Fort Lauderdale, Fla., 33307. Editor Allen Willette pays 5 cents a word, on publication, for articles to 900 words on commercial and fine art. Uses how-to articles on art techniques, profiles on artists, and new ideas. Pays $5 per photo.

High Fidelity, Great Barrington, Mass., 01230. Editor Leonard Marcus pays good rates, on acceptance, for articles 2,500 to 3,000 words about music, recordings, tapes, and sound equipment for knowledgeable readers. Query.

Industrial Photography, 200 Madison Ave., New York, N.Y., 10016. Buys illustrated articles 500 to 1,500 words, for industrial photographers and executives. Prefers case histories with technical information. Pays good rates, on publication. Query.

Leica Photography, 15 Columbus Circle, New York, N.Y. 10019. Buys articles on 35mm photo techniques using Leica cameras and accessories, from 750 to 1,500 words. Pays on acceptance. Query.

Opera News, Metropolitan Opera Guild, 1865 Broadway, New York, N.Y., 10023. Editor Frank Merkling pays 8 cents a word and up for articles on the world of opera. Also uses humor and unusual associations between operatic writers and their subject. Lengths run 600 to 3,500 words.

Playbill, 3 E. 54th St., New York, N.Y., 10022. Editor Joan Rubin pays $100 to $300 for short, lively articles on theatre for sophisticated readers. Lengths run 800 to 2,300 words. Uses photos.

Popular Ceramics, 6011 Santa Monica Blvd., Los Angeles, Calif., 90038. Editor and publisher William Geisler buys instructional articles on ceramic hobbies, from 800 to 1,000 words. Uses photos. Rates vary.

Popular Photography, One Park Ave., New York, N.Y., 10016. Pays $75 and up for illustrated articles 500 to 2,000 words on subjects of interest to amateur photographers. Pays $10 for illustrated photo tips. Prefers queries with short outline and a few photos.

Revue des Beaux Arts, Box 23505, Fort Lauderdale, Fla., 33307. Editor Marie Stilkind pays 5 cents a word, on publication, for articles to 900 words, of interest to art lovers, including profiles of famous artists, and methods and techniques of art.

Stereo Quarterly, State Rd., Great Barrington, Mass., 01230. Pays 10 cents a word, on acceptance, for articles to 4,000 words on stereo music equipment. Query.

Education Markets

"Publish or perish" is still the unhappy way of it at many colleges and universities. Professors who publish articles in academic journals, or books if they're luckier, remain the faculty darlings from term to term. Those who don't publish regularly may find themselves sitting in a corner or out in the cold.

Elementary and high school teachers also can enjoy the success that publishing brings, especially if they are reporting favorably on new teaching methods at their school, thus bringing it national attention in educational circles.

Payment to educational publications is generally poor or none at all. Still, this should not deter educators from writing for these markets. The prestige of a by-lined article in these journals can push them up the ladder to academic success.

American School & University, 134 N. 13th St., Philadelphia, Pa., 18107. Editor Georgette Manla uses articles 1,200 to 1,500 words related to design, construction, maintenance, and other aspects of running a school and college. Usually no payment. Query.

American School Board Journal, National School Boards Assn., 1233 Central St., Evanston, Ill., 60201. Uses articles on problems of school administration. Query.

Athletic Journal, 1719 Howard St., Evanston, Ill., 60202. Editor John Griffith pays $20, on publication, for articles to 1,500 words, by coaches and athletic directors, describing interscholastic athletics. Uses photos.

Catholic School Journal, 22 W. Putnam Ave., Greenwich, Conn., 06830. Pays $20 per printed page for articles 500 to 2,000 words on educational projects and trends, for teachers and administrators in Catholic elementary and high schools.

Children's House, P.O. Box 111, Caldwell, N.J., 07006. Editor Margaret Clarke Torres uses articles about Montessori method of education. Lengths run 800 to 2,000 words, covering child development, trends in education for average, gifted, and handicapped children.

College Management, 22 W. Putnam Ave., Greenwich, Conn., 06830. Editor Campbell Geeslin pays various rates, on or before publication, for case histories of college management problems and their solutions. Query.

Educate, Gellert Publishing Corp., 33 W. 60th St., New York, N.Y., 10022. Pays $30 per printed page for articles on new trends in education, from pre-school through 12th grade. Lengths run 1,200 to 3,000 words. Query.

Forecast for Home Economics, 50 W. 44th St., New York, N.Y., 10036. Editor Eleanor Adams buys articles of interest to home economics teachers, by specialists in the field. Rates vary. Uses photos.

Industrial Arts and Vocational Education, 22 W. Putnam Ave., Greenwich, Conn., 06830. Editor John Feirer pays $10 to $15 per magazine page, on publication, for articles about administration and instruction for vocational, industrial arts, and technical education classes. Lengths run 1,000 to 2,000 words. Uses photos and drawings.

Nation's Schools, 1050 Merchandise Mart, Chicago, Ill., 60654. Articles on school administration, on assignment only.

HOW TO SELL TO SPECIAL INTEREST MARKETS

Scholastic Teacher, Scholastic Magazines, 50 W. 44th St., New York, N.Y., 10036. Editor Loretta Hunt Marion pays $40 to $150, on acceptance, for articles on trends and new methods in education, from 1,000 to 1,500 words.

School Management, 22 W. Putnam Ave., Greenwich, Conn., 06830. Editor James E. Doherty pays 5 cents a word and up, for articles on solutions to school management problems. Query.

Spectrum/International Journal of Religious Education, Room 724, 475 Riverside Dr., New York, N.Y., 10027. Editor Bert Tippit buys articles, photos, and news about new educational projects in churches, particularly ecumenical material. Payment varies. Query.

Today's Catholic Teacher, 38 W. 5th St., Dayton, Ohio, 45402. Editor Ruth Matheny pays $20 to $80, on acceptance, for articles of interest to Catholic elementary and high school teachers and administrators. Lengths run 600 to 800 words for shorts, and from 1,500 to 3,000 words for longer subjects. Sample copy on request.

Agriculture Markets

How are you going to keep them down on the farm, after they've sold to *Playboy*? Well, you probably won't. But if they, or you, haven't yet sold to the big markets, and your community is dotted with farms, why not pick up some extra money writing for the agricultural journals?

Here again, however, you are writing for a specialized market. If you don't know enough about farming, be sure you interview someone who can speak as an authority. Often, your local county agent will be willing to read your article, to confirm its authenticity.

Farm markets pay well, as a general rule. In addition to feature pages and Sunday supplements of local newspapers, these are the best agriculture markets:

American Agriculturalist-Rural New Yorker, Savings Bank Bldg., Ithaca, N.Y., 14850. Editor Gordon Conklin buys articles on farm topics in New York, New Jersey, northern Pennsylvania, and the New England states. Payment varies, on acceptance.

American Fruit Grower, Willoughby, Ohio, 44094. Pays 2 cents a word, on acceptance for articles to 750 words, on how a commercial fruit grower overcomes specific problems in production or marketing. Pays $3 and up per photo. Same requirements, rates, for *American*

Vegetable Grower.

Big Farmer, Big Farmer, Inc., 131 Lincoln Hwy., Frankfort, Ill., 60423. Editor Royal Fraedrich buys articles for and about high income commercial farmers. Lengths run to 1,500 words. Uses photos. Payment varies, on acceptance.

Business Farming, Box 4480, Monroe, La., 71201. Buys articles of interest to the commercial farmer in New Jersey, Delaware, Maryland, Virginia, and West Virginia. Uses photos. Payment varies, after publication. Query.

The Cattleman, 410 E. Weatherford, Fort Worth, Tex., 76102. Editor Paul W. Horn buys articles on cattle-raising. Payment varies, on publication.

The Farm Quarterly, 22 E. 12th St., Cincinnati, Ohio, 45210. Editor Bill Barksdale pays 10 cents a word for articles on practical farm subjects with human interest appeal. Lengths run 1,500 to 5,000 words. Buys photos.

Farm Supplier, Mt. Morris, Ill., 61504. Editor Ray Bates pays 7 cents a word, on acceptance, for articles and photos on selling and servicing feed, fertilizer, farm supplies, agricultural chemicals, etc., through retail farm trade outlets. Lengths run 600 to 1,200 words. Also buys articles on small business management subjects related to farm suppliers.

The Furrow, Deere & Co., John Deere Rd., Moline, Ill., 61265. Managing Editor George Sollenberger prefers to be queried for articles of interest to farmers. Pays good rates, on acceptance.

The Georgia Farmer, 476 Plasamour Dr., N.E., Atlanta, Ga., 30324. Editor Elmo Hester buys illustrated articles to 750 words, about Georgia farming and subjects of interest to Georgia farm families. Pays on publication.

The Kentucky Farmer, 1407 Laurel Ave., Bowling Green, Ky., 42101. Payment varies, on publication, for how-to farming articles about Kentucky farmers. Uses photos.

Nation's Agriculture, 1000 Merchandise Mart Plaza, Chicago, Ill., 60654. Editor Delmer Groves uses articles on farm production, management, and economics, for members of the American Farm Bureau Federation.

National Future Farmer, Box 15130, Alexandria, Va., 22309. Editor Wilson Carnes pays 4 cents a word, on acceptance, for features of interest to high school students of vocational agriculture, who are members of the Future Farmers of America. Likes success stories about members.

Organic Gardening and Farming, (see listing under Ecology-Conservation, earlier in this chapter).

Poultry Meat, The Magazine for the Broiler Business, Mt. Morris, Ill., 60105. Editor Rex Parsons pays up to 5 cents a word, on acceptance, for articles with photos, on broiler production, processing, and marketing.

Poultry Tribune, Mt. Morris, Ill., 61054. Editor Milton R. Dunk pays up to 5 cents a word, on acceptance, for features on egg production, processing, and marketing. Lengths run 200 to 1,000 words.

Successful Farming, 1716 Locust St., Des Moines, Iowa, 50303. Editor Dick Hanson buys articles on farm management, operation, and farm experience. Also helpful hints for farm shop. Pays various rates.

Wallaces Farmer, Des Moines, Iowa, 50305. Editor Alvin F. Bull pays 4 to 5 cents a word for articles on Iowa farming, including farming methods, equipment. Pays $7.50 to $15 per black and white photo, $50 to $100 for color.

The Wyoming Stockman Farmer, 110 E. 17th St., Cheyenne, Wyo., 82001. Editor Russell Fawcett buys articles on ranch and farm subjects, both current and historic, for readers in Wyoming, western Nebraska, and the Rocky Mountain area. Lengths run to 500 words. Uses black and white photos. Rates vary, on publication.

5

HOW TO SELL TO TRAVEL AND OUTDOOR MARKETS

"To freelancers imaginative enough to take advantage of every opportunity, writing for travel and outdoor markets is like taking a paid vacation."

James Joseph, one of the top travel writers in the business, says that with understandable conviction. He adds from $150 to $300 to his income regularly by taking "weekend vacations," selling his articles to a wide variety of markets. And he says any good writer can do the same.

Joseph, who lives in Los Angeles but travels the globe writing for *Family Weekly,* trade journals, camping and trailer magazines, and even has a medical book coming out soon, says he earns over $20,000 a year in travel and outdoor writing. Similar figures are banked annually by Richard Dunlop, Len Hilts, Pat Snook, and many others.

MULTIPLE ASSIGNMENTS

The secret of making the most of travel and outdoor writing is in lining up as many assignments as you can on the same or nearby areas. And if you can tie them in with a business trip, perhaps writing on a non-travel subject for another client, a richer one who may pay your expenses, so much the better.

James Joseph is a master at that. A good example of how he gets the most out of his trips is one he took to the Imperial Valley desert near Palm Springs, Calif. He wrote three unrelated stories for three different markets, earning a total of $750 while having himself an all-expenses-paid vacation. He wrote on hiking into the wilderness along a tramway for a diesel engine magazine, did a

HOW TO SELL TO TRAVEL AND OUTDOOR MARKETS 71

story on desert agriculture, and wrote a *Mechanix Illustrated* piece on a trout farm in the desert!

Of course, like many travel and outdoor writers, James Joseph makes himself doubly useful to editors and clients by taking his own photos (and adds about double to his sales). In these days of automatic cameras, there is really no reason why every writer should not take his own photos. Writers often double their sales and can even make subsequent sales with "stock photos" if they shoot several frames of the same subject. Advertising agencies will pay several hundred dollars for the right travel or outdoor color slide, while magazines and text book houses will pay from $50 to $250 per slide.

"Travel and outdoor writing is one of the best and most rewarding markets for freelancers," says Richard Dunlop, who besides being a very successful freelancer is national president of the Society of American Travel Writers (SATW). In one year, Dunlop travelled throughout the United States, to Russia, Bali, Australia, Canada, Finland, Greece, Mexico, and twice to Germany. He has been to fifty countries in his sixteen years of freelancing and knows how to stretch an assignment.

Dunlop says most SATW members earn at least $5,000 a year in travel writing alone, many make $20,000 and up, and one member banks $75,000.

Membership in the SATW is not necessary to become a successful freelancer in the travel field, but like the initials of a member of the Professional Photographers of America, it can be impressive when querying an editor. Membership is no easy matter, however. Two active members must co-sponsor you, and you must submit samples of your travel writing, then wait a year while you prove you are making a sufficient amount of your living by freelance travel writing. If this sounds like work, remember that membership and market information from the Society can open doors and help you to land assignments. (For more information about the Society, write the general secretary at 1146 16th St. N.W., Washington, D.C., 20036.)

"Travel and outdoor writing, like other specialities of freelancing, depends a great deal on knowing what to write and where to market it," says Len Hilts, of Hinsdale, Ill., who has been a writer for thirty years and knows the business from both sides of the desk as writer and editor.

I first met Hilts five years ago, when he was in charge of publications at a Chicago advertising agency and he hired me to edit a general feature trade magazine for Goodyear Tire and Rubber Company. Called *Progress Magazine*, a bimonthly with a 5 million circulation, it contained at least one travel article per issue. When Hilts left the agency to freelance, he asked me, almost tearfully, to be fair to the freelancer, "because it's a rough life and freelancers are people."

I've never forgotten that advice, and since I believe as an editor I have been fair to freelancers, and apparently Len feels I have been too, he offered me some advice to pass on to freelancers in general, but those writing travel in particular:

NEW SLANTS ON TRAVEL WRITING

"The 'cutting edge' in travel writing is *what is it*? What's the *angle*?" Hilts says. "You can have a very readable style, and know all about the city or area you're writing about, but you've got to have an angle!"

Later, as associate editor of *Discovery*, travel magazine of the Allstate Motor Club, I learned how true that advice was.

"Most editors don't want *another* story about Atlanta," Len says. "But they *will* buy a story about *Underground* Atlanta (a restored turn-of-the-century neighborhood). They don't want *another* story about Virginia, but they *will* buy a story on the *caves* around Harrisonburg." (Don't write about them; Len is.)

Another tip Hilts gives freelancers is: "Specialize. Get to know your field."

He is an expert at doing profiles of cities. Today he can arrive at a city he's never been in before and after three days can write as comprehensive a profile as if he was a native. But his first time out profiling a city, Len said it took him three weeks! Now he knows how to do his preliminary groundwork, line up contacts, do prior reading and research, and to look for new angles in an otherwise old story. His new guide book on Canada ought to make interesting reading.

REWRITE AND RESUBMIT

Another tip I've learned is, never let a story die. I once sold an article on Little Norway, a restored 19th century Norwegian farm settlement in Wisconsin, to two midwest newspaper Sunday travel supplements and struck out on selling a rewrite of it to the sophisticated *New York Times*. I put the story in my file cabinet and forgot about it until two years later, when I read that the *New York Times* had a new travel editor. This one liked human interest travel stories, so I rewrote the Little Norway article emphasizing the people who had lived in the settlement, and sold it (along with some 8 x 10 black and white photos I took) for another $195. So dusting off a story once sold, and polishing it up with a new slant, can earn you extra sales.

Pat Snook, another Midwestern writer, specializes in outdoor subjects. He's a camper, wilderness canoer, aficionado of snowmobiling, and admittedly doesn't work as hard at freelancing as he could. Yet he attributes over $20,000 of his annual income to travel and outdoor writing. He prefers adventure, told in the first-person, accounts of his own dare-deviling. Or, as in the case of a very popular two-part article for *National Wildlife*, his and his wife's dare-deviling. In that article Mr. and Mrs. Snook recounted a man-and-wife two-week survival trip on the Apostle Islands off Wisconsin's Lake Superior.

Snook, who also takes his own pictures, has lived with a Lapland family and hunted polar bears north of Russia. But even for him, it isn't all just adventure. He knows that to make a trip pay, he has to think of how many articles he can write from one location and how many assignments he can get in advance of a trip.

If you're content to earn $25 to $150 for a weekend "vacation," sold to a Sunday travel section of a newspaper or one of the controlled-circulation magazines, fine. That isn't hard to take any weekend. But if you want to double or triple that, you'll line up more than one assignment in advance of your trip.

Perhaps you know you can sell a travel article about Hudson's Bay to your local newspaper travel editor. But, with a little imagination and planning, you may also be able to sell an article on the history and present operation of the Hudson's Bay Company to a trade journal specializing in retail store management. And maybe another article on how a local northwoods Indian tribe is managing to survive (or not managing to survive) in the Hudson's Bay area. And perhaps another article on a conservation theme to magazines hungry today for stories on ecology.

With a little planning and letter-writing, you might line up half a dozen stories to do while you're wandering through God's Country, having yourself the vacation of a lifetime. And if the clients can't pay your way, you can always claim travel and living deductions on your income tax, as business expenses.

Yes, travel and outdoor writing *can* be like taking a paid vacation *if* you look for a new angle, *if* you study your markets, and *if* you can line up more than one assignment. That is what makes the difference between a weekend writer, who is content to pick up an occasional extra $150, and the professional who takes advantage of every opportunity to double, triple, or sextuple his income from one trip. That fellow who banks $75,000 a year from travel writing alone plans his trips well, you can bet on that!

Travel Magazines and General Travel Markets

National travel magazines have undergone major changes in recent years. Some, like *Venture,* have folded, while others have changed size and format. There are still plenty of sales for travel freelancers, but the market has changed and doubtlessly will continue to change. It is always best to study the big national magazines carefully to see what they are using and what direction they are going.

The big five in the travel field are:

Holiday, published by the Ser Vass family at 1100 Waterway Blvd., Indianapolis, Ind., 46202. Issued monthly except for combined issues Dec.-Jan., May-June, and July-Aug. Editor and publisher Beurt SerVass is buying a variety of domestic and foreign travel articles from 1,500 to 3,000 words, but mostly from regular contributors or well-known travel writers. Rates are among the best in the business. Extensive color photography is used. Query first.

National Geographic, 17th and M Sts., N.W., Washington, D.C., 20036. More than half of the articles used are by non-staff members, but you must know your subject and write convincingly. Editor Gilbert M. Grosvenor prefers first-person narratives with an emphasis on human interest, direct quotations, and humor when appropriate. Major articles run to 8,000 words, while shorts are from 2,000 to 4,000. Rates are from $1,500 to $3,000 and up. Minimum payment for color transparencies is $50 per slide and $200 per page. Unsolicited material is welcomed, but queries are preferred, with a generous selection of slides and brief descriptive captions and one to two pages of synopsis about the proposed article. Article ideas and manuscripts should be sent to Assistant Editor James Cerruti.

New York Times Travel Section, Times Square, New York, N.Y., 10036. Editor Al Marlens prefers queries in the form of a brief description of the subject and the article approach. He is interested in lively, anecdotal writing in the magazine style that puts the reader "in the scene." Use humor, personal reactions, conversation, and quotes to bring a story alive. Articles should be on a particular subject such as St. Thomas, rather than one on the Virgin Islands. Length runs from 750 to 2,500 words. Payment varies but averages about 10 cents a word, on acceptance. Minimum photo payment is $35 per picture. Authors should include data on when they visited the place they are writing about, to assure timeliness. Writers new to the *New York Times* travel section should include samples of their published works.

Travel, Travel Bldg., Floral Park, N.Y., 11001. Editor Malcolm McTear Davis buys personal experience travel articles only. New approaches are sought on places to visit, what to see and do, with costs and expenses included where possible. Current needs are especially for off-beat areas in the United States or abroad. Photos should accompany manuscript, if possible. Article lengths run from 1,000 to 3,000 words, with 2,500 preferred. Payment is from $50 to $100 on acceptance, including black and white photos; up to $250 with color transparencies.

Travel and Leisure, 132 W. 31st St., New York, N.Y., 10001. (Formerly *Travel & Camera* magazine.) Caskie Stinnett, editor-in-chief, intends the magazine to be for people who really travel and can afford to live "the good life." Published bimonthly for the three million United States and Canadian holders of American Express Money Cards, the magazine also is sold on newsstands and by subscription. Content is sophisticated, worldly, and stylish. Manuscripts and queries will be read, but most articles will be assigned to established freelance writers and photographers. Articles run from 2,500 to 3,000 words. Payment for short articles is $500; major article as high as $4,000. Usual rate of pay for 2,500-word article is about $1,500.

Other magazines using one or more travel or outdoor articles per issue are:

Chicago Tribune Travel Section, Tribune Tower, Chicago, Ill., 60611. Editor Kermit Holt buys descriptive travel articles from 800 to 1,200 words, with black and white photos. Payment is $35 for inside articles, $60 to $75 for page one article. Photo payment is $5 inside; $10 on page one; $50 for page one color, on publication.

Cosmopolitan, 1775 Broadway, New York, N.Y., 10019. Editor Helen Gurley Brown prefers first-person narratives about places single girls can vacation. Candid 35mm photos should accompany article. Length: 2,000 to 2,500 words. Payment varies but rates are good. Query Roberta Ashley, articles editor.

Friends, 4-213 General Motors Bldg., Detroit, Mich., 48202. Editor Alexander Suczek uses articles on travel, with route and recreation information. Query first with outline and photo descriptions and for information sheet on submitting freelance material. Pays $75 a page up to $150, including photos.

Kiwanis Magazine, 101 E. Erie St., Chicago, Ill., 60611. Human interest travel features bought by Editor Dennis Moore. Payment is $250 to $500 for articles of 2,000 to 4,000 words.

Posh, 712 Steiner St., San Francisco, Calif., 94117. Editor Ernest Beyl buys sophisticated, off-beat travel articles of from 1,000 to 5,000 words, with photos. Payment varies, on publication.

Signature Magazine, 660 Madison Ave., New York, N.Y., 10021. Editor Kenneth Gould Thorpe and Articles Editor Norman Smith produce this magazine for the Diners Club. Travel articles should include the culture, economy, politics, and people of a place, along with information on food, fashions, accomodations, and art. Maximum length, 2,500 words; minimum payment, $600.

Today's Health, 535 N. Dearborn St., Chicago, Ill., 60610. Editor Byron Scott likes clear, concise, thorough writing. Travel articles with health slant receive most attention. Length from 1,000 to 2,500 words. Payment up to $600.

Motor Club, Auto Markets

Canadian Motorist, 2 Carlton St., Toronto 102, Ontario, Canada, Editor George Ostermann buys travel articles on Canada, the U.S., and abroad. Lengths from 1,000 to 1,500. Payment is 5 cents a word for articles; $7.50 for black-and-white photos, $35 for color transparencies.

The Continental Magazine, Room 950, Central Office Bldg., Ford Motor Company, Dearborn, Mich., 48121. Editor Robert M. Hodesh buys service articles on travel and sport for the well-to-do. Length: 1,300-1,700 words. Payment varies, on acceptance. Query first.

Discovery Magazine, Allstate Motor Club, Allstate Plaza, Northbrook, Ill., 60062. Editor David L. Watt uses about six travel articles per quarterly issue, almost entirely from freelancers. Prefers first-person narratives with human interest side of travel. Use of the family car on weekend or longer vacations should be emphasized. Payment varies from $150 to $300 for articles from 1,000 to 3,000 words. Quality photography considered, both black-and-white and color. Payment on acceptance.

Dodge News Magazine, 5435 W. Fort St., Detroit, Mich., 48209. Editor William Hinds buys travel articles to 2,200 words of special interest to young adult readers. Pays top rates. Query.

Ford Times, Ford Motor Co., The American Road, Dearborn, Mich., 48121. Managing Editor Hal Butler is interested in articles of 1,500 words or less, on recreation and travel related to auto ownership and little-known places to visit. Slant should be to interest young adults, 25 to 35 years of age. Pays 10 cents a word and up, on acceptance. Query preferred.

Minnesota AAA Motorist, 7 Traveler's Trail, Burnsville, Minn., 55378. Managing Editor Ron D. Johnson buys articles of 800 to 1,500 words on domestic and foreign travel. Pays $150 and up, on acceptance; $10 and up for photos.

Motor News, 150 Bagley Ave., Detroit, Mich., 48226. Buys articles on American tourist objectives with information on cost, tips on what to see and what to avoid. Especially interested in articles about Michigan. Length, 800 to 2,000 words. Pays $70 and up, on acceptance.

National Motorist, 65 Battery St., San Francisco, Calif., 94111. Editor Jim Donaldson buys articles from 500 to 1,500 words for the California motorist and motoring in the western states. Also interesting people and places in the West and motor travel stories, outdoor features. Pays 10 cents a word, $10 and up for black-and-white photos, on acceptance.

In-Flight Magazine Markets

Aloft, 4025 Ponce de Leon Blvd., Coral Gables, Fla., 33146. Editor Karl Y. Wickstrom buys travel articles giving fresh approaches to cities along the route of National Airlines. Articles on off-beat places to go and sports to see run about 1,300 words. Payment is $150 to $200. Query first.

Braniff International Magazine, 300 E. 42d St., New York, N.Y., 10017. Editor Barbara Johnson uses "jet-set" travel articles from 750 to 1,750 words, on Braniff destination-cities in North and South America. Study issues first (obtainable at any Braniff ticket office) for style and trends. Pays about $150 for articles, separate for photos. Query first.

Flightime, 3540 Wilshire Blvd., Suite 503, Los Angeles, Calif., 90005. Bill Simar edits this magazine for Pacific Southwest Airlines and also *Yellowbird* for Northeast Airlines. He buys articles of interest to Continental Airlines passengers in flight. Payment varies, on publication.

Mainliner, United Air Lines, P.O. Box 66100, Chicago, Ill., 60666. Uses travel articles from 800 to 1,800 words; pays $250 and up; $75 and up per color photo. Query first.

Mohawk Airlines Gateway Magazine, Anderson, Davis, & Seeds, Inc., First National Bank Bldg., Utica, N.Y., 13501. Editor Derek E. Sparks uses articles on travel, recreation, and sports, all aimed at business and professional people. Articles should be on northeast cities and seasonal attractions. Pays from $50 to $100 for articles up to 2,000 words, on acceptance.

TWA Ambassador, 1999 Shephard Rd., St. Paul, Minn., 55116. Editor Roy J. Dunlap buys travel, humor, and personality articles from 1,500 to 2,000 words. Pays $150 to $500 on acceptance. Queries preferred. Editorial fact sheet sent on request.

Outdoor Markets

For outdoor markets, including travel, camping, trailer and mobile home living, hunting, fishing, etc., be sure to also review the markets elsewhere in this book. Especially check on men's magazines, city and regional magazines, Sunday supplements, and book publishers who produce travel and recreation guides. Major markets listed below pay from 2 to 10 cents a word and up. Lesser markets were not selected.

American Forests, 919 17th St., N.W., Washington, D.C., 20006. Editor James B. Craig buys articles on environmental needs, how to take camping trailer vacations, horseback trips, hiking, and other outdoor subjects. Payment is from 3 to 5 cents a word, on publication, for articles to 1,800 words.

Archery World, 534 N. Broadway, Milwaukee, Wisc., 53202. Editor Glen Helgeland pays good rates for articles 1,000 to 3,000 words on all aspects of archery, for hunters and competitive shooters. Pays on acceptance.

Argosy, 205 E. 42d St., New York, N.Y., 10017. Editor Milt Machlin buys first-person adventure articles of interest to men. Outdoor

HOW TO SELL TO TRAVEL AND OUTDOOR MARKETS 79

action articles especially needed. Payment is from $400 to $750, extra for photos, two weeks after acceptance.

Arizona Highways, 2039 W. lewis Ave., Phoenix, Ariz., 85009. Editor Raymond Carlson prefers articles of a specific place rather than a general area. Rarely buys stories on events such as rodeos, art shows. Pays from 5 to 10 cents a word for articles about 2,500 words. Subjects should be in Arizona and the Southwest. Query first.

Arizona Wildlife Sportsman Magazine, 1103 N. Central, Phoenix, Ariz., 85004. Uses features about outdoor Arizona and the Southwest. Payment is on publication. Rates vary.

Better Camping, 500 Hyacinth Pl., Highland Park, Ill., 60035. Editor Katie McMullen uses articles on camping, tent trips, camping trailers, and all camping vehicles. Travel articles must include information on campgrounds. Payment is 4 cents a word, on acceptance. Query first. Writer's fact sheet sent on request.

Bon Voyage, 4700 Belleview, Kansas City, Mo., 64112. Managing editor Jane Rosenthal buys articles on world travel for the sophisticated traveler. Prefers color transparencies to accompany a query letter with outline and sample of writer's style.

Camper Coachman, 10148 Riverside Dr., North Hollywood, Calif., 91602. Editor Bill Estes wants articles to 1,500 words on camping coaches hauled on light trucks. He also uses travel, human interest, and how-to-do articles related to camping. Photos should accompany manuscript. Pays from $50 to $125, on publication.

Camping Guide, 319 Miller Ave., Mill Valley, Calif., 94941. Editor George S. Wells buys articles on practical aspects of family camping and trailering. Prefers first-person accounts. Also how-to articles and accounts of boating and wilderness trips. Payment is $25 for shorts, $40 and up for longer features.

Camping Journal, also *Camping Yearbook* and *Hunting Guide,* 229 Park Ave. S., New York, N.Y., 10003. Editor-in-Chief Fred Sturges buys camping articles with a strong element of adventure, including hunting and fishing. Articles should include information on routes, campsites, facilities, etc. Also buys articles on camping skills. Payment for articles from 2,500 to 3,000 words is $100 and up, on acceptance. Send manuscripts and slides or black and white photos to Managing Editor Kenneth G. Grant, who suggests writers study recent issues before submitting.

Desert Magazine, Palm Desert, Calif., 92260. Editor Jack Pepper buys illustrated articles about the West, including travel. Payment is 2 cents a word, on publication, for stories from 500 to 2,500 words. Pays $5 and up for photos.

The Eagle Magazine, 2401 W. Wisconsin Ave., Milwaukee, Wisc., 53233. Editor Arthur S. Ehrmann buys sports, outdoor life, and travel features. Pays 5 cents a word, $5 per photo, on acceptance.

European's Guide to Camping North America, 319 Miller Ave., Mill Valley, Calif., 94941. Editors of this new annual publication are buying family camping articles about camping in Europe, the U.S., Canada, and Alaska. Prefers queries with outline of camping and writing experience and availability of photos.

Field and Stream, 383 Madison Ave., New York, N.Y., 10017. Editor Jack Samson fills his pages with a wide range of articles on hunting, fishing, camping, travel, nature, flying, sky diving, snowmobiling, cooking, workshop, and other outdoor subjects. Samson emphasizes that the magazine is an outdoor service publication, so features should contain a lot of helpful information that is either new or has a new approach. Prefers queries rather than completed manuscripts. Articles run about 2,500 words, and payment is 16 cents a word, on acceptance, to beginning authors. Rates increase for frequent contributors. If photos are purchased with article, payment rates are $25 for black-and-white, $25 to $100 for color.

Fish and Game Sportsman, P.O. Box 1654, Regina, Sask., Canada. Editor Red Wilkinson pays from $40 to $100, on publication, for articles to 2,000 words on fishing, hunting, camping, and outdoor trips in Alberta and Saskatchewan.

Fishing World, 21 Vernon St., Floral Park, N.Y., 11001. Editor Keith Gardner buys articles for sports fisherman, told in the first person. Stories should run from 2,500 to 3,000 words, on outstanding fishing experiences, including information on methods and tackle, in both fresh and salt waters. Payment is from $150 to $200.

Florida and Tropic Sportsman, 4025 Ponce de Leon Blvd., Coral Gables, Fla., 33146. Articles wanted from 800 to 1,500 words on outdoor sports in Florida and the Islands. Payment is from $50 to $100, on publication.

Motor Coach Travel, 319 Miller Ave., Mill Valley, Calif., 94941. Editor Bill Shepard buys articles from 1,500 to 2,000 words on travel with motor homes, truck and van campers, houseboats, and technical articles. Payment is $50 and up, on acceptance.

Motor Home Life, 10148 Riverside Dr., Toluca Lake, N. Hollywood, Calif., 91602. Editor Art Rouse buys articles to 2,000 words about motor homes, including how-to-do articles. Payment is from $50 to $150, on publication.

National Mobile Home Journal, 1815 E. Minnezona, Phoenix, Ariz., 84016. Editor Ron Aleamoni buys articles on mobile living. Payment is from 3 to 4 cents a word, on publication.

HOW TO SELL TO TRAVEL AND OUTDOOR MARKETS

National Police Gazette, 520 Fifth Ave., New York, N.Y., 10036. Editor Nat K. Perlow pays 5 to 10 cents a word, on publication, for sports, male adventure stories, fishing and hunting experiences. Articles run from 1,500 to 2,000 words. Query first..

National Wildlife, 534 N. Broadway, Milwaukee, Wisc., 53202. Also *International Wildlife.* Query editors first, with articles on wildlife, conservation, and recreation. Payment is $25 to $100 per magazine page; $35 and up for color photos.

Natural History Magazine, Central Park West at 79th St., New York, N.Y., 10024. Editor Alfred Meyer buys articles and photography in the natural sciences, geology, anthropology, astronomy, and environment. Payment is up to $600 for stories 4,000 words in length, well-researched by authorities. Pays $75 a page for color, $100 for cover photos.

Northeast Outdoors, 90 Church St., Naugatuck, Conn., 06770. Editor Ira Bartfeld buys camping, hunting, fishing, skiing, conservation, recreation, travel, nature, and other outdoor articles printed in newspaper format for readers in the northeastern states. Payment varies, on publication, $25 and up.

Northliner and *Best Western Way* magazines, 1999 Shepard Rd., St. Paul, Minn., 55116. Two new quarterly controlled-circulation magazines edited by Don Picard. *Northliner* is the in-flight magazine for North Central Airlines, and *Best Western Way* is distributed in Best Western Motel rooms in the U.S., Canada, and Mexico. Both use 1,000 to 2,000 word articles on travel, business, and personalities. Specific subjects preferred rather than city profiles or general areas. Payment is from $50 to $400, on acceptance. Query first.

Outdoor Life, 355 Lexington Ave., New York, N.Y., 10017. Editor William E. Rae wants hunting and fishing, camping, firearms, motorboats, woodcraft articles from 3,500 to 4,500 words. Prefers a combination of how-to and personal experience. Also uses picture stories with short captions. Pays $350 and up, on acceptance.

Outdoor World, 1645 Tullie Circle, N.E., Atlanta, Ga., 30329. Editor Ernest Booth buys articles on wildlife, outdoor activities associated with nature, conservation, ecology. Prefers outline and photos with article. Payment is $125 for articles 1,200 to 2,500 words.

Outdoors, Outdoors Bldg., Columbia, Mo., 65201. Editor Lee Cullimore wants recreational articles with emphasis on boating. Manuscripts to 1,200 words. Payment is $75 to $100, on acceptance.

Pacific Discovery, California Academy of Sciences, Golden Gate Park, San Francisco, Calif., 94118. Editor Bruce Finson buys natural history articles from 1,500 to 3,200 words and pays 5 cents a word and

$10 a picture, on publication. Articles are read by scientists and well-informed laymen. Query first.

Points, 465 W. Milwaukee, Detroit, Mich., 48202. Pays from $100 to $400 for articles and photos on travel, sports, and hobbies. Lengths run 700 to 900 words. Stories must be accompanied by color transparencies. Query first.

Popular Science, 355 Lexington Ave., New York, N.Y., 10017. Editors want consumer-aimed articles on products for the home, yard, car, boat, workshop, and outdoor recreation. Good market for picture stories and short features, as well as full-length articles. Complete package wanted: article and illustrations, black-and-white only. Payment on publication. Queries welcome.

Publication Management Newsletter, 5 Mountain Ave., North Plainfield, N.J., 07060. New trade book publishing division is in the market for book-length manuscripts on camping and outdoor subjects. Director Bill Henderson is especially interested in nature subjects, conservation, and ecology. Payment by standard royalty rates or an outright fee. Query first.

Quest Magazine, 527 Madison Ave., New York, N.Y., 10022. Feature Editor Andrew Ettinger says most of the magazine is written by its own regular contributors, but freelance material is considered in the travel field. *Quest* is read by well-educated families of more than $15,000 income. Pays $200, on publication, for articles up to 1,000 words. Query first.

Saga, 333 Johnson Ave., Brooklyn, N.Y., 11206. Editor Martin M. Singer wants first-person adventure features from 4,000 to 5,000 words. In-depth articles on sports personalities or aspects of a game. Also hunting and fishing, especially big game here or abroad. Photos should be sent with manuscript. Pays from $250 up, with bonus for exceptional articles.

Scouting Magazine, Boy Scouts of America, North Brunswick, N.J., 08902. Editor Walter Babson buys articles on outdoor activities of Scouting, unit conversation projects, family camping. Pays $50 to $100 per magazine page, on publication. Articles should be aimed at adult leaders of Scouts. Query first.

Sports Afield, 250 W. 55th St., New York, N.Y., 10019. Executive Editor Norbert Darga buys articles on fishing, hunting, camping, small boats, and guns, but they must be written with authority. Most contributors are experts in their fields. How-to and personal experience stories welcomed. Photos must accompany manuscripts. Similar articles also needed for *Sports Afield Fishing Annual* and *Hunting Annual.* Pays $400 and up for 3,000-word articles.

HOW TO SELL TO TRAVEL AND OUTDOOR MARKETS

Trailer Life, 10148 Riverside Dr., N. Hollywood, Calif., 91602. Editor Arthur J. Rouse buys articles to 1,500 words on trailering, truck campers, motor homes, and pays up to $150, on publication. Photos should accompany manuscripts. Send for editorial fact sheet.

Vacations Unlimited, 112 N. University Dr., Fargo, N.D., 58102. Editor Leslie Watson pays $50 for articles 1,000 to 1,500 words long, first-person accounts of outdoor experiences. Subjects can be on sports, vacation, travel, recreation, camping, and recreational vehicle experiences. Uses color transparencies.

Western Gateways, Box 269, Palm Desert, Calif., 92260. Editor Walt Arendale pays 3 to 6 cents a word for 1,000 to 2,000 word articles on Arizona, Colorado, New Mexico, and Utah, emphasizing interesting places and people. Prefers photos with articles. Query first.

Westways, 2601 S. Figueroa St., Los Angeles, Calif., 90054. Editor Larry L. Meyer pays 10 cents a word, on acceptance, for articles 700 to 2,500 words, on western U.S., Canada, Mexico. Primarily wants activities in those locales, but also uses natural science, travel, history. Query first.

Sports and Recreation Markets

Many of the above markets also use sports articles, if they are about the sport and not the player. Those markets that follow are interested in both sport and player, and the list includes many recreational activities and hobbies.

Aero Magazine, 499 E. Rowland Ave., Suite 455, Covina, Calif., 91722. Editor Marvin Patchen pays from $25 to $50 per printed page for articles on aircraft ownership, from single engine to light business jet and general aviation aircraft. Query first.

American Field, 222 W. Adams St., Chicago, Ill., 60606. Editor William F. Brown buys first-person accounts of hunting trips and upland bird-shooting experiences. Also short articles to 1,500 words on breeding and training hunting dogs and pointer and setter field trials. Major articles run to 3,500 words. Also buys articles on conservation of game resources and restoration of game and preserves. Payment varies, on acceptance.

Bow and Arrow, 116 E. Badillo, Covina, Calif., 91722. Editorial Director Jack Lewis pays up to $125 for 1,500 to 2,500 words on bowhunting, target archery, do-it-yourself activities, and historic subjects. Query first.

Bowling, 1572 E. Capitol Dr., Milwaukee, Wisc., 53211. Editor

Stephen K. James pays 3 to 5 cents a word for articles to 1,000 words on bowling, especially league or tournament bowling in ABC competition. Pictures necessary with manuscript. Query.

Country Club News, Box 1533, Harrisburg, Pa., 17103. Editor Mrs. Elsie Deller pays 5 cents a word, on publication, for articles aimed at affluent, well-traveled and sports-minded people of the country club set. Articles may be on golf, sports, travel, leisure activities.

Dog Fancy and *Cat Fancy,* 3 W. 57th St., New York, N.Y., 10019. Editors want articles for dog and cat lovers, aimed at health, grooming, and care. Pays 3 cents a word, on publication.

Golf Digest, 88 Scriber Ave., Norwalk, Conn., 06856. Editor Dick Aultman pays up to 25 cents a word (15 cents minimum), for features on prominent and unusual golfers or events. Also uses historical golf articles. Up to 3,000 words.

Golf Magazine, 235 E. 45th St., New York, N.Y., 10017. Editor Ross Goodner pays $50 to $150 for short articles and up to $350 for full-length articles on golf, personalities, special events, instruction. Query first.

Gun Digest and *Handloader's Digest,* 20604 Collins Rd., Marengo, Ill., 60152. Editor John T. Amber pays 4 to 10 cents a word for articles up to 5,000 on guns and other shooting equipment. Query.

Guns, 8150 N. Central Park Blvd., Skokie, Ill., 60076. Editor J. Rakusan buys articles from 1,500 to 2,500 words, on shooting for target, self-defense, hunting, and military. Also history and design of firearms and tips to owners of guns. Wants good photos or illustrations. Pays 5 cents a word, on publication. Query.

Guns and Ammo, 8490 Sunset Blvd., Los Angeles, Calif., 90069. Editor George Martin pays up to $50 for articles from 1,500 to 2,000 words, of technical nature, on guns and ammunition, target shooting, gunsmithing. Photos should accompany manuscript and be well-captioned.

Gunsport, Box 116, Hughesville, Md., 20601. Pays up to $125 for illustrated articles on new sports equipment related to guns, scopes, etc., on publication.

Hockey Times, Box 547, Lexington, Mass., 02173. Editor J. Robert Sherman wants brief features and articles on hockey; its players and managers, principally in New England. Youth and women's articles welcome. Payment varies, on publication.

Horseman, 5314 Bingle Rd., Houston, Tex., 77018. Editor Bob Gray pays 3 cents a word for in-depth articles of 500 to 3,000 words for owners, trainers, and breeders of race horses. Payment varies.

Mechanix Illustrated, 1140 Avenue of the Americas, New York, N.Y., 10036. Editor Robert G. Beason pays up to $500 for articles of interest to male readers, such as new inventions, recreational vehicles, transportation, hunting, fishing, mobile homes. Query is essential.

National Sportman's Digest, 4229 N. Central Freeway, Dallas, Tex., 75221. Pays up to $125, after publication, for articles on big game hunting in North America, emphasizing good sportsmanship and conversation. Uses color and black-and-white photos.

Private Pilot, 641 Lexington Ave., New York, N.Y., 10022. Editor Leslie Smith pays $150 and up, on publication, for articles of 2,500 words on light-plane flying.

Pro Football Guide, 20 E. 53d St., New York, N.Y., 10022. Pays $50, on publication, for articles and human interest features on professional football players and teams. Maximum length 1,000 words.

Railroad Magazine, 205 E. 42d St., New York, N.Y., 10017. Editor Freeman Hubbard pays 5 cents a word for articles to 3,000 words, on aspects of railroading. Features should combine technical information with human interest slant. Query first.

Rx Sports and Travel, 200 S. Main St., Hillsboro, Ill., 62049. Controlled circulation magazine for physicians. Editor Tom D. Harris pays from $25 to $300 for articles 1,500 to 3,000 words, on sports and travel with a medical doctor involved. Uses profiles on physicians with unusual sports achievements. Prefers queries.

Shooting Times, News Plaza, Peoria, Ill., 61601. Editor R.A. Steindler buys articles from 2,000 to 2,500 words in length, on guns and pistols, hunting and shooting. Pictures should accompany manuscript. Pays on acceptance; rates vary. Query.

Ski Magazine, Universal Publishing and Distributing Corp., 235 E. 45th St., New York, N.Y., 10017. Editor John Fry wants articles on skiing, illustrated with photos or drawings. Query.

Skiing Magazine, Ziff-Davis Publishing Co., One Park Ave., New York, N.Y., 10016. Editor Al Greenberg pays from $100 to $500 for articles 1,000 to 3,000 long, on travel, personality profiles of skiiers, humor, history, technique. Query.

Sport, 205 E. 42d St., New York, N.Y., 10019. Editor Fred Katz pays $200 to $750, on acceptance, for articles about top sports figures. Prefers human iterest and controversy. Query.

Sportfishing, Yachting Publishing Corp., Room 600, 50 W. 44th St., New York, N.Y., 10036. Executive Editor Frank T. Moss pays up to 10 cents a word for articles about salt and fresh water fishing, including how-to, new or little-used fishing areas, tackle and equipment, conservation, fishing profiles. Query.

Sport Digest, Suite 1706, 999 S. Bayshore Dr., Miami, Fla., 33131. Executive Editor Douglas Lang pays from $110 to $140 for articles from 1,300 to 1,900 words, with illustrations, that entertain and inform fans of both amateur and professional sports. Prefers articles on well-known sports figures and events. Also buys articles on conservation, recreation, health. All material should be for family reading, though subjects may be controversial. Also publishes reprints of articles from smaller magazines. Prefers completed manuscript to a query.

Sports Illustrated, Time & Life Bldg., Rockefeller Center, New York, N.Y., 10020. Articles Editor Ray Cave pays from $250 to $750 and up for articles on sports, major sports figures, personal reminiscence of sports, etc. Pays top rates for color sports and outdoor photography. Emphasis is on timely sports happenings. Accepts articles, outlines, or queries.

Surfer Magazine, Box 1028, Dana Point, Calif., 92629. Editor John Severson uses articles on surfing anywhere in the world, from 500 to 3,000 words. Color and black-and-white photos can be sent with or without articles.

True, 1 Astor Plaza, New York, N.Y., 10003. Executive editor Melvin Shestak pays $500 to $2,000 for articles on sports, personality profiles, adventure. Likes lively prose with anecdotes. Prefers queries, sent to James H. Endsley, associate editor. Roger Hall pays $150 for cartoons. Also publishers of *True's Fishing Yearbook* (fishing spots, trips, techniques, personal experiences) and *True's Hunting Yearbook* (same aspects of hunting). Peter Barrett edits both. Send queries, with outlines and photos. Payment is $300.

Woman/Golfer, 131 Lincoln Hwy., Frankfort, Ill., 60423. Editor Len Richardson pays 10 cents a word and up, on acceptance, for articles of interest to women golfers.

Car and Motorcycle Markets

Auto and motorcycle racing markets are lucrative ones, for those who know their subject. Besides sales to Sunday Supplements, men's, and outdoor markets, there are these leaders in the field:

Auto Racing, 211 W. 58th St., New York, N.Y., 10019. Editor Lyle Kenyon Engel prefers queries from writers who know about cars and have had features published on them. The same is true for photographers. Payment varies, but rates are good.

Car and Driver, One Park Ave., New York, N.Y., 10016. Editor Gordon Jennings pays up to $500 for articles of interest to well-informed auto enthusiasts. Articles, to 2,500 words, can be on new

HOW TO SELL TO TRAVEL AND OUTDOOR MARKETS

developments in autos, safety, top designers, what's new in Detroit, and what foreign manufacturers are doing.

Car Craft, 8490 Sunset Blvd., Los Angeles, Calif., 90069. Editor Sal Fish pays $50 a page and up, on acceptance, for illustrated features on hot rods, drag cars, events. Especially likes color drag race action photos. Query first.

Cars, 1560 Broadway, New York, N.Y., 10036. Editor Martyn L. Schorr pays from $40 to $75 a page for articles emphasizing the technical aspects of cars, with black-and-white or color photos. Query.

Cycle, Ziff-Davis Publishing Co., 1 Park Ave., New York, N.Y., 10016. Editor Sally Wimer buys quality articles to 3,000 words, on motorcycling. Payment is up to $250.

Cycle World, 1499 Monrovia Ave., Newport Beach, Calif., 92663. Editor Ivan Wagar pays 5 to 10 cents a word for technical articles of interest to motorcycle owners. Query.

Enthusiast, Harley-Davidson Motor Co., P.O. Box 653, Milwaukee, Wisc., 53201. Editor Barry Hammel pays 5 cents a word for articles to 2,000 words on motorcycle racing, tours, etc., featuring Harley-Davidson motorcycles. Pays up to $15 per photo.

Hot Rod, 8490 Sunset Blvd., Los Angeles, Calif., 90069. Publisher Dick Day pays up to $75 per page for how-to articles on hot rods and auto mechanics. Also likes picture stories on custom or modified cars, track and drag racing, hill climbing, and other hot rod events. Uses black-and-white and color photos.

Modern Cycle, 7950 Deering Ave., Canoga Park, Calif., 91304. Editor Gordon Karrel pays good rates, on publication, for articles and photos with broad interest to motorcycle fans. Uses trail articles with maps and action photos. Query.

Motor, 250 W. 55th St., New York, N.Y., 10017. Editor Bill Wolfe pays up to $100 for short articles to 1,200 words on how garages and auto service stations attract customers and increase sales. Pays $7.50 per photo. Query.

Motor Trend, 8490 Sunset Blvd., Los Angeles, Calif., 90069. Publisher Eric Dahlquist pays $250 and up for articles on foreign and domestic automobiles and profiles on colorful drivers and manufacturers. Uses black-and-white and color photos.

National Motorist, 65 Battery St., San Francisco, Calif., 94111. Editor James Donaldson pays 10 cents a word for articles of interest to California motorists. Magazine is issued bimonthly for members of the National Automobile Club, who live in California. Articles can be about travel in California and the Western states, history, outdoor events, hobbies, hunting and fishing. Lengths run from 500 to 1,000 words. Black-and-white and color photos used. Payment on acceptance.

Popular Hot Rodding, Argus Publishers Corp., 131 S. Barrington Pl., Los Angeles, Calif., 90049. Editor Lee Kelly pays top rates, on publication, for features on cars and mechanics.

Sports Car Graphic, 8490 Sunset Blvd., Los Angeles, Calif., 90069. Editor Robert Kovacik pays $50 and up, on acceptance, for articles on sports cars, performance cars, or racing cars. Likes a breezy style and unusual approaches to subjects. Also uses technical articles on all aspects of sports cars. Uses black-and-white and color photos, rates to $100 for full-page color.

Wheels Afield, 8490 Sunset Blvd., Los Angeles, Calif., 90069. Editor Ken Fermoyle pays up to $175 for articles of interest to owners of recreational vehicles from tent or camping trailers to motor homes. Likes how-to material and tips on how to have more fun mobile camping. No travel or accounts of a trip or articles on the joys of camping. Prefers query first.

World Car Guide, (formerly *Foreign Car Guide*), 4207 Palos Verdes Dr. S., Palos Verdes Peninsula, Calif., 90274. Editor Don Mac Donald pays $50 to $125 for articles to 2,000 words of interest to owners of foreign cars. Uses black-and-white photos.

Boating Markets

Like auto and camping markets, boating articles can be sold to most outdoor and men's markets. Again, sufficient knowledge of this specialized field is essential. Leaders in the field are:

Boating, One Park Ave., New York, N.Y., 10016. Editor Moulton Farnham pays good rates, on acceptance, for articles on boating, especially adventure, navigation, and how-to projects. No fishing, water-skiing, skin-diving stories. Prefers articles to run 1,000 to 1,500 words, illustrated.

Family Houseboating, 10148 Riverside Dr., Toluca Lake, N. Hollywood, Calif., 91602. Editor Art Rouse pays from $50 to $150, including photos, for articles on houseboats, including how-to, personal accounts of trips, and new waterway routes. Lengths to 2,000 words.

Motor Boating, 959 Eighth Ave., New York, N.Y., 10019. Editor Peter R. Smyth pays good rates, on acceptance, for articles to 2,500 words, on motor boating, sailing, yachting, cruising. Important to include illustrations.

Rudder, Fawcett Publications, Inc., 1 Astor Plaza, New York, N.Y., 10003. Editor Stuart James pays good rates, on acceptance, for boating articles to 2,000 words. Photos should accompany articles.

The Skipper, Riverview Bldg., Rowayton, Conn., 06853. Editor T.F. Norton pays 3 cents and up a word, on publication, for articles to 3,000 words on yachting or the sea. Also buys picture stories and fiction on the sea.

Yachting, 50 W. 44th St., New York, N.Y., 10036. Editor William W. Robinson pays 6 cents a word, on acceptance, for articles on recreational boating (both sail and power), and technical articles dealing with yachting.

6

HOW TO SELL TO MEN'S MARKETS

The top of the men's market, of course, is *Playboy*, with its tantalizing rates of $3,000 for a lead short story, and $2,000 for articles and middle-of-the-book short stories. How difficult is it to sell to *Playboy*? Jack Sharkey, who writes regularly for *Playboy*, believes he has the secret:

"When I first tried to sell to *Playboy*, I asked myself, what do they have a plethora of? I answered: sex! Then I asked myself, what do they have a dearth of? And I answered: nutsy humor! So I proceeded to write nutsy humor for them, and they proceeded to send me beautiful money.

"So my secret to success (and it's not bad—now when *Playboy* needs humor, their editor contacts *me*, instead of vice-versa) is to give them what they *want*, not what they *print!*"

Of course *Playboy*, and other men's magazines, buy articles and fiction with a good dose of sex, but like the boy who ate too much ice cream, editors and readers both prefer a little balance to their reading diet. Sharkey's secret can work for you, too, in the men's market and other markets, if you follow a few important rules:

Study the magazine you are aiming for, and then submit something entirely different from what they are running. But always keep your reader in mind. If you don't give the editor the typical type of story or article he is running, be certain your story would interest his average reader. Men like to read about sports, automobiles, science, science-fiction, politics, travel, adventure, history, mystery, and humor. Keep your subjects in these areas and you may be in Jack Sharkey's enviable shoes: the editor will call *you*!

Playboy is especially responsive to new and unpublished writers, though you will find the names of some of the best-known novelists, short story writers, and nonfiction authors between their covers. The emphasis is not on name but on quality writing, since some of the men's magazines balance their girlie material with fiction comparable to that found in literary publications. As in other markets, all men's magazines are not alike. Study those you wish to write for, and aim your material at their audience.

SEX OR NO SEX?

The case against sex in men's magazines is put even more strongly by Douglas Allen, editor of *Cavalier*:

"We won't buy sex. We're not even interested in sex. The main mistake most writers make is assuming we want articles on how to have a wild time in Sin City.

"We use cheesecake sex only, in some of our photo features. Otherwise, our material is aimed at the fairly intelligent young man. His interests go beyond sex and include all subjects that help him enjoy a lively, interesting, good life.

"*Cavalier* runs articles of contemporary interest, sports, entertainment, travel, personal adventures (though not in fields of hunting and fishing), and we like articles about interesting men doing interesting things. We do not buy articles on politics or social problems.

"Freelancers have a good chance of selling to *Cavalier*. We're always open to new writers. It's a good idea to look at several recent issues, to see just what we are running."

Allen pays $200 and up, on acceptance, for articles averaging 2,500 words. He prefers queries for articles.

Cavalier's Fiction Editor, Maurice DeWalt, also advises writers to forget about sex and he-man antics, unless they are an important part of the story.

It is important to study the men's magazine field by reading or at least leafing through the many that are published, to distinguish the girlie magazines from the more general men's magazines such as *Playboy* and *Cavalier*. The girlie magazines are predominantly picture magazines displaying lots of bosom and little in the way of articles or fiction to interest the average intelligent young man. If you prefer to sell to the girlie magazines, you'd fare better if you turned to photography.

The market list that follows includes both girlie magazines and general interest men's magazines.

Other related men's markets, such as detective, mystery, science fiction, and sports markets, can be found in other chapters.

Men's Magazine Markets

Adam, Publisher's Service Inc., 8060 Melrose Ave., Los Angeles, Calif., 90046. Editor Merrill Miller pays from $50 to $400, on publication, for articles and fiction from 1,000 to 5,000 words. Prefers fiction with male-female relationship, sexy humor, and satire. Articles can be on social subjects, human sexuality, personalities, and other subjects of interest to men. Also publishes *Adam Bedside Reader,* with same requirements and rates. David Hine, editor.

Adventure, 205 E. 42d St., New York, N.Y., 10017. Editor Carson Bingham pays $250 for fiction adventure stories such as sea, air, jungle, mystery, and suspense stories of interest to men.

American Art Enterprises, 7311 Fulton Ave., North Hollywood, Calif., 91605. Pays $75 and up for articles and short stories 2,000 to 3,000 words, of general interest to men. Likes witty and controversial articles that report or comment on aspects of today's society. Short stories should have strong male-female relationship, eroticism, physical conflict, or be action-packed. Buys photos, cartoons, jokes. Send material to George Bemos, manuscript editor.

Argosy, see Chapter 5.

Best for Men, Camerarts Publishing Co., 2715 N. Pulaski Rd., Chicago, Ill., 60639. Editor Frank Sorren pays from $20 to $100, on acceptance, for articles to 2,000 words and for fiction from 2,000 to 5,000 words. Fiction should have man-woman relationship and contain a surprise ending. Articles should cover range of subjects of interest to men. Also publishes *Men's Digest* and *Rascal,* with same requirements and rates.

Bluebook, 201 Park Ave., S., New York, N.Y., 10003. Editor B.R. Ampolsk pays from $100 to $300, on acceptance, for articles only. Bimonthly magazine is slanted to men's adventure, with true war and adventure stories that contain a strong personality development and has authentic background. Also uses expose articles and exotic places to vacation. Photos bought for $12.50 each. Also publishes *Man's Illustrated* and *Man's Conquest,* with same requirements, rates.

Broadside, 7311 Fulton Ave., North Hollywood, Calif., 91605. Editor Arthur S. Long pays $75 and up for articles 2,000 to 3,000 words, and fiction. Articles should be outspoken and factual, on sex, drinking, gambling, and other male subjects. Fiction should contain lots of action, physical conflict, and scenes with beautiful women.

Cavalier, 236 E. 46th St., New York, N.Y., 10017. Editor Douglas Allen pays up to $300 for articles and fiction, from 3,000 to 4,000 words, on acceptance. Slant is for hip young men, and writers should study recent issues before submitting.

Esquire, 388 Madison Ave., New York, N.Y., 10022. Editor Harold Hayes pays from $350 to $1,000 for fiction and articles for men. Emphasis is on sophisticated male readers. Articles should be controversial and of high literary merit on personalities in the news, insights into life, morals, trends, events of interest to men. Query first for articles. Fiction must be of high literary quality, about 3,000 words. Pays $25 for photos; $100 to $150 for picture pages. Always needs humor.

Fling, Box 151, Evanston, Ill., 60204. Editor Arv Miller pays from $125 to $250 for fiction and articles. Readers are from 18 to 38 years old. Likes controversy and off-beat articles with adult male viewpoint of life, and should contain a sexual statement. Articles should be well-researched, contain strong case histories, and have lots of quotes. Study magazine's style and query first. Buys fiction with unusual and/or man-woman themes, from 3,000 to 4,000 words; shorter if humor or satire. Buys no science fiction, westerns, mysteries.

For Men Only, 625 Madison Ave., New York, N.Y., 10022. Editor Ivan Prashker pays from $275 to $400 for true adventure stories with lots of action, exposes, and articles of general interest to men. Lengths run to 6,000 words. Pays $10 to $25 for photos; to $50 a page for picture essays.

Gallery, 632 N. Dearborn St., Chicago, Ill., 60610. New men's magazine for successful young men 18 to 35. Buys quality articles on everything to interest intelligent men, controversial interviews, action sports. Pays top rates. Query James Spurlock, editor.

Gem, 303 W. 42d St., New York, N.Y., 10036. Editor Will Martin buys articles and short stories with comtemporary slant, preferably containing sex. Lengths run 500 to 1,500 words. Payment varies according to length and is made after assignment to an issue.

Gentleman's Quarterly, 488 Madison Ave., New York, N.Y., 10022. Editor Jack Haber accepts queries only, for articles of interest to sophisticated male reader. Buys no fiction.

Gourmet, 777 Third Ave., New York, N.Y., 10017. Managing Editor (Mrs.) Justine Valenti prefers to be queried first, on articles for sophisticated male readers, with emphasis on fine foods and wines. Uses articles from 2,500 to 3,000 words, on travel, adventure, hunting, fishing, with a light, sophisticated style that also would interest women.

Hughes Rigway, Hughes Tool Co., Box 2539, Houston, Tex., 77001. Mark Eversole prefers queries about oil and drilling stories for unsophisticated male readers. Pays 10 cents a word for articles to 2,500 words.

Knight, Publisher's Service, Inc., 8060 Melrose Ave., Los Angeles, Calif., 90046. Editor Jared Rutter pays from $75 to $3,000 for fiction and articles for men. Fiction should be for sophisticated men, with male-female relationships. Articles should be of contemporary interest to men. Lengths run 1,000 to 5,000 words. Payment on publication.

Male, 625 Madison Ave., New York, N.Y., 10022. Editor Carl Sifakis buys articles only, from 4,000 to 6,000 words: true adventures set in exotic locales, World War II and current international cold war stories. No history or western stories. Also buys profiles of unusual men and exposes. Pays up to $600 for lead articles, on acceptance. Same requirements for *Men.*

Man's Magazine, 444 Madison Ave., New York, N.Y., 10022. Editor Phil Hirsch pays $175 to $500, on acceptance, for articles on war, espionage, sex, adventure, crime. Lengths run 4,500 to 6,000 words. Likes action and dialogue.

Man's World, 625 Madison Ave., New York, N.Y., 10022. Editor Martin Sage pays up to $400, on acceptance, for articles 4,000 to 5,000 words. Likes hard-hitting exposes, true adventure, profiles of unusual men, and general male subjects. Prefers query first.

Modern Man, 8150 N. Central Park Ave., Skokie, Ill., 60076. Editor Donald Stahl pays $200 for articles exploring sex in all its aspects, treated in documentary, dramatic, or humorous style. Lengths run to 2,500 words. Buys no fiction.

National Police Gazette, 520 Fifth Ave., New York, N.Y., 10036. Editor Nat Perlow pays 5 to 10 cents a word, on publication, for articles 1,500 to 2,000 words, of general male interest: adventure, sports, true detective, fraud exposes, fishing and hunting experiences. Also buys profiles on sports and theatre personalities.

Oui, Playboy Bldg., 919 N. Michigan Ave., Chicago, Ill., 60611. Editor Jon Carroll pays top rates for articles to interest intelligent young men. Slant is toward younger, more "hip" male than its parent magazine, *Playboy.*

Penthouse, 1560 Broadway, New York, N.Y., 10036. Pays 10 cents a word for articles and sexy fiction from 4,000 to 6,000 words. Slant is toward sophisticated male audience. Articles of interest to men, covering range from sex to sports. Pays thirty days after acceptance.

HOW TO SELL TO MEN'S MARKETS 95

Playboy, 919 N. Michigan Ave., Chicago, Ill., 60611. Managing Editor Sheldon Wax. Articles Editor David Butler pays $2,000 for articles about 4,000 words, for the young, urban male reader. Buys well-written and well-researched articles running the gamut of interest to sophisticated males, including sports, politics, new developments in science, medicine, etc. Also buys short humor and satire (about 2,000 words). Prefers one-page query and sample of author's published writing. Fiction Editor Robie Macauley buys quality short stories, suspense, science-fiction, adventure, mystery, that are well-written and well-constructed, with strong male interest. Pays $3,000 for lead short story, $2000 for others. Short-shorts pay $1,000, and Ribald Classics, $400. Humor and satire always in demand.

Rogue, Captain Publishing Co., 95 Madison Ave., New York, N.Y., 10002. Query first, for articles and short stories. Buys general male-interest articles and fiction. Pays competitive rates.

Saga. (See Chapter 5.)

Sea Classics, 7950 Deering Ave., Canoga Park, Calif., 91304. Editor James Scheetz pays up to $150 for historical articles on ships and men of the sea. Lengths run from 1,000 to 3,500 words. Payment on publication.

Sir!, 21 W. 26th St., New York, N.Y., 10010. Editor Everett Meyers pays $75 and up for fiction and $100 and up for articles, on or before publication. Fiction should be of interest to the modern man. Lengths run from 1,500 to 5,000 words. Articles, from 2,000 to 5,000 words, should be on contemporary subjects of interest to men. Pays $50 to $100 extra for photos, both black and white and color. Same requirements and rates for *Man to Man* and *Mr. Magazine.*

Stag, 625 Madison Ave., New York, N.Y., 10022. Editor Noah Sarlat pays up to $500 for articles, on acceptance, for male readers. Uses true adventure, expose, social commentary, personalities in the headlines. Pays $10 to $25 per photo, up to $50 per page for photo essays.

The Swinger, 303 W. 42d St., New York, N.Y., 10036. Editor Will Martin buys articles on current themes, fiction, and satire, for sophisticated men. Lengths run from 750 to 1,500 words.

True. (See Chapter 5.)

True Adventures, 205 E. 42d St., New York, N.Y., 10017. Editor Peter Hill Gannett pays $100 to $250, on acceptance, for articles of male interest: adventure, travel, girls, etc. Lengths from 2,000 to 4,000 words. No fiction.

True West, Western Publications, Inc., P.O. Box 3668, Austin, Texas 78704. Editor Pat Wagner pays 2 cents a word, on acceptance, for articles dealing with true events of the Old West (1830 to 1910). Lengths run 750 to 7,000 words. Photos help sell the article, and are returned after publication. Query first. Same requirement, rates, for *Frontier Times* and *Old West.*

Western Fiction Magazine, P.O. Drawer L, Conroe, Texas, 77301. Editor John Latham pays 3 cents a word, and up, on acceptance, for short stories about the Old West. Likes action-packed, tightly-written stories from 1,000 to 15,000 words. Does not want sex. Prefers old-time action western stories.

Whisper, 8060 Melrose Ave., Los Angeles, Calif., 90046. Pays $100 and up, on publication, for entertaining articles for men. Likes personalities and exposes, but no sex. Lengths run 1,000 to 3,000 words.

Wildcat, 108 S. Franklin Ave., Valley Stream, N.Y., 11580. Editor Dan Sontup pays up to $125, on acceptance, for fiction and articles about modern sexual relationships between men and women. Lengths run 2,000 to 3,000 words. Same rates and requirements for *Charger* and *Daring.*

Other Men's Markets

A most intelligent young woman once told me: "The subject women are most interested in is Men." She learned this several ways, but one of the most observant was something she noticed while sitting under the dryer at a beauty parlor. She reached down to select a magazine from a table and found, among the ladies' journals, such magazines as *True, Argosy, Stag,* and *Playboy.*

"It seems," my lady friend told me, "that the owner of the hair salon realized that women want to know all they can about men. What better way of spending an hour under the hair dryer than researching about Men. So the salon owner stocked the men's magazines and the women gobbled them up."

So it is also true with women's magazines. Editors have learned that women readers want to know about three main subjects: sex, children, and Men.

A word to the wise is always sufficient: try your man's story on a woman's magazine.

In addition to which, there are Sunday women's pages of newspapers. I once sold a humorous article on how men are spending big money these days getting their hair cut (or stylized), buying wigs and having them combed, getting facials, manicures, and the works. I got $50 for the article and the barber shop owner picked up the tab for my "beauty treatment": $15 including cocktail.

It is said in the children's writing field that what will interest a boy usually will interest a girl, so therefore write for boys. But while it generally follows that what will interest a man will interest a woman, it decidedly does not follow that what will interest a woman will interest a man. So do not submit your women's stories to men's markets. Try your men's article or short story on a woman's market—but only if it is rejected by the men's field, or you can sell it for more money to a woman's market.

If women are unpredictable, so too, it seems, is the men's market. And for the freelancer, it all means more extra sales.

7

HOW TO SELL TO WOMEN'S MARKETS

Abortion and veneral disease once were subjects only for the sensational weekly tabloids. Today they're as important a part of the article line-up of women's magazines as recipes and gardening.

Chuck and Bonnie Remsberg, a young suburban Chicago husband-and-wife writing team, are earning extremely attractive annual incomes from writing about controversial social problems for *Good Housekeeping, Family Weekly*, and other top women's magazines. What's more, they got their start in the true detective market, reporting on slices of life that gave them the insight and experience to write for the women's slicks.

"It's very rewarding, both financially and as interesting work, to write for the women's market today," Chuck reports. "Women's magazine editors want in-depth articles on all important and controversial social problems involving men, women, and children, and want them well-written, well-researched, and with a compelling women's angle.

"In such a market, of course, the standards are high. Writers who work in this field will be competing with professionals who regularly produce what the editors want. Many of the writers have impressive backgrounds on newspapers, either as general assignment feature writers, women's page writers, and columnists who can write with authority on pollution, hunger, medicine, and the whole spectrum of subjects of interest to women."

Though the Remsbergs each do separate stories at times, most of their work is done together. One does the research and writing while the other edits, or both will share the research and compose together.

Most of their assignments come from query letters they submit to editors, following the same general approach that a novice will. They will write a brief outline of their proposed article, submitting any suitable photos or other illustrations they may have. Then they wait to see if the editor is interested in the subject. Several times a year they go to New York to talk with editors about article ideas, but they have first lined up their appointments. About a quarter of their work comes in on assignments directly from an editor.

Women's markets are excellent ones for housewives and career women who have some new insight into subjects to interest women. The best writer in the world can not sell an old idea. The woman writer who does not sell regularly, but comes upon a fresh approach to an old idea, can break into the leading women's magazines.

Specialization is also important in the women's market. Women who know about needlepoint, gardening, or food can add substantially to their income by writing on their specialty for the women's market.

Cynthia Scheer, a college friend now happily freelancing in San Francisco, is parlaying her knowledge and experience in home economics into top-paying assignments. One job, for the Amana company, had her traveling all over the western states and Hawaii, demonstrating radar ovens, writing about them, and talking about them on women's television shows. She is also testing French cookware and writing reports on them for women's pages of newspapers. And she is smart enough to capitalize on her travel by writing travel articles for magazines and Sunday supplements. Besides which, she gets to keep all the French cookware she tests!

Most of the top women's magazines buy articles on homemaking, family care, gardening, women in the news, cooking, successful families, inspirational stories, new developments in medicine, and recreation and travel. Many also buy how-to articles of interest to both men and women. Humor is always in demand, and some of the leading magazines also buy short stories to interest women, from light romance to dramas with insight into problems that concern women.

In most cases, query the editors first with nonfiction. You do not have to query an editor with fiction. And always study the magazine first, to see what the editor is buying, and what tone and direction the magazine is taking.

Whether you write as a husband-and-wife team or alone, the

women's field is a changing and a challenging one, with rewards of being among the best-paying and most interesting markets.

In addition to the women's magazines listed below, keep in mind that local newspaper women's pages and Sunday supplements are excellent markets for articles for and about women. Manufacturers or distributors of women's products also frequently need freelance writers to promote the articles. A blanket query letter to manufacturers or shops in your area, informing them of your experience and availability to do freelance work, could bring extra assignments.

Women's Magazines

Allied Publications, Inc., P.O. Box 23505, Fort Lauderdale, Fla., 33307. Editor Marie Stilkind pays 5 cents a word, on acceptance, for noncontroversial articles on home and family, travel, decorating, beauty, art, how-to home and hobby projects, and other general subjects to interest women. Prefers black and white photos. Pays $5 per photo. Also uses articles and photos on famous women, secretaries, and beauticians.

American Home, 641 Lexington Ave., New York, N.Y., 10022. Also publishes California edition (425 California St., San Francisco, Calif., 94104; Editor Mrs. Nancy Carpenter Gray). Buys short articles on the home, its maintenance, food, family travel, decorating, building and remodeling, gardening, as well as human interest articles. Likes articles of equal interest to men and women. Pays good rates, on acceptance. No fiction or poetry. Query.

Antiques Journal, Box 88128, Dunwoody, Ga., 30338. Editor John Mebane buys articles and photos about antiques. Lengths to 1,800 words (prefers shorter articles). Query.

Apartment Ideas, published by *Better Homes and Gardens,* Meredith Corp., 1716 Locust St., Des Moines, Ia., 50303. Editor James Hufnagel buys articles of interest to apartment renters and owners, from decorating to entertainment ideas. Query.

Baby Care, 52 Vanderbilt Ave., New York, N.Y., 10017. Distributed free in hospitals and pediatricians' offices for mothers and expectant mothers. Editor Mrs. Maja Bernath pays from $50 to $125, on acceptance, for articles to 1,800 words on basic infant care, emotional and physical development, family relationships, travel with infants. Also buys short humorous features to 1,000 about infants and motherhood. Pays $25 for contributions to "Focus On You," a department of brief essays to 500 words that are personal accounts of being a new parent or family relationships in connection with a new baby, and $10 for "Family Corner" items 100 words or less, which are unusual or humorous anecdotes about the family and the new baby.

Baby Talk, 149 Madison Ave., New York, N.Y., 10016. Editor Eve Hammerschmidt buys true experience articles from 500 to 1,000 words, by mothers or fathers, on baby care and family relationships.

Better Homes and Gardens, 1716 Locust St., Des Moines, Iowa, 50303. Editor James A. Autry pays top rates for articles about the home and family. Submit query and short outline to department editor. Best freelance areas are travel, health, automobiles, money management, home and family entertainment. Lengths from 250 to 1,000 words. Also buys how-to-do-it-yourself articles about home projects for middle-income family readers. Remodeling stories should be accompanied by "before" and "after" photos and complete information on cost, time involved, and why the remodeling was done.

Bride's Magazine, 420 Lexington Ave., New York, N.Y., 10017. Editor Barbara Donovan pays $75 to $500 for articles 1,000 words and up, of interest to brides-to-be and newlyweds. Subjects range from marital adjustment and entertaining to money handling and setting up a home or apartment. Query first, to Ann Diamond, features editor.

✓ *The Christian Home,* 201 Eighth Ave., S., Nashville, Tenn., 37203. Editor Helen F. Couch pays 2 cents a word, on acceptance, for articles 1,000 to 2,000 words, of interest to parents. Likes humor. Also buys fiction from 2,500 to 3,500 words. Pays 50 cents a line for poetry. Query.

✓ *Christian Science Monitor,* One Norway St., Boston, Mass., 02115. Women's Editor Nan Trent pays good rates for articles on homemaking, food, fashion, and successful women.

Cosmopolitan, 221 W. 57th St., New York, N.Y., 10019. Editor Helen Gurley Brown. Fiction Editor Junius Adams. Articles and fiction aimed at young career women. Pays $1,000 to $1,500 for full-length articles about 4,000 words, that tell an intelligent modern woman 18 to 34 years old how to have a more rewarding life. Also top rates for shorter features 2,000 to 3,500 words, on careers, part-time jobs, dieting, food, fashion, men, emotions, life styles, medicine, entertainment, and other subjects of interest to young women married or single who lead a life of their own. Pays $1,000 for short stories to interest sophisticated women, especially contemporary man-woman relationships. Study magazine for articles and fiction before submitting query or story.

Expecting, 52 Vanderbilt Ave., New York, N.Y., 10017. Editor

Mrs. Maja Bernath pays $50 to $125 for articles from 700 to 2,000 words, on acceptance, to interest expectant mothers. Subjects include prenatal development, husband-wife relationships, medical articles by registered nurses and doctors. No fiction.

Family Circle, 488 Madison Ave., New York, N.Y., 10022. Articles Editor Babette Brimberg pays $1,000 and up for articles about 2,500 words about family life, especially emphasizing service. Query first, with outline and statement of your background and qualifications. Uses material on family relationships, finances, health. Study several issues before submitting query.

Family Handyman, 235 E. 45th St., New York, N.Y., 10017. Pays $40 to $100, on acceptance, for step-by-step, non-technical articles to 1,000 words on home improvement, repairs and maintenance, do-it-yourself. Black and white photos should accompany query or manuscript. Pays $5 to $15 for tips or short-cuts for do-it-yourselfers.

Family Houseboating, 10148 Riverside Dr., North Hollywood, Calif., 91602. Editor Art Rouse pays good rates, on publication, for articles on houseboating, family trips, maintenance, remodeling, etc. Lengths from 500 to 2,000 words. Uses color transparencies and black and white photos.

Family Weekly, 641 Lexington Ave., New York, N.Y., 10022. Editor-in-Chief Mort Persky pays good rates, on acceptance, for short, lively articles on family help and advice, and features on people in the news. Study publication and query first.

Flower & Garden Magazine, 4251 Pennsylvania, Kansas City, Mo., 64111. Editor-in-Chief Rachel Snyder pays 3 cents a word and up, on acceptance, for articles on indoor and outdoor gardening. Good photos should accompany manuscript or query.

Forecast for Home Economics, 50 W. 44th St., New York, N.Y., 10036. (Teacher edition of *Co-ed* magazine published by Scholastic Publications). Payment varies, on publication, for articles of interest to home economics teachers, home demonstration agents, and home economists in business. Writers should be educators or experts in the home economics field. Lengths to 1,500 words.

Girl Talk, 230 E. 44th St., New York, N.Y., 10017. Pays good rates for articles and fiction of interest to women. Lengths run to 2,000 words. Likes personality features on men and women in entertainment or the news. Also likes humor. Query first. Accepts only one manuscript per month from the same writer.

Glamour, 420 Lexington Ave., New York, N.Y., 10017. Editor-in-Chief Ruth Whitney pays $300 to $700 for articles of interest to young women, serious or humorous. Subjects include social and emotional problems, travel, man-woman relationships, family, medicine, unusual careers, successful or happy women. Also short first-person articles of opinion or experience. Lengths from 1,500 to 3,000 words.

Good Housekeeping, 959 Eighth Ave., New York, N.Y., 10019. Articles Editor Betty Frank, Fiction Editor Naome Lewis. Buys wide range of articles of interest to women. Subjects can be on vital problems concerning the woman and family, articles should be comprehensive, well-written, well-researched, and contain the human element. Lengths run from 3,000 to 5,000 words. Rates range up to $5,000 for lead story, on acceptance. Query first with outline. Also buys true-life incidents in the lives or careers of well-known people. Short stories run to 5,000 words and must contain reader identification, with practical and believable solutions to problems. Pays $1,250 for a first short story. Short short stories bring $1,000 and up.

Gourmet, 777 Third Ave., New York, N.Y., 10017. Managing Editor Mrs. Justine Valenti buys articles for sophisticated male readers interested in fine foods and fine wines (see Chapter 6), but articles also should appeal to women who live, or aspire to live, "the good life" of fine dining and travel.

Harper's Bazaar, 717 Fifth Ave., New York, N.Y., 10022. Long known primarily as a literary magazine, *Harper's Bazaar* now uses less fiction and more articles. Subjects deal with the problems of modern women. Readers are between 25 and 40, in the upper income bracket. Articles should be brief, up to 2,000 words. Fiction should be shorter. Betsy Freund, literary and articles editor, pays about $300 for articles. Good rates for fiction, but competition is very keen.

Hair Do & Beauty, 750 Third Ave., New York, N.Y., 10017. Editor Dorothea Hanle uses mostly staff-written articles on hair styling and beauty, but occasionally buys from freelancers. Query with outline.

Home Garden Magazine: Flower Grower, 235 E. 45th St., New York, N.Y., 10017. Editor William Meachem pays 5 cents a word for short how-to articles and picture stories for the suburban and hobby gardener. Lengths run 500 to 1,000 words.

Horticulture, 300 Massachusetts Ave., Boston, Mass., 02115. Editor Edwin Steffek pays 3 cents a word, after publication, for authoritative articles 500 to 1,200 words, on gardening or horticulture.

House and Garden, 420 Lexington Ave., New York, N.Y., 10017. Most articles are assigned to regular contributors. Query first, with outline.

House Beautiful, 717 Fifth Ave., New York, N.Y., 10022. Editor Wallace Guenther assigns most articles to regular contributors but will accept queries with outline for articles of interest to the male or female homeowner. Also buys short articles on the art of living. Pays good rates, on acceptance.

Ladies' Home Journal, 641 Lexington Ave., New York, N.Y., 10022. Most articles staff-written or assigned through literary agents. Managing Editor Richard Kaplan accepts queries for nonfiction. Fiction editor is Wesley Price.

Lady's Circle, 21 W. 26th St., New York, N.Y., 10010. Editor Betty Etter pays $125 and up, on publication, for articles to interest homemakers. Lengths run 2,500 to 3,500 words. Uses black and white photos.

Ladycom, 520 N. Michigan Ave., Chicago, Ill., 60611. Editor Ann Nelson pays from $30 to $75, after acceptance, for articles to interest military and embassy wives living overseas. Age of readers is from 21 to 35 years. Lengths of articles runs to 2,000 words.

Living Now, 383 Madison Ave., New York., 10017. Formerly *Home Modernizing Guide.* Query with photos on unusual new homes. Pays on acceptance.

McCall's, 230 Park Ave., New York, N.Y., 10017. Study the magazine for recent changes in editorial requirements. Pays tops rates, on acceptance, for articles of interest to the modern woman. Average length, 4,000 words. Also pays up to $300 for short pieces on women doing interesting, worthwhile things for "Right Now" department. Send query on these to Miss Carole Garibaldi. Send longer article queries to Miss Helen Markel, articles editor. Also buys well-written, distinguished fiction.

Mademoiselle, 420 Lexington Ave., New York, N.Y., 10017. Magazine aimed at women 18 to 25 years old. Buys articles for the college and post-college woman, which means their variety is almost unlimited. Controversial articles welcome if tastefully written. Likes personal experience and humor, as well as experiences living, working, or studying in a foreign country. Lengths run 2,000 to 3,500 words. Prefers query but accepts finished manuscripts. Send queries or articles to Mary Cantwell, managing editor, who pays $400 to $850 for articles. Fiction Editor Ellen Stoianoff buys short stories from 2,500 to 6,500 words and pays $300. Also buys poetry under 65 lines long, for $25 and up.

Modern Bride, One Park Ave., New York, N.Y., 10016. Editor Robert Houseman pays good rates, on acceptance, for articles of interest to both bride and groom: marriage, home and/or apartment living, honeymoon travel, etiquette. Lengths run 1,500 words and up.

Modern Girl, 235 Park Ave., S., New York, N.Y., 10003. Editor Rena Adler pays from $50 to $75 for articles and $75 for short stories, 2,000 to 4,000 words, on all aspects of interest to the modern woman aged 18 to 35. Looking for new subjects with new approaches, told in a fresh, interesting way. Payment on acceptance.

Modern Maturity, 215 Long Beach Blvd., Long Beach, Calif., 90802. Editor Hubert Pryor pays from $50 to $500 for articles and short stories, on acceptance, of interest to men and women over 55. Subjects should be service articles on health, food, housing, employment, hobbies, or nostalgia, inspirational articles, or personality stories on happily and successfully retired men and women. Pays $15 and up for black and white photos, $50 and up for color.

Modern Screen, 750 Third Ave., New York, N.Y., 10017. Editor Joan Thursh buys interviews and third person articles on movie stars, television personalities, and others well-known in the entertainment business. Stories must be factual, not fiction, and preferably exclusive. Lengths to 2,000 words. Pays $200 and up, on acceptance. Pays $20 and up for photos. Query first.

Mothers' Manual, 420 Lexington Ave., New York, N.Y., 10017. Editor Beth Waterfall pays 2 to 5 cents a word, on publication, for articles of interest to mothers of babies six weeks to six years old, from 1,000 to 1,500 words. Send articles or queries to Miss Waterfall at 176 Cleveland Dr., Croton-on-Hudson, N.Y., 10520.

Mothers-to-be/American Baby, 10 E. 52d St., New York, N.Y., 10022. Formerly *American Baby.* Editor Judith Nolte pays good rates for articles of help to new and expectant mothers, and child care for infants to age three. Lengths run 400 to 1,500 words. Query first.

Movie Mirror Yearbook, Sterling Group, Inc., 315 Park Ave., New York, N.Y., 10010. Pays $200 and up, on acceptance, for stories or photo essays on top Hollywood, television, or recording artists.

Ms., 207 E. 32d St., New York, N.Y., 10016. Editor Gloria Steinem pays good rates for articles of interest to the new woman. While not to be considered a magazine specifically for the new liberated woman, articles will be topical and offer an alternative to the more established women's magazines.

New Woman, Box 24202, Fort Lauderdale, Fla., 33307. Articles Editor Thetis Powers pays good rates for subjects to interest modern young women.

The PTA Magazine, 700 N. Rush St., Chicago, Ill., 60611. Editor Mrs. Eva Grant buys articles on parent education, parent-teacher-student cooperation. Lengths to 1,800 words.

Parents' Magazine, 52 Vanderbilt Ave., New York, N.Y., 10017. Editor-in-Chief Mrs. Genevieve Millet Landau pays top rates for well-researched articles about family and marriage relationships, children and adolescents, baby care, new developments in education, mental and physical health, and major social problems. Prefers conversational, personal approach, but documented with examples and opinions of authorities. Query first with outline. Lengths run 2,000 to 3,000 words. Payment varies, on acceptance.

Perfect Home, 427 6th Ave., S.E., Cedar Rapids, Iowa, 52400. Editor Donna Nicholas Hahn pays $50 for photo essays with brief captions on remodeling projects in the home, ideas for built-in cabinets, unusual decorating ideas. Also 500-word essays on "What Home Means to Me," by prominent, well-known people.

Popular Science Monthly, 355 Lexington Ave., New York, N.Y., 10017. Editor Hubert Luckett pays $25 and up, on acceptance, for short tips for the homeowner: easier ways of doing indoor and outdoor chores, and clever repair jobs.

Progressive Woman, Box 510, Middlebury, Ind., 46540. Editor Rosalie Corson pays 8 cents a word for articles and 4 cents a word for fiction, aimed at the working woman. Buys a wide variety of articles of from 1,000 to 2,000 words. Fiction runs about 1,500 words. Payment on publication.

Redbook, 230 Park Ave., New York, N.Y., 10017. Pays top rates for practical articles on the home, family, health. Also fiction with themes of love, marriage, parenthood, social and moral problems. Pays $1,000 and up for short stories, $600 to $850, for short-short stories from 1,400 to 1,600 words, and from $5,000 to $10,000 for novels of from 25,000 to 35,000 words.

The Secretary, 616 E. 63d St., Kansas City, Mo., 64110. Editor Mrs. Shirley Englund pays good rates, on publication, for articles 800 to 1,200 words, of interest to secretaries: office procedures, skills administrative tips, and human relations.

Sunset Magazine, Menlo Park, Calif., 94205. Editor Proctor Mellquist buys freelance ideas and research as background material for staff-written articles on food, homes, travel, gardening, and other subjects of interest to people living in the western states. Payment varies, on acceptance. Query.

Today's Secretary, 330 W. 42d St., New York, N.Y., 10036. Editor Donna Zack pays $25 for fiction and from $35 to $150 for articles to help young secretaries, including new office techniques, self-improvement, and preparing for a new job. Fiction should interest readers age 16 to 21, but emphasis should not be on romance. Fiction lengths run 500 to 1,000 words; articles from 1,000 to 1,500 words. Buys candid photos.

TV and Movie Screen, 315 Park Ave. S., New York, N.Y., 10010. Editor Beryl Basher pays $200 on acceptance for articles about television and movie personalities. Stories must be factual, from personal interviews or experience with the stars, and have strong dramatic appeal. Lengths about 2,000 words. Query.

T.V. Guide, Radnor, Pa., 19088. Pays top rates, on acceptance, for lively articles and humor on television and its stars. Most articles are staff-written, but queries are accepted. Lengths run 1,000 to 1,500 words. Managing Editor is A.H. Joseph.

TV Picture Life, 315 Park Ave. S., New York, N.Y., 10010. Editor Lyla Aubry pays $220 for articles and picture stories on the private lives of the top television stars, preferably from interviews. Prefers human angles such as romance, inspiration, dramatic events in their personal life or career. Approach is always sympathetic to the star. Lengths run from 2,000 to 3,000 words. Photo essays should picture stars at home, dating, on vacation, or other informal situations. Query essential.

TV Radio Talk, 750 Third Ave., New York, N.Y., Editor Barbara Schrank pays $300 and up, on acceptance, for interviews and third-person stories on television, movie, and recording stars. Articles must be factual, lively, and sympathetic to the star. Lengths to 2,000 words. Pays $20 and up for photos. Query.

Vogue, 420 Lexington Ave., New York, 10017. Feature Editor Kate Lloyd prefers queries for articles of general interest to women readers. Study magazine before submitting. Pays good rates, on acceptance. Lengths to 2,500 words.

Weight Watchers Magazine, 635 Madison Ave., New York, N.Y., 10022. Feature Editor Edythe Kopman does not want diet or overweight stories; these she assigns to regular contributors. She does accept ideas and outlines for articles of general interest to women, such as travel, personalities, humor. Also buys some fiction. Pays on acceptance.

The Woman, 235 Park Ave. S., New York, N.Y., 10003. Editor Diana Lurvey pays $50, on acceptance, for articles written in the first-person, about everyday problems of women. The solution should help readers with similar problems. No fiction.

Woman/Golfer, 131 Lincoln Hwy., Frankfort, Ill., 60423. Editor Len Richardson buys articles on golf instruction, stories on women golfers both pro and amateur, and instruction by top women golf pros. Travel stories should be about golf in an area.

Woman's Day, 1 Astor Pl., New York, N.Y., 10003. Editor Geraldine Rhoads pays top rates, on acceptance, for articles 1,500 to 3,000 words, of interest to women: family, family health, marriage, human interest, travel, bringing up children. Buys fiction, about 3,000 words. Send article queries to Rebecca Greer, articles editor.

Woman's World, Editor Diana Walton pays $35 for articles to 1,000 words on subjects of interest to women. Likes humor. No fiction. Uses black and white photos. Also humorous fillers.

The Workbasket, 4251 Pennsylvania, Kansas City, Mo., 64111. Editor Mary Ida Sullivan pays 2 cents a word, on acceptance, for articles 500 to 700 words on women who have improved their home environment, such as how-to articles on women's crafts around the home. Also 200-word shorts on how women can make extra money.

The Workbench, 4251 Pennsylvania, Kansas City, Mo., 64111. Editor Jay Hedden pays $20 to $50 per published page, $75 and up for assigned articles, on home workshop, home improvement, home maintenance.

You, 261 5th Ave., New York, N.Y., 10016. Editor Rochelle Larkin pays good rates for articles to interest modern young women.

Your New Baby, 52 Vanderbilt Ave., New York, N.Y., 10017. Editor Mrs. Maja Bernath pays $100 to $125, on acceptance, for articles for new and expectant mothers: pregnancy, baby care, family relations, etc. Lengths from 1,200 to 1,500 words.

True Confession and Romance Magazines

These are actually fun to write, and lucrative. But they're not as easy to write as they may appear. The best thing to do is read several copies of the best-paying confession and romance magazines, to see who their audience is. Then you have a choice: either give them what they're running or, probably better, something close to it but just a little different. In other words, a new approach to an old, familiar story.

Most true confession magazine editors are responsive to new writers. Since bylines do not appear on the stories (they're supposed to be autobiographical, by the suffering person—usually a woman but sometimes a man), unknown writers have just as good a chance of selling. It all depends on the story. And of course it's fiction, but it should be about a believable situation or problem.

There is good money in the true confession and romance market. One writer makes $18,000 a year writing confessions. A husband and wife writing team sold 88 stories in one year (at $150 to $300 a story). And many writers use true confessions as their "bread and butter" job, keeping them in rent and food money while they work on other projects.

There is a formula to writing for the true confessions. It

involves studying the market as a whole, each magazine individually, and learning how to write a complete confession drama. Many writers fail at this market because their stories are not quite complete. They have a good "soap opera" plot, and their characters suffer enough, but either they have not taken a new look at the problem or found a new solution. The confession magazines do not keep running the same story over and over, though it may seem so to the beginning writer for the market. Like editors of any other magazine, confession editors want to read something *new*. And their readers want to read something new. Each magazine has its own particular needs, as you can see from the list that follows.

Some general rules apply to selling to the confessions: stories should have a modern approach and attempt to solve some of the problems facing the modern woman, girl, and man. A narrator must suffer, must make a big mistake, or grope for a better life. She must look forward to a happier life for her suffering. All need not be sweetness and light and rainbows at the end, but there must be some sunlight breaking through the clouds of gloom. After all, readers turn to confessions to experience (or share) the suffering, but they're mainly looking for some hope. Perhaps your heroine (or hero) will give them an idea of how to solve their own personal problem. At least, if your narrator survives, and has a better future to look forward to, perhaps the reader will too. Reader identification is one of the strongest plusses in selling to the confessions.

Most confession stories are about man-woman relationships, although some are parent-child, some are about teens' problems of growing up or overcoming an emotional crisis, birth defects, and other problems that can stand in the way of happiness.

Some confession magazines are aimed at teen-age girls, some at matrons, others at blue collar girls, and some aim at all of them, even picking up some male readers. Only by studying each magazine will you learn who their audience is, at what level to write your story, and what subjects are selling and what are not. And, as one editor says, "If you make me cry, you'll make me buy!"

Confession and Romance Magazines

Confidential Confessions, 17 W. 44th St., New York, N.Y., 10036. Editorial Director Jean Sharbel pays 3 cents a word, on acceptance, for confession stories from 2,000 to 6,000 words. Also some longer stories to 8,500 words.

Daring Romances, 17 W. 44th St., New York, N.Y., 10036. Editorial Director Jean Sharbel pays 3 cents a word, on acceptance, for confessions emphasizing marriage and dating, strong on emotion and realism. Lengths from 2,000 to 8,500 words.

Exciting Confessions, 17 W. 44th St., New York, N.Y., 10036. Editorial Director Jean Sharbel. Same requirements and pay rate as for two above magazines.

Hers, George Newnes, Ltd., 300 E. 42d St., New York, N.Y., 10017. British romance magazine with New York office, pays good rates, on acceptance, for first-person romances. Likes emotional, realistic stories. Lengths from 5,000 to 8,000 words.

Intimate Confessions and *Thrilling Love Stories,* 108 S. Franklin Ave., Valley Stream, N.Y., 11580. Editor Lorraine Zuckerman pays $100 and up, on acceptance, for confessions involving teen-agers, mature women, and occasionally, men. Prefers modern approaches to solving sex problems and other themes. Lengths from 3,000 to 6,000 words. Realism and realistic solutions to problems are a must.

Intimate Story, 295 Madison Ave., New York, N.Y., 10017. Editor Bessie Little pays 3 cents a word, on acceptance, for man-woman confessions, parent-child stories, and teen-age problems. Also buys articles based on exciting new events that can be made into confessions. Lengths from 2,000 to 6,500 words. Likes stories to be believable, have strong emotional appeal, have a moral, and show some character change in the narrator, ending with some encouragement for a happier future.

Modern Romances, 750 Third Ave., New York, N.Y., 10017. Editor Henry Malmgreen pays 4 cents a word for the first two stories bought; 5 cents a word afterward. Magazine is primarily aimed at wives and daughters of blue-collar class. Strong, new plot or twist on familiar themes, and good characterization are required. Lengths run from 5,000 to 7,000 words. Malmgreen welcomes stories by new writers and gives capsule comments on rejections. Also publishes a newsletter of advice to confession writers, available on request.

My Love Secret Confession, 21 W. 26th St., New York, N.Y., 10010. Editor Ardis Sandel pays $100 to $150, 30 days after acceptance, for confessions of interest to teen-agers and young married women. Lengths run to 7,000 words.

My Romance, Romantic Confessions, True Secrets, Secret Story, and *My Confession,* 625 Madison Ave., New York, N.Y., 10022. Editors use only staff-written stories. If you are a regularly selling confession writer, you may query them for possible assignments.

HOW TO SELL TO WOMEN'S MARKETS

Personal Romances, 295 Madison Ave., New York, N.Y., 10017. Editor Johanna Ronan Smith pays 3 cents a word, on acceptance, for problems of teen-agers and young married women. Solutions should be positive, helping readers to solve their problems. Romances should have a moral to them. Lengths from 1,500 to 6,500 words.

Real Confessions and *Modern Love,* 315 Park Ave. S., New York, N.Y., 10010. Editor Ruth Beck pays prevailing rates, on acceptance, for realistic, modern, action-filled stories about love, marriage, parent-child problems, and other stories reflecting the current scene. Prefers action and dialogue rather than long narrative passages.

Real Romances, 21 W. 26th St., New York, N.Y., 10010. Editor Ardis Sandel pays $100 to $150, 30 days after acceptance, for true-life stories of interest to modern young women.

Real Story, 21 W. 26th St., New York, N.Y., 10010. Editor Ardis Sandel pays $100 to $150, 30 days after acceptance, for confessions to 7,000 words, about problems of young marrieds. Stories involving older women and men also occasionally used.

Secret Romances, 17 W. 44th St., New York, N.Y., 10036. Editorial Director Jean Sharbel pays 3 cents a word, on acceptance, for dramatic romances on marriage and dating. Lengths from 2,000 to 6,500 words, and novelettes to 8,500 words.

Secrets, Dauntless Books, Inc., 17 W. 44th St., New York, N.Y., 10036. Editorial Director Jean Sharbel pays 3 and 4 cents a word, on acceptance, for all types of first-person confessions involving teens, young married and single women, and even stories of older courtship and family situations. Most stories have girl or women narrators, but also buys stories told by a man. Same requirements and rates for *Revealing Romances.*

True, George Newnes, Ltd., 300 E. 42d St., New York, N.Y., 10017. New York office of British romance magazine. Pays good rates, on acceptance, for first-person stories with lots of drama and emotion. Lengths from 3,000 to 8,000 words.

True Confessions, 205 E. 42d St., New York, N.Y., 10017. Editor Florence Moriarty pays top rates, on acceptance, for confessions of young married women of the blue collar class. Lengths from 2,500 to 7,000 words, plus novelettes to 18,000 words.

True Experience, 205 E. 42d St., New York, N.Y., 10017. Editor Bruce Elliott pays up to $250 for dramatic first-person stories of love, dating, health, religion, and other subjects that give the reader an insight into living a full, enriching life. Lengths from 4,000 to 8,000 words.

True Love, 205 E. 42d St., New York, N.Y., 10017. Editor Bruce Elliot, pays 3 cents a word, on acceptance, for first-person stories usually narrated by a woman, for women readers aged 18 to 34. Does not buy the typical confession story read in most confession magazines. Lengths from 5,000 to 7,000 words.

True Romance, 205 E. 42d St., New York, N.Y., 10017. Editor Jean Press Silberg pays from 3 to 5 cents a word, on acceptance, for stories narrated by women and teens. Accepts wide range of subject matter, including romance, adventure, suspense, as well as typical confession subjects of dating, sex, marriage. Lengths from 6,000 to 8,000 words.

True Story, 205 E. 42d St., New York, N.Y., 10017. Editor Suzanne Hilliard pays 5 cents a word and up, on acceptance, for confessions of interest to teens and blue collar women. Stories range from provocative sex to warm family stories. Narrator usually is a woman, but also buys male-written stories. Also buys general women's articles. Lengths from 1,500 to 3,000 words for articles; 1,500 to 8,000 words for confessions.

Uncensored Confessions, 21 W. 26th St., New York, N.Y., 10010. Editor Ardis Sandel pays $150, 30 days after acceptance, for topical confessions slanted for teen-agers and young marrieds. Lengths run from 1,500 to 7,500 words.

8

HOW TO SELL TO DETECTIVE, MYSTERY, AND SCIENCE FICTION MARKETS

Many a name novelist and successful nonfiction writer cut his writing teeth by selling true detective and mystery stories to pulp magazines. You can do it too, for an average of about $200 a story, if you have a good nose for a sensational murder or other crime story, or know how to invent one with a little twist.

Charles Remsberg, a high-income Chicago freelancer now writing for the top national magazines, explains how he got his start by writing true detective stories, and comments on today's market:

"I was just out of Medill journalism graduate school at Northwestern and wanted to freelance. I figured that true detective stories would bring in some money and, in the meantime, I would be learning how to report and write, both in a hurry.

"Most of the true detective magazine editors have a stable of writers in various parts of the country. If a sensational murder happens in Madison, Wisconsin, the editor's man in Chicago might be assigned to cover it. Usually this man is a crime reporter on a newspaper in the area. Editors do buy stories from untried freelancers, but the story would have to be a good one and their regular writers would have to be either too far away or too busy to cover it.

"I happened to luck out, because one of the true detective magazines' regulars, a Chicago crime reporter, was retiring. I got his 'beat.'

"I had to learn the true detective business fast, so I read everything there was on the magazine stands and studied the style of the stories. I learned that the bulk of stories were on how murder cases were solved, although some stories are on aspects of crime detection, like hypnosis.

"I also learned that I had to work fast to make the $200 worth it. If I had to spend more than two days on the assignment, researching and writing it, it wouldn't pay." Of course, if you're just interested in an occasional extra $200, it wouldn't matter to you if you spent a few more days working on the story. And, as Remsberg says, it gets you started toward full-time freelancing by providing steady income.

Besides murder and crime stories, the true detective magazines also buy articles about interesting policemen or detectives in this country, usually for "Police Officer of the Month" features.

True detective stories must, of course, be true. Real names are not used, but facts must be accurate. Other publications like true adventure stories, which range from happenings in the old West to modern James Bond-type escapades involving intrigue and perhaps some sex. Still other magazines buy fictional detective and adventure stories. Study each magazine carefully to learn what they are using.

Besides the magazines that follow, keep in mind that many men's and outdoor magazines also use true detective and adventure stories, both fiction and nonfiction.

Alfred Hitchcock's Mystery Magazine, 2441 Beach Ct., Riviera Beach, Fla., 33404. Editor Ernest Hutter pays from 3 to 5 cents a word, on acceptance, for mystery and suspense stories. Subjects include spy and supernatural and science fiction, if written for mystery and suspense readers. Does not buy true crime stories. Lengths from 1,000 to 10,000 words.

Armchair Detective, 3656 Midland, White Bear Lake, Minn., 55110. Editor Allen Hubin uses nonfiction mystery and detective stories. No payment.

Confidential Detective Cases, 201 Park Ave. S., New York, N.Y., 10003. Editor B.R. Ampolsk pays good rates, on acceptance, for true detective cases about 3,500 words. Principal character must be a woman. Likes action and emotion. Uses photos.

Crime Detective. Same requirements, address as *Confidential Detective Cases.*

Ellery Queen's Mystery Magazine, 229 Park Ave. S., New York, N.Y., 10003. Managing Editor Eleanor Sullivan pays 3 to 8 cents a word, on acceptance, for detective, crime, mystery, and spy fiction.

DETECTIVE, MYSTERY, AND SCIENCE FICTION MARKETS

Likes detective stories with lots of suspense and straight detection. Lengths run 4,000 to 6,000 words.

Front Page Detective, 750 Third Ave., New York, N.Y., 10017. Editor James Bowser pays $200 and up, on acceptance, for true detective stories of suspense with good detective work and emotional conflict. Lengths run 3,500 to 4,500 words. Also pays $25 to $50 for true crime shorts, to 1,500 words.

Inside Detective. Same requirements, address, as *Front Page Dectective.*

Master Detective, 205 E. 42d St., New York, N.Y., 10017. Editor A.P. Govoni pays up to $200 for true detective stories with good detective work and strong human motivation. Actual photos of case must be available. Lengths run 5,000 to 6,000 words. Query first.

Mike Shayne Mystery Magazine, Renown Publications, 56 W. 45th St., New York, N.Y., 10036. Editor Cylvia Kleinman pays 1 cent a word and up, on acceptance, for detective and mystery stories. Uses 1,500-word shorts and stories up to 12,000 words.

Official Detective Stories, 205 E. 42d St., New York, N.Y., 10017. Editor A.P. Govoni pays $200, on acceptance, for true detective stories. Stories must be current and told from the investigator's point of view. Lengths from 5,000 to 6,000 words. Query.

Startling Detective, 67 W. 44th St., New York, N.Y., 10036. Editor Joseph Corona pays 5 cents a word, on acceptance, for true murder cases, emphasizing police work. Lengths run to 6,000 words. Query.

True Detective, 205 E. 42d St., New York, N.Y., 10017. Editor A.P. Govoni pays up to $200, on acceptance, for current true detective stories. Strong human elements must be present, as well as detailed detective work. Also buys some older detective cases. Lengths run from 5,000 to 6,000 words. Extra payment for photos. Query.

True Police Cases, 67 W. 44th St., New York, N.Y., 10036. Editor Joseph Corona pays 5 cents a word, on acceptance, for true detective stories, articles about crime experts, and articles by law-enforcement officers about aspects of crime and crime detection. Lengths from 4,000 to 6,000 words. Query.

SCIENCE FICTION AND FANTASY

Jack Sharkey, who commented in Chapter 6 on the men's market, makes a lot of his sales to the science fiction market. Again, he chooses to give the editor something different and finds it pays off.

"Humor is my secret in science fiction," says Sharkey. "I read everything on the market and decided the stories were deadly serious, so I thought I'd try some nutsy humor.

"I invented a new kind of alien, and came up with Martians made of candy (red-hued sugar crystals which the early settlers on Mars held off with water pistols). The result was *The Secret Martians,* put out by Ace paperbacks and nicely received in the sci-fi magazine reviews.

"I did the same thing for the hardcover mystery market. I analyzed private eyes—what did they all have in common? The best ones had an avocation which meant more to them than crime-solving (Hercule Poirot's gardening, Nero Wolfe's orchid-growing, Sherlock Holmes' violin-playing). So I concocted George Herbert Henry, a private eye who is a frustrated song-writer (he answers his phone with, 'Private Investigations and songs for all occasions.'), and proceeded to sell *Murder, Maestro, Please* and *Death for Auld Lang Syne.*"

Beyond trying to give the science fiction editor something different, as Sharkey does, the writer for this market must know his field. Science fiction fans are very sophisticated about their Martians and galaxies and zap guns. So before you decide to write for this market, read as many current science fiction stories as you can, to become familiar with technical aspects and for insight into what editors are buying.

Science Fiction and Fantasy Magazines

Analog: Science Fact and Fiction, 420 Lexington Ave., New York, N.Y., 10017. Editor Benjamin Bova pays up to 5 cents a word, on acceptance, for science fiction stories. He prefers characters to be human, against a futuristic setting. Lengths run from short stories 3,500 to 7,500 words, up to novelettes 10,000 to 20,000 words. Also buys short factual articles about science fiction subjects such as space exploration and unidentified flying objects. Query only on novels and factual articles.

Fantasy and Science Fiction, 347 E. 53d St., New York, N.Y., 10022. Editor E. Ferman pays 2 cents a word, on acceptance, for supernatural and science fiction, from short-shorts to serialized novels. Also pays 1 cent a word for reprints of stories run in any but science fiction magazines. Special needs are for fiction with strong science material and well-plotted fantasy. Humor always welcome.

Galaxy Magazine, 235 E. 45th St., New York, N.Y., 10017. Editor Ejler Jakobsson pays good rates, on acceptance, for adult science fiction intelligent readers can enjoy. No fantasy. Lengths from 5,000-word short stories, to novelettes 10,000 words, and novellas from 17,000 to 20,000 words.

If Science Fiction, 235 E. 45th St., New York, N.Y., 10017. Editor Ejler Jakobsson pays 2 cents a word and up, on acceptance, for science fiction up to 20,000 words. No fantasy.

Magazine of Horror, 140 Fifth Ave., New York, N.Y., 10011. Editor Robert A.W. Lowndes pays 1 cent a word, on publication, for horror stories. No science fiction. Uses mainly reprints. Stories run from 1,000 to 5,000 words.

Weirdbook, Box 601, Chambersburg, Pa., 17201. Editor W. Paul Ganley pays $1 per printed page, on publication, for supernatural fiction to 6,000 words, poetry to 15 lines, and photos and drawings.

9

HOW TO SELL TO JUVENILE
AND TEEN-AGE MARKETS

I sold my first published short story for children to a mobile home magazine for $37.50, and it is still my favorite sale. The magazine's secretary said she was so moved while typing up the story for the printer that she cried. I've been trying to find another story that would move my readers so, but they're not that easy to come by.

Tom McGowen, a prolific writer of children's books, agrees that a children's story should touch an adult as well as a child. If you need examples or proof of that, just consider the Dr. Seuss books, the Oz series, or *Charlotte's Web*.

In about four years, McGowen, who is an editor of educational material for Field Enterprises, has sold nine books. His success story is one from which all writers, but especially writers of children's fiction and nonfiction, can profit.

"Don't get discouraged. Keep writing and sending out your manuscripts." That is McGowen's main advice, and he had to learn it himself before he made his first sale.

"I wrote for three years and submitted one story after another before I finally got one accepted," McGowan recalls. "I was ready to quit, when my first book was accepted. The next week, a second book was accepted, by a different publisher. I still write books for those two publishers and, in fact, now they assign books to me."

McGowen's specialty is humorous fantasy. Two of his books, *Dragon Stew* and *Apple Strudle Soldier*, are still very popular with young readers, providing him with an annual annuity better than many retirement income policies.

"Write what interests and pleases *you*," McGowen advises.

"Don't try to write something that is temporarily popular on the market, unless you sincerely enjoy writing that type of story. And don't write up or down or preach to your reader. Entertain him, and you've sold a book. Even factual, nonfiction books should entertain. The 'lasting' books are those that entertain, whether they contain a message or moral or not. My *Apple Strudle Soldier* is an anti-war book, but it got its message across by entertaining the reader."

"*To whom should I send my book?*" McGowen has good advice on that:

"It's a fact of literary life in the children's book market that most books for young readers are not sold through book stores or bought by parents, grandparents, or children, although of course many are. Most books, however, are sold to public and school libraries, through buyers who know what students, librarians, and teachers want. But trying to second-guess what they want is futile for the writer. It's best to simply write what *you* like, and then find the publisher who buys that type of book.

"All publishers have special preferences; books that buyers for public and school libraries learn to look for from them. Some publishers buy fantasy, some won't touch fantasy. Some buy picture books, others prefer mystery and adventure. Some only buy nonfiction. You have to look for the right publisher for your story. Once you sell to that 'right' publisher, you're likely to sell him more, because he knows you can write what he, and his buyers, want."

THE PUBLISHER'S "LIST"

"*We liked your book, but it is just not quite right for our list.*" This is a phrase many writers of children's books get from editors. What exactly does it mean, and is it a legitimate excuse for turning down your manuscript?

The answer is yes: it *is* a legitimate excuse, and if you get such a reject from an editor, consider yourself on the way to selling.

When an editor says a book is not quite right for his list, he means that he has a subject quota to fill for the publisher. He may need one adventure novel, an animal picture book or two, a biography, a rhyme book, a beginning reader, a young people's science book, and a mystery story. He may like your book a lot, but have no opening for it on his list. Often reluctantly, he will be forced to reject your story, not because it wasn't well-written, but because he had no place for it on his list.

"*Is it necessary to have a teaching background in order to write children's books?*" The answer to that is, No. But, as McGowen puts it, "It helps to have a childlike mind. I'm 44 on the outside, but on the inside, I'm 10. I write books *I* would like to have read when *I* was 10 or 12."

"*Should I collaborate with an artist in order to get a picture book sold?*" Again, the answer to that is, No. Unless you are a skilled artist, don't try illustrating your own children's book, and you can sell a book whether or not you team up with an artist. Most editors prefer to assign an artist to illustrate a book. He will be someone the editor knows can bring out the best visual possibilities in a story.

"*Must I be a parent to write children's books that sell?*" Once again, the answer is No. But you must like children and like what they like to read. It isn't essential that you observe and love children of your own, as long as you observe and love children. (And it helps to keep a keen ear open for their current jargon.)

THE MONEY SIDE

"*Can I make a living writing children's books?*" The answer to that is No and Yes.

"*No,* you can't make a living as a writer of children's books," McGowen says, as a father of four children and a writer of children's books who also is employed full-time as an editor. "Most writers do other allied things. I'm fortunate in that I write and edit educational material for young readers. I was in advertising, before that, and just didn't belong. If you want to write books for children, find a full-time job writing or editing for young readers, and you'll gain experience while you enjoy security, plus a good extra income. And what you write and publish on your own is bound to improve your skill in your job, thus pleasing your boss."

"*Yes,* you can make a living writing children's books," says Cliff Hicks, a prolific writer of fiction and nonfiction for the 9 to

12 age group. "I've kept time records of my work on books for children, and records of what I've made on the books. Hour for hour, writing children's books is the most lucrative writing I've ever done!"

Hicks, an editor of *Popular Mechanics*, divides his freelance writing between children's books and adult articles for science magazines. He also has written a children's science book.

"My best sellers are a series of boy adventure novels," Hicks says. "They all have the boy's name in the title: Alvin Fernald. He gets involved in science adventures and, in one book, was mayor for a day. To my great pleasure, Walt Disney Productions recently bought television rights to the series, and I went out to Hollywood to watch them make a movie of it. It was a real thrill to see my fictional characters come to life on the set. And I admit, it was lucrative. Having Disney Productions pick up the books was just like 'found money!' "

If Hicks is so successful writing children's books, why doesn't he quit his job and write them full-time?

"I guess I still don't have that much confidence," he admits. "Raising a family requires steady income. But writing children's books, for me, is a very lucrative sideline. Most children's books have a life of several years, unlike adult novels. You may not make much money on a book during its first year, but if it's a good book, it will remain on the market three or four years or longer. Over a period of time, you will make good money on it. I write one children's book a year. But if you have two or three going in a year, there is no doubt in my mind that you can make a good living writing children's books."

Hicks' advice to writers of children's books parallels McGowens: write what you like to read, make yourself stop procrastinating and sit down and actually write, keep writing and sending out manuscripts, and find the right publisher for your type of writing.

HOW TO GET STARTED

For the writer aspiring to write books for young readers, a good start is to sell fiction and articles to magazines published for juvenile, teen-age, and young adult readers. The material bought by this market is vast and varied, so it is best to study recent issues to determine just what the editors are buying.

Generally, the magazines for younger readers have not changed much in their requirements. They still publish predominately stories and articles to entertain and inform beginning readers. On the other hand, magazines for teen-agers and young adults are progressively seeking more mature, sophisticated material, aimed at readers who are growing up much faster than the authors did when they were young, and who are more concerned with social problems and their solutions. Writers can debate whether this is good or not, but if they want to sell to this market, they will have to give the editors what they think the readers want. Studying each magazine is the best way of learning what the market wants.

Religious and educational markets are important ones in the children's magazine field. Many are weekly publications, using up material almost as fast as television. Authors should note that even in these fields, they should be careful not to preach to their readers. If a message is to be gotten across, it must be easy to swallow and well-disguised.

If you are writing seasonal material, submit your story or article to a publication at least four months in advance of the season.

Upon request, some editors will send a fact sheet detailing their magazine's requirements.

Following are the best markets in children's magazines and books. In addition, many women's and general magazines buy fiction and nonfiction for and about children and teen-agers. The writer for this market should also read the current magazines and best-selling books in the children's field. He also should study newspaper reviews of children's books, such as those the *New York Times* and *Christian Science Monitor* publish each week, and especially their special seasonal book section supplements on children's books. *Horn Book Magazine* also reviews children's books.

Juvenile Magazines

Adventure, Baptist Sunday School Board, 127 Ninth Ave., Nashville, Tenn., 37203. Editor Muriel Blackwell pays 2½ cents a word, on acceptance, for short stories 900 to 1,200 words, and articles to 900 words for children ages 8 to 11. Also buys puzzles, cartoons, and poetry. Likes articles to be illustrated.

Adventure Magazine, Harvest Publications, 5750 N. Ashland Ave., Chicago, Ill., 60626. Editor David Olson pays 3 cents a word and up, on acceptance, for articles of Evangelical Christian adventure and activities for ages 9 to 12. Lengths run 1,000 to 1,500 words. Also buys picture stories. Query first. Sample of magazine and fact sheet sent on request.

Ambassador Life (see *Crusader*).

American Red Cross Youth News, American National Red Cross, Washington, D.C., 20006. Pays $50 to $125, on acceptance, for stories on children of other countries, national holidays, and activities of children in America today. Wants 600-word stories for young readers, and 1,000-to-1,200-word stories for children through sixth grade.

The Annals of the Holy Childhood, P.O. Box 6758, Pittsburgh, Pa., 15212. Managing Editor Fred McCool pays $25 and up for articles about Catholic missions for elementary school children. Also buys stories with religious or moral lessons. Lengths run 600 to 800 words.

Child Life, 1100 Waterway Blvd., Indianapolis, Ind., 46202. Editor Beth Thomas pays 3 cents a word for short stories to 900 words and beginning reading material from 400 to 500 words for children ages 7 to 12. Also buys short plays for classroom and home production, games, puzzles, and verse. Payment on publication.

The Children's Friend (see *The Friend*).

Children's Playmate Magazine, 1100 Waterway Blvd., Indianapolis, Ind., 46202. Editor Mrs. Beth Thomas pays about 3 cents a word, on publication, for short stories to 600 words for children ages 3 to 8. Also buys poetry, puzzles, science for children, and easy projects for home or classroom.

Christian Science Monitor, One Norway St., Boston, Mass., 02115. Editor John Hughes pays $30 for short stories 600 to 900 words for children 10 years and younger. Runs one story a week, and does not buy serials. Send stories to "Editor for Children."

Climb, Box 2499, Fifth and Chestnut Sts., Anderson, Ind., 46011. Editor William A. White buys religious and character-building stories for children ages 8 to 11. Lengths run 900 to 1,200 words; also 3- to 5-chapter serials. Pays $7.50 per 1,000 words, on acceptance.

Crusader (formerly *Ambassador Life*), 1548 Poplar Ave., Memphis, Tenn., 38104. Editor Lee Hollaway pays 2 cents a word, on acceptance, for fiction and articles for boys ages 6 to 11. Magazine is published by the Brotherhood Commision of the Southern Baptist Convention. Lengths run to 1,000 words. Also buys short articles on games, hobbies, crafts.

Discovery, Light and Life Press, Winona Lake, Ind., 46590.

Formerly *Story Trails*. Editor Helen Hull pays 2 cents a word, after acceptance, for short stories 2,000 to 2,500 words for ages 8 to 11. Also how-to-do features 500 to 1,000 words, and pays 20 cents a line for poetry.

Explore, Christian Board of Publication, Box 179, St. Louis, Mo., 63166. Editor Rosalie Logan pays good rates, on acceptance, for short stories to 600 words for grades 1 and 2. Also articles to 400 words and poems to 12 lines. Sample copy and fact sheet sent on request (enclose 25 cents).

Five/Six, 201 Eighth Ave. S., Nashville, Tenn., 37203. Pays from 2 to 4 cents a word for short stories to 1,250 words, for fifth and sixth graders. Also pays $1 a line for poetry.

The Friend (formerly *The Children's Friend*), 79 S. State St., Salt Lake City, Utah, 84111. Monthly magazine published by the Church of Jesus Christ of Latter-Day Saints. Managing Editor Mrs. Lucille Reading buys short stories and articles of general child interest as well as religious articles. Pays up to 4 cents a word for stories to 1,000 words. Likes adventure, suspense, character-building situations, and humor. Also uses "Tiny tot" stories from 300 to 500 words and stories about children in this country and other countries. Pays 25 cents a line for poetry. All payment on acceptance. Sends free copy of magazine on request.

Fun for Middlers, American Baptist Board of Education and Publication, Valley Forge, Pa., 19481. Editor Nina Booth pays up to 2 cents a word, on acceptance, for short stories to 1,200 words for children ages 8 to 9. Also biographies, interesting activities of children, poetry, puzzles, cartoons.

Highlights for Children, 803 Church St., Honesdale, Pa., 18431. Editor Garry Cleveland Myers pays 6 cents a word and up, on acceptance, for short stories for children ages 3 to 12, under 1,000 words. Likes characters who struggle to achieve an ideal, easy-to-read stories with strong plot from 400 to 600 words, and humor. Also stories of people from ethnic or urban backgrounds. Also buys verse.

Humpty Dumpty's Magazine, 52 Vanderbilt Ave., New York, N.Y., 10017. Managing Editor Thomas S. Roberts pays $50 on acceptance for stories for beginning readers, 600 to 850 words; read-aloud stories to 900 words with third or fourth grade vocabulary; and stories intended to be read by the parent and retold to the child, up to 1,000 words.

Jack and Jill, P.O. Box 528, Indianapolis, Ind., 46206. Editor Nelle Keys Bell pays good rates, on publication, for short stories and articles from 300 to 1,500 words. Also buys puzzles, riddles, plays, songs, games, jokes, poems, and arts and crafts for children.

Jet Cadet (formerly *Junior Life*), 8121 Hamilton Ave., Cincinnati, Ohio, 45231. Sunday school weekly for children ages 9 to 12. Editor Dana Eynon pays 1½ cents a word, on acceptance, for short stories 900 to 1,200 words about children in situations involving adventure, sports, travel, mystery, animals, human relationships. Also articles 400 to 500 words on hobbies and handicrafts (with illustrations), famous people, holidays, hobbies, life in other countries. Material should have some Christian emphasis, but not preachy. Also buys previously-published material. Poetry bought for up to 35 cents a line. Sample copy sent free upon request.

Junior Discoveries, 6401 The Paseo, Kansas City, Mo., 64131. Editor Maureen H. Box pays 1½ cents a word, on acceptance, for short stories and articles for Sunday School children ages 9 to 11. Fiction runs 1,000 to 1,400 words, with Christian emphasis. Articles on nature, travel, history, crafts, science run 500 to 800 words. Pays 10 cents a line for poetry.

Junior Trails, 1445 Boonville Ave., Springfield, Mo., 65802. Editor Dorothy Morris pays good rates on acceptance for stories for boys and girls 10 to 12 years old emphasizing how Bible principles can be put into practice in their lives. Lengths 1,200 to 1,500 words.

Kids, P.O. Box 30, Cambridge, Mass., 02139. A magazine with articles and stories written solely by children under 15, not adults writing for children. Editors Jenette Kahn and Jim Robinson pay $5 and a year's free subscription, on publication, for stories, articles, drawings, photos, poetry. Sample copy sent for 50 cents. Young contributors are reminded to enclose self-addressed, stamped envelope for return of material not accepted.

The Kindergartner, Graded Press, 201 Eighth Ave. S., Nashville, Tenn., 37202. Editor Mrs. Ernestine Calhoun pays good rates, on acceptance, for stories to 300 words to interest Methodist kindergarten pupils.

Merry-Go-Round, Scholastic Magazines, Inc., 50 W. 44th St., New York, N.Y., 10036. Pays from $75 to $100, on acceptance, for stories about 280 words for early second grade readers, and about 375 words for upper second graders. Address Editor, Manuscript Department.

More, Baptist Sunday School Board, 127 Ninth Ave. N., Nashville, Tenn., 37203. Editor Muriel F. Blackwell pays 2½ cents a word, on acceptance, for stories and articles to 500 words for beginning readers. Also buys poems to 16 lines and simple puzzles.

News Explorer, Scholastic Magazines, Inc., 50 W. 44th St., New York, N.Y., 10036. Pays $75 and up, on acceptance, for short stories 900 to 1,000 words and two-part serials to 2,000 words, for children 9 and 10 years old. Likes suspense, adventure, legends, mystery, humor, pets, in current or historic setting. Send to Editor, Manuscript Department.

NewsTime, Scholastic Magazines, Inc., 50 W. 44th St., New York, N.Y., 10036. Pays $50 and up for stories to interest children ages 11 to 12. Lengths about 600 words; 1,200 to 1,500 words; and 2,000 words. Likes mystery, humor, action, folklore, family dramas. Send to Editor, Manuscript Department.

News Trails, Scholastic Magazines, Inc., 50 W. 44th St., New York, N.Y., 10036. Short stories for children 8 and 9 years old, including school subjects and situations, children of interest in this country or abroad, pets, holidays. Vocabulary for average third grader. Pays $75 and up, on acceptance. Send to Editor, Manuscript Department.

Nursery Days, Graded Press, 201 Eighth Ave. S., Nashville, Tenn., 37202. Editor Miss Evelyn Andre pays on acceptance for stories on the Methodist church for nursery children ages 2 and 3. Lengths 300 words. Also poetry.

One/Two, 201 Eighth Ave. S., Nashville, Tenn., 37202. Editor Jean Buchanan pays 3 cents a word, on acceptance, for short stories to interest Methodist church young readers age 6 and 7. Lengths run 100 to 500 words.

Our Little Friend, Pacific Press Publishing Assn., 1350 Villa St., Mountain View, Calif., 94040. Editor Louis Schutter pays 1 cent a word for stories aimed at children ages 2 to 6 who are members of the Seventh-day Adventist religion. Lengths run 800 to 1,500 words. Also verse from 8 to 12 lines, at 10 cents a line. Also buys puzzles, photos, drawings.

Presbyterian Life, Witherspoon Bldg., Philadelphia, Pa., 19107. Editor Robert J. Cadigan buys some stories for children for this adult magazine. Age range is 6 to 10 years; lengths from 700 to 800 words. Payment on acceptance.

Primary Treasure, Pacific Press Publishing Assn., 1350 Villa St., Mountain View, Calif., 94040. Editor Louis Schutter pays 1 cent a word for stories to interest children 7 to 9 who belong to the Seventh-day Adventist church. Lengths run 800 to 1,500 words. Also pays 10 cents a line for verse from 8 to 12 lines, and buys puzzles, photos, drawings.

Quest, Christian Board of Publication, Box 179, St. Louis, Mo., 63116. Editor Lee Miller pays on acceptance for short stories to 1,200 words and articles to 600 words, for grades 5 and 6. Sample copy sent on request, for 25 cents.

Ranger Rick's Nature Magazine, Publisher's Services, Inc., 1518 Walnut St., Philadelphia, Pa., 19102. Editor Trudy Dye Farrand pays from $5 to $200, shortly before publication, for articles to help young readers enjoy and appreciate nature. Slant must be on nature, natural science, or conservation. Lengths to 800 words. Published by the National Wildlife Federation.

Roadrunner, American Baptist Board of Education and Publication, Valley Forge, Pa., 19481. Editor Nina M. Booth pays up to 2 cents a word, on acceptance, for short stories, articles, and biographies from 200 to 700 words, of interest to children age 6 and 7. Also poetry, puzzles, activity projects.

Search, Christian Board of Publication, Box 179, St. Louis, Mo., 63166. Editor Lee Miller pays on acceptance for short stories to interest children in grades 3 and 4. Lengths to 1,000 words. Also articles to 600 words and poetry to 16 lines. Sample copy sent on request, for 25 cents.

Story Friends, Mennonite Publishing House, Scottdale, Pa., 15683. Editor Alice Hershberger pays up to 1½ cents a word, on acceptance, for stories and articles relating faith to everyday life, aimed at children ages 4 to 8. Subjects include nature, family, school, church, courage, friendship, and harmony among races. Lengths from 400 to 800 words.

Story Trails (see *Discovery*).

SummerTime, Scholastic Magazines, Inc., 50 W. 44th St., New York, N.Y., 10036. Pays $50 and up, on acceptance, for short stories to interest children ages 11 to 13. Subjects range from mystery and sports to folklore, family life, humor. Send to Editor, Manuscript Department.

Three/Four, 201 Eighth Ave. S., Nashville, Tenn., 37203. Editor Betty Buerki pays 4 cents a word for short stories about 1,000 words for third and fourth graders. Also pays 50 cents to $1 a line for poetry, and buys puzzles, quizzes, and short informational articles.

Trails, Box 788, Wheaton, Ill., 60187. Editor Jane Sorenson pays up to $50, on acceptance, for short stories and articles for girls, emphasizing Christian teaching. Published by Pioneer Girls for girls age 8 to 12. Also buys photos and cartoons.

Treasure Chest, P.O. Box 726, Dayton, Ohio, 45401. Comic magazine for children age 8 to 14. Published in comic book format, and pays $10 per printed page. Material can be comic treatments of history, biography, mystery, adventure, and humor. Artists will be assigned to illustrate the stories if the writer does not illustrate them himself (only writer-artists should attempt to illustrate their own material). Also publishes one non-comic story or article per issue, to 1,000 words, for 5 cents a word. Query.

Vacation Fun, Scholastic Magazines, Inc., 50 W. 44th St., New York, N.Y., 10036. Pays $75 and up, on acceptance, for short stories to interest children ages 8 to 10. Subjects range from adventure and legends to pets and contemporary life. Lengths to 1,000 words, and two-parts if suspense warrants. Send to Editor, Manuscript Department.

Wee Wisdom, Unity Village, Mo., 64063. Editor Thomas N. Hopper pays 2 cents a word and up for stories and articles emphasizing character-building for boys and girls. Wants lively short stories, articles on science, nature, projects, crafts. Do not sermonize. Also buys short, seasonal poems at 50 cents a line, and pays $3 for puzzles and games.

Whenever Whatever, American Baptist Board of Education and Publication, Valley Forge, Pa., 19481. Editor Gracie Adkins pays up to 2 cents a word, on acceptance, for short stories, biographies, and articles on current events, for children aged 10 to 11. Also activities of boys and girls, poetry, how-to projects, puzzles, cartoons. Lengths of fiction and articles to 1,800 words.

Witness, George A. Pflaum, Publisher, Inc., 38 W. 5th St., Dayton, Ohio, 45402. Pays up to $75 for short stories and articles for children 10 to 15 years old, on people living the Christian life. Also buys picture stories, photos without stories, and cartoons. Prefers query.

Wonder Time, 6401 The Paseo, Kansas City, Mo., 64131. For Sunday school children under 9 years old. Editor Elizabeth B. Jones pays 1½ cents a word, on acceptance, for short stories and articles on nature, travel, crafts, Bible stories. Fiction lengths 200 to 750 words, articles 200 to 500 words. Also pays 12 cents per line and up for poetry.

Woodmen of the World Magazine, 1700 Farnam St., Omaha, Nebr., 68102. Editor Leland Larson pays 2 cents a word, on acceptance, for stories to interest girls and boys aged 8 to 19. Lengths 400 to 1,200 words.

Young Crusader, 1730 Chicago Ave., Evanston, Ill., 60201. Editor Lillian Luney pays half a cent a word, on acceptance, for character-building stories for readers ages 6 to 12. Lengths run 600 to 850 words.

Young World, 1100 Waterway Blvd., Indianapolis, Ind., 46202. Associate Editor Ellen Taggart pays from 3 to 6 cents a word, on publication, for articles and short stories for boys and girls ages 8 to 13. Likes short stories to be suspenseful or adventure, involving 9- to 13-year-olds. Likes humor but not fantasy or talking inanimate objects. Short articles can be on any subject of interest to young readers, but especially history, nature, little-known events in lives of famous people, with their identity left to the end. Also buys puzzles, how-to projects. Pays $3 for photos; $15 and up for poetry.

Teen-Age and Young Adult Markets

Much the same rules apply in writing for teen-agers and young adults that apply in writing for younger readers: entertain them, inform them, but don't preach to them. Important contemporary issues such as ecology and better human understanding are extremely serious to many teen-agers, but they prefer not to be hit over the head with the message. They also enjoy romance, adventure, mystery, humor, and all the other good-reading subjects that children and adults like.

Leading markets for teens and young adults follow:

Accent on Youth (formerly *Twelve/Fifteen*), 201 Eighth Ave. S., Nashville, Tenn., 37203. Editor Margaret Barnhart pays 3 cents a word and up, on acceptance, for articles and short stories for readers in their early teens. Lengths for short stories run to 2,500 words. Articles of about the same length range from the outdoors to hobbies and from biography to family relationships. Also buys photo features.

Ambassador Life (see *Probe*).

American Girl, 830 Third Ave., New York, N.Y., 10022. Editor Pat di Sernia, published by the Girl Scouts for girls aged 10 to 16. Pays good rates, on acceptance, for short stories of adventure and mystery, school, and family life, careers, sports, romance, etc., and articles of interest to teen girls. Fiction lengths from 1,000 to 3,000 words; nonfiction from 500 to 1,500 words. Query for articles.

American Newspaper Boy, 915 Carolina Ave. N.W., Winston-Salem, N.C., 27101. Editor Charles Moester pays $10 to $25 for fiction to interest newsboys aged 14 to 17: mystery, humor, adventure, character-building. Lengths to 2,000 words. Also buys inspirational stories about boys who were helpful or courageous while on their newspaper route.

American Red Cross Youth Journal, American National Red Cross, Washington, D.C., 20006. Pays good rates, on acceptance, for articles of interest to junior high and high school students: science, self-development, problems and interests of teen-agers. Lengths from 1,000 to 1,500 words.

Blast, 209 Dunn Ave., Stamford, Conn., 06905. Editor Al Forman pays good rates, on acceptance, for material that can be used in comic strip style, like *Mad Magazine,* aimed at both young and old people "with young ideas." Emphasis is on satire and humor on practically everything. Sample copy sent on request for 50 cents. Material should be sent in script form, from which a staff artist can turn it into cartoon format.

Boys' Life, North Brunswick, N.J., 08902. Editor Robert E. Hood pays from $150 to $300 for short articles 750 to 1,200 words; $500 to $1,000 for feature articles 2,500 words; and $500 and up for short stories to 2,500 words. Magazine is aimed at Boy Scouts and Cubs from 8 to 17 years old. Subjects include sports, adventure, history, science, personalities. Articles should be sent to Stan Pashko; fiction to Mrs. Deming Small.

Campus Life, Box 419, Wheaton, Ill., 60187. Editor Harold Myra pays 2 cents a word and up for articles and fiction about 1,500 words for teens 16 to 19. Stories and features should reflect wholesome activities of teens, be about outstanding Christian young people, or be helpful "how-to" articles. Also buys teen-slanted cartoons. Query first.

Catalyst, Christian Board of Publication, Beaumont and Pine Blvd., St. Louis, Mo., 63166. Editor Jerry O'Malley pays 1½ cents a word and up for stories and articles to 2,000 words slanted for high school readers, emphasizing religion and social issues. Also pays 25 cents a line for poetry. $6 and up for cartoons. Sample copy sent on request, for 25 cents.

Co-Ed, Scholastic Magazines, 50 W. 44th St., New York, N.Y., 10036. Pays $150 and up, on acceptance, for short stories to 5,000 words for girls 14 to 18. Subjects include boy-girl situations, problems of teen-agers, home, family, romance. Humor welcome. Stories should have fall, winter, or spring settings rather than summer. Send stories to Editor, Manuscript Department.

Conquest, 6401 The Paseo, Kansas City, Mo., 64131. Editor Paul Miller pays 1½ cents a word, on acceptance, for articles and fiction with Christian emphasis, for teen-agers. Fiction lengths run to 2,500 words; nonfiction, 500 to 1,200 words. Poetry, to 20 lines.

Contact, 302 U.B. Building, Huntington, Ind., 46750. Editor Stanley Peters buys articles and fiction for teens and adults of the United Brethern in Christ.

Earth, Agricultural Bldg., Embaracadero at Mission, San Francisco, Calif., 94105. Editor James Goode pays $100 per magazine page for in-depth articles on people and events of interest to readers aged 17 to 26. Not specifically an ecology magazine, but does buy articles on that subject, as well as other subjects of interest to concerned young readers. Pays $200 per page for photos and is especially interested in color and black and white photo essays. Also buys some fiction.

Lengths for articles and fiction run from 1,000 to 5,000 words. Query first.

Encounter (formerly *Venture*), Editor of Sunday School Magazines, The Wesleyan Church, Box 2000, Marion, Ind., 46952. Published for older teens age 15 to 18. Pays 2 cents a word for fiction including serials 6 to 8 chapters, 800 to 2,500 words per chapter, and articles 500 to 1,500 words, with Christian emphasis. Subjects include nature, travel, history, science, humor. Also poetry 4 to 6 lines for 25 cents a line.

Event, Baptist Sunday School Board, 127 Ninth Ave. N., Nashville, Tenn., 37203. Editor Billie Pate pays 2½ cents a word, on acceptance, for stories and articles to interest Southern Baptist youth, ages 12 to 17. Stories run 1,000 to 3,000 words; articles to 1,500 words. Pays slightly higher rates for poetry, any length.

Exploring, Boy Scouts of America, New Brunswick, N.J., 08903. Editor Robert E. Hood pays good rates for articles aimed at older boys, aged 15 to 20. Subjects include careers, sports, adventure, science. No fiction. Query Articles Editor Louis Sabin before submitting manuscript.

Face-to-Face, 201 Eighth Ave. S., Nashville, Tenn., 37203. Editor Kenneth Winston pays 2 cents a word and up, on acceptance, for fiction and articles of interest to older teens of the United Methodist church. Fiction runs 2,500 to 3,000 words; articles 1,500 to 1,800 words. Query.

For Teens Only, 235 Park Ave. S., New York, N.Y., 10003. Editor Rena Adler pays $50 for articles and fiction to interest girls aged 12 to 16. Situations and dialogue must be realistic. Lengths run 1,500 to 4,000 words. Payment on acceptance. Sample copy sent for 50 cents. Send completed manuscript, not a query.

HiCall, 1445 Boonville Ave., Springfield, Mo., 65802. Editor Dorothy Morris pays good rates, on acceptance, for fiction and articles with evangelical slant, for ages 12 to 21. Fiction runs 1,000 to 1,500 words; articles 500 to 1,000 words. Buys true stories of mission activities, biographies of leading Christians, and general subjects of interest to teen-agers.

High, Harvest Publication, 5750 N. Ashland Ave., Chicago, Ill., 60626. Editor David Olson pays 3 cents a word and up, on acceptance, for articles and fiction with Evangelical Christian emphasis. Articles run 500 to 1,500 words; fiction 500 to 1,500 words. Prefers illustrated articles. Samples and fact sheet sent on request. Query for articles.

Impact, American Baptist Board of Education and Publication, Valley Forge, Pa., 19481. Editor Janice M. Corbett pays up to 2 cents a word for articles to 2,000 words, and stories to interest senior high youth.

Ingenue, Dell Publishing Co., 750 Third Ave., New York, N.Y., 10017. Editor-in-Chief Joan Wynn prefers queries for articles. Send them to Articles Editor Henrietta Schlanger. Magazine is aimed at teen girls aged 13 to 19, with most material slanted at age 15. Articles must relate to her world, but not in a hip style. Readers are intelligent and want quality and service. Article lengths run from 700 to 4,500 words. Payment is from $75 to $500, on acceptance. Fiction Editor Myrna Blyth wants romance and problem stories with a teen-ager in a dominant role in the story, but it can be either a girl or a boy. Stories should be on contemporary subjects: problems of growing up, relationships with family and friends, romance, school, etc. Fiction runs 1,500 to 5,000 words; ideal length, 3,500 words. Payment ranges from $175 to $500.

Junior Hi Challenge, 922 Montgomery Ave., Cleveland, Tenn., 37311. Editor Martha Wong buys fiction and articles to 1,200 words for students in junior high school: youth news, activities, character-building stories, camp and school life, biography, preferably with Christian emphasis, without sermonizing. Also picture stories, humor, puzzles, cartoons, poetry. Pays half a cent a word, on acceptance; $1 for poems; $1 to $2 for photos.

Junior Scholastic, Scholastic Magazines, Inc., 50 W. 44th St., New York, N.Y., 10036. Magazine for students in grades 7 and 8 (ages 12 to 14). Buys fiction and original plays from 1,000 to 2,000 words, and articles 500 to 2,000 words about young teen-agers' hobbies, community activities, achievements. Pays from $50 to $100 and up, on acceptance. Send material to Editor, Manuscript Department. Query.

Literary Cavalcade, Scholastic Magazines, Inc., 50 W. 44th St., New York, N.Y., 10036. Pays $150 and up for reprints only for short stories for young adults (they must be a complete story, no mood pieces, and no high school romances). Lengths from 1,500 to 3,500 words.

The Mother Earth News, Box 38, Madison, Ohio, 44057. Editor John Shuttleworth pays up to $100 for how-to articles for hip young adults. Likes features that tell how people can save the ecology of the world and save money besides. Buys articles on organic gardening, starting a home business, and in general, dropping out of the rat race and living your own life. Sample of magazine and fact sheet sent on request.

National Future Farmer, Box 15130, Alexandria, Va., 22309. Editor Wilson Carnes pays up to 4 cents a word, on acceptance, for articles to 1,000 words, of interest to high school students of vocational agriculture. Average age of reader is 17. Buys features on new developments in agriculture, leadership and activities of members of Future Farmers of America. Also pays $7.50 for cartoons.

National Lampoon, 1790 Broadway, New York, N.Y., 10019. Editor Douglas C. Kenney pays 10 cents a word and up for satire, parody, and humor from 1,000 to 3,500 words for college-age readers, predominantly male. Send manuscripts to Mary Martello, articles editor.

On the Line (formerly *Words of Cheer*), 610 Walnut Ave., Scottdale, Pa., 15683. Editor Helen Alderfer pays up to 2 cents a word for stories and articles 750 to 1,000 words, for weekly paper for children 9 to 14. Stories and articles should point up Christian belief that God is at work in the world. Also poetry, puzzles, quizzes, cartoons. Sample and fact sheet sent free on request.

Probe (formerly *Ambassador's Life*), 1548 Poplar Ave., Memphis, Tenn., 38104. Editor Everett Hullum pays 2 cents a word, on acceptance, for fiction and articles to interest boys aged 12 to 17, members of the Southern Baptist church. Lengths run to 1,000 words. Also hobbies, crafts, games.

Reachout (formerly *Teen Time*), Light and Life Press, Winona Lake, Ind., 46590. Editor Helen Hull pays 2 cents a word for short stories to 3,000 words, and articles 800 to 2,000 words on careers, hobbies, human interest for teen-agers. Fiction must be religious in tone. Buys seasonal material; also poetry.

Reflection (formerly *Trails*), Box 788, Wheaton, Ill., 60187. Editor Jane Sorenson pays up to $50, on acceptance, for stories and articles to 2,000 words with Christian teaching slant for Pioneer Girls ages 13 to 18. Also photos, cartoons.

Rolling Stone, 625 Third St., San Francisco, Calif., 94107. Newspaper which reports on rock music and its stars. Editor Jann Wenner pays 5 cents a word, on publication, for articles aimed at young adults and those under 30 who are rock music fans. Timely articles can be submitted directly; query on other features. Buys photos and drawings; no fiction or poetry.

Scholastic Scope, Scholastic Magazines, 50 W. 44th St., New York, N.Y., 10036. Pays $50 to $150 for stories and articles for 4th and 6th graders (age 15 to 18). Stories from 400 to 1,200 words, and plays to 3,000 words, should be on problems of urban students (job, racial, teen-adult). Emphasis is on realism, action, good characterization. No crime. Articles 400 to 800 words should interest mid-teens. Pays $10 per photo used.

Scholastic VOICE, Scholastic Magazines, 50 W. 44th St., New York, N.Y., 10036. Pays from $100 to $150 for stories and plays; aimed at readers age 14 through 17. Fiction must be well-plotted with strong characters, on adventure, mystery, science fiction, family, sports, problems. Short-shorts run 500 to 1,000 words; stories and plays from 1,500 to 3,000 words. Payment on acceptance. Send manuscripts to Editor, Manuscript Dept.

Science World, Scholastic Magazines, 50 W. 44th St., New York, N.Y., 10036. Pays $125 for articles 1,000 to 1,800 words for grades 7 through 12. Buys material only for two departments: "Today's Scientists," a progress report of important contemporary scientific work; and "Science World Takes You There," reporting on laboratories and other scientific places and expeditions. Photos should accompany manuscripts. Query. Address Eric Berger, Science Division.

Senior Hi Challenge, 922 Montgomery Ave., Cleveland, Tenn., 37311. Editor Martha Wong pays half a cent a word for true stories with Christian emphasis. Subjects include character-development, missionary work, camping, adventure, biography. Also poetry and humor.

Seventeen, 320 Park Ave., New York, N.Y., 10022. Editor-in-Chief Enid A. Haupt pays top rates, on acceptance, for well-written articles of interest to young girl and women readers. Fiction Editor Babette Rosmond pays $400 and up for quality short stories about 3,000 words that emphasize characterization and tell a good story, especially involving those in their late teens. "Growing-up" stories always welcome.

Spirit, Concordia Publishing House, 3558 S. Jefferson Ave., St. Louis, Mo., 63118. Pastor Walter Reiss, editor, pays from $20 to $200, on publication, for articles about teen-agers active in Christian activities. Lengths run to 2,000 words. Prefers black and white photos to accompany article.

Straight, 8121 Hamilton Ave., Cincinnati, Ohio, 45231. Editor Mrs. Bee Nelson pays up to $35 for fiction and articles to interest teen-agers. Stories to 1,500 words should be character-building, about Christian athletes, school-family stories, teen problems, church work, etc. Articles to 1,200 words should emphasize Christian approach to contemporary life and its problems, especially as they concern teens.

Surfer Magazine, Box 1028, Dana Point, Calif., 92629. Editor John Severson pays good rates for articles on surfing, from 500 to 3,000 words, anywhere in the world. Also short stories related to surfing, from 1,000 to 3,000 words. Pays good rates for color and black and white photos of surfing, with or without article.

Teen Magazine, 8490 Sunset Blvd., Los Angeles, Calif., 90069. Managing Editor Carole Ann Tucker pays $150 and up for short stories 2,500 to 4,000 words, and illustrated articles under 1,500 words, for teen-agers. Material should reflect current interests and trends of active teens.

HOW TO SELL TO JUVENILE AND TEEN-AGE MARKETS

Teens Today, 6401 The Paseo, Kansas City, Mo., 64131. Editor Wesley Tracy pays 1½ cents a word, on acceptance, for contemporary fiction and articles with Christian slant, to challenge teens. Stories run to 2,500 words; articles to 1,500 words. Also buys poetry for the same rate.

Union Gospel Press, Box 6059, Cleveland, Ohio, 44101. Publishes Sunday School material for teens and young adults. Pays 2 cents a word, for articles with religious emphasis, from 300 to 1,400 words. Sample sent on request.

Venture, Christian Service Brigade, P.O. Box 150, Wheaton, Ill., 60187. Editor Daniel Jessen pays from $25 to $100, on publication, for articles and fiction for boys 8 to 18, to help them develop as Christian men. Also Biblical stories of Christian boys and men. Lengths run 1,000 to 1,500 words.

Win Magazine, Youth Publication of the Wesleyan Church, Box 2000, Marion, Ind., 46952. Editor Robert Zuhl pays half a cent per word for religious and educational articles for teens. Lengths to 1,500 words. Also photos and cartoons for $2.50 each.

World Over, 426 W. 58th St., New York, N.Y., 10019. Co-editors Ezekiel Scholoss and Dr. Morris Epstein pays 4 to 5 cents a word for stories of Jewish interest for children 9 to 14. Stories can be historic or contemporary. Also buys serials for from $175 to $225; lengths to 5 chapters, 1,200 words per chapter. Query first.

Young Ambassador, Box 233, Lincoln, Nebr., 68501. Associate Editor Ruth Johnson Jay pays 1½ cents a word for stories with Christian emphasis, for young teen-agers. Lengths to 1,800 words.

Young Judaean, 116 W. 14th St., New York, N.Y., 10011. Editor Doris B. Gold pays 2 cents a word for articles to interest young Jewish readers 12 to 14. Subjects include Jewish youth activities, music, Israel-U.S. news, etc. Also poetry and humor. Copy sent on request, for 25 cents.

Young Miss, 52 Vanderbilt Ave., New York, N.Y., 10017. Editor Rubie Saunders pays $50 to $100 for short fiction and $100 to $150 for novelettes to 6,500 words, for girls 10 to 14. Also pays $10 to $50 for articles to 2,000 words on sports, careers, crafts, problems of young girls. Query on articles.

Youth Alive, (formerly *Christ's Ambassadors Herald*), 1445 Boonville Ave., Springfield, Mo., 65802. Christian magazine for readers in their mid- and late teens. Buys some fiction, mainly articles 800 to 1,000 words on activities of teens in Christian life, interviews, profiles, humor, biography. Pays 1 cent a word, on acceptance. Free copy and fact sheet on request.

Youth in Action, Winona Lake, Ind., 46590. Official publication of Free Methodist Youth. Pays 1 cent a word for articles and stories 500 to 2,500 words, helping teen-agers to lead confident Christian lives. Also articles to give Christian courage to servicemen. Buys black and white photos.

Book Markets for Children, Teen, and Young Adult Fiction and Nonfiction.

Chapter 15 will deal with book markets in greater detail, but for the convenience of those writing for the vast children's market, publishers of books for children, teens, and young adults are listed in this chapter.

Some hardcover book publishers also publish paperback books for young readers, as noted in the following list. Those only publishing paperback follow the hardcover list.

Book publishers pay mainly on a royalty basis, the author earning a percentage of the book's sales (usually 10 per cent). Most publishers pay an advance against royalties, before publication. Royalty rates usually increase if the book becomes popular.

Two new pamphlets on writing for children are available free from the Children's Book Council: "Writing Children's Books" and "Illustrating Children's Books." Send a stamped, self-addressed envelope (8 cent stamp for one pamphlet, 16 cent stamp for both), to Children's Book Council, 175 Fifth Ave., New York, N.Y., 10010.

Childrens Book Publishers

Abelard Schuman Ltd., 257 Park Ave. S., New York, N.Y., 10010. Mrs. Frances Schwartz, senior editor, Children's Books, buys fiction and nonfiction, juveniles, mysteries.

Abingdon Press, 201 Eighth Ave. S., Nashville, Tenn., 37203. Juvenile Editor Katherine Fite prefers query and sample chapters for juvenile books.

Addison-Wesley Publishing Co., Reading, Mass., 01867. Editor Ray Broekel buys picture books and fiction and nonfiction for ages 4 to 16. Pays by standard royalty basis.

Allyn and Bacon, Inc., 470 Atlantic Ave., Boston, Mass., 02210. Publishes textbooks for students in kindergarten through college. Philip Parson is editor for elementary through high school texts; Wayne Barcomb for college texts. Pays on royalty arrangement.

HOW TO SELL TO JUVENILE AND TEEN-AGE MARKETS

American Book Company, a division of Litton Educational Publishing, Inc., Litton Industries, 450 W. 33d St., New York, N.Y., 10001. Publishes textbooks and other educational materials.

American Heritage Press, 330 W. 42d St., New York, N.Y., 10036. Kathleen N. Daly, editor of children's books, buys fiction and nonfiction for ages up to 12. Pays by royalty. Query.

Amis Publishing Co., 38 W. 32d St., New York, N.Y., 10001. Harold Miller, president. Buys juvenile nonfiction with Jewish and Israeli themes. Pays by royalty. Query.

Astor-Honor Inc., 114 Manhattan St., Stamford, Conn., 06904. Publishes juvenile line under title Astor Books and quality paperbacks under title Honor Books. Query.

Atheneum Publishers, 122 E. 42d St., New York, N.Y., 10017. Editor of Children's Books Jean Karl. Buys fiction and nonfiction juvenile books. Also quality paperbacks. Pays by royalty. Query on nonfiction.

Atlantic Monthly Press, 8 Arlington St., Boston, Mass., 92116. Mrs. Emile McLeod, editor of children's books, buys juvenile books. Prefers query for nonfiction, with outline and sample chapters. Publishes books in association with *Little, Brown.*

Augsburg Publishing House, 426 S. Fifth St., Minneapolis, Minn., 55415. Roland Seboldt, director of Book Department, buys juvenile fiction and nonfiction with a Christian theme. Pays on regular royalty basis.

Aurora Publishers, Inc., Suite 619, 170 Fourth Ave., N., Nashville, Tenn., 37219. Publishes hardcover and paperback books including juveniles from earliest ages through young adult. Pays by royalty contract. Query.

Avon Books, division of Hearst Corporation, 959 Eighth Ave., New York, N.Y., 10019. Publishes juvenile books. Catalog sent on request. Pays by royalty contract. Query.

Barnes and Noble, Inc., 105 Fifth Ave., New York, N.Y., 10003. E. P. Epler, administrative editor. Publishes educational paperback books for college use. Query.

Basic Books, Inc., 404 Park Ave. S., New York, N.Y., 10016. Publishes science and general nonfiction for readers 14 years and up. Query.

Charles A. Bennett Co., Inc., 809 W. Detweiller Dr., Peoria, Ill., 61614. Senior Editor Paul Van Winkle buys books on high school and junior college home economics and industrial education.

Bobbs-Merrill Company, Inc., 3 W. 57th St., New York, N.Y., 10019. Miriam Chaikin, children's book editor, buys juvenile fiction and nonfiction for all age levels. Standard royalty. Query.

Thomas Bouregy and Company, Inc. (Avalon Books), 22 E. 60th

St., New York, N.Y., 10022. Editor Reva Kindser buys fiction for teens and young adults including romances, career stories, westerns. Query.

Bradbury Press, Inc., 2 Overhill Rd., Scarsdale, N.Y., 10583. Richard W. Jackson, editor-in-chief. Publishes fiction for children aged 2 to 12. Royalty basis. Query.

Broadman Press, 127 Ninth Ave. N., Nashville, Tenn., 37203. Juvenile Editor Lane Esterly buys juvenile fiction, biography, and picture books for ages 1 to 14 years. Prefers material to reflect Christian principles and be character-building.

Bruce Publishing Co., 866 Third Ave., New York, N.Y., 10022. Publishes textbooks of religious education, vocational education, and industrial arts for elementary, high school, and college. Buys hobby and craft books, contemporary religious and social questions, and theological studies. Also high school and college text books in social studies, languages, humanities, industrial arts, and vocational education. Royalty basis. Query.

Children's Press, 1224 W. Van Buren St., Chicago, Ill., 60607. Mrs. Margaret Friskey, editor, buys juvenile books; more nonfiction than fiction.

Chilton Book Company, 401 Walnut St., Philadelphia, Pa., 19106. Editor John F. Marion buys young adult books of 60,000 words, both fiction and nonfiction, including arts and crafts. Send query and sample chapters plus outline. Royalty basis.

Concordia Publishing House, 3558 S. Jefferson Ave., St. Louis, Mo., 63118. Juvenile fiction and nonfiction and teen-age books, with moral or religious tone. Regular royalty basis.

Coward-McCann, Inc., 200 Madison Ave., New York, N.Y., 10016. Ferdinand Monjo, editor of juvenile books, buys fiction and nonfiction for nursery school age to teen-age. Royalty. Query.

Thomas Y. Crowell Co., 201 Park Ave. S., New York, N.Y., 10003. Mrs. Ann Beneduce, juvenile book editor, buys fiction and nonfiction for all ages, plus college and secondary school text books. Royalty payment. Query.

Crown Publishers, 419 Park Ave. S., New York, N.Y., 10016. Morrell Gipson, editor of juvenile books, buys all types of fiction and nonfiction. Send query letter with outline and sample chapters.

Jonathan David Publishers, Inc., 68-22 Eliot Ave., Middle Village, N.Y., 11379. Editor-in-Chief Alfred Kolatch buys juveniles and texts of interest to Jewish book-buying market. Royalty

John Day Company, 257 Park Ave. S., New York, N.Y., 10010. Publishes juveniles (history, biography, science, arts; no mysteries, thrillers, or science fiction). Juvenile books are primarily educational or exceptional story books. Send query letter with outline and sample chapters.

T.S. Denison & Co., 5100 W. 82d St., Minneapolis, Minn., 55431. Buys children's stories for school reading.

The Dial Press, 750 Third Ave., New York, N.Y., 10017. Mrs. Phyllis Fogelman, editor of Children's Books, buys general fiction and nonfiction (no mysteries, romance, western). Royalty and advance payment. Query.

Dimension Books, Inc., P.O. Box 811, Denville, N.J., 97834. Editor Thomas Coffey buys nonfiction and fiction children's books. Query.

Dodd, Mead & Company, Inc., 79 Madison Ave., New York, N.Y., 10016. Publishes juvenile fiction and nonfiction of all types. Send query to Mrs. Jo Ann Daly, juvenile editor. Payment on royalty basis.

Doubleday & Co., Inc., 277 Park Ave., New York, N.Y., 10017. Buys juvenile nonfiction. Royalty payment.

E.P. Dutton & Co., 201 Park Ave. S., New York, N.Y., 10003. Publishes children's books on royalty basis.

Elk Grove Press, 17420 Ventura Blvd., Encino, Calif., 91316. Editor Ruth Shaw Radlaver publishes social studies books for kindergarten through 8th grade. Also fiction with easy-to-read vocabulary. Royalty. Query.

Follett Publishing Company, 1010 W. Washington Blvd., Chicago, Ill., 60607. Mrs. Sandra Greifenstein, Children's Book Editor, buys quality fiction and nonfiction ranging from picture books to young adult books. In fiction, there must be a strong plot and well-developed characterization. Prefers contemporary themes to historical. Likes good science fiction. Also nonfiction sports books and beginning science books. Prefers to read complete manuscript for fiction, but queries for nonfiction with outline and sample chapters. Payment is on royalty basis.

Four Winds Press, Scholastic Magazines, Inc., 50 W. 44th St., New York, N.Y., 10036. Juvenile and young adult fiction and nonfiction. Send manuscript for fiction; outline and sample chapters for nonfiction. Pays on royalty basis.

The Free Press, 866 Third Ave., New York, N.Y., 10022. A division of *The MacMillan Company.* Mrs. Valery Webb buys nonfiction college text books. Payment by royalty.

Ginn and Company, Statler Bldg., Park Square, Boston, Mass., 02117. Publishes text books for elementary, high school, and college readers. College Division queries should be sent to Xerox College Publishing, 275 Wyman St., Waltham, Mass., 02154.

Golden Gate Junior Books, 8344 Melrose Ave., Los Angeles, Calif., 90069. Publishes juvenile books. Query.

Golden Press, 850 Third Ave., New York, N.Y., 10022. Fiction and nonfiction for children.

Grosset & Dunlap, Inc., 51 Madison Ave., New York, N.Y., 10010. Publishes picture story and activity books for young children and also fiction, history, biography, and informational books for teen-agers.

Harcourt Brace Jovanovich, Inc., 757 Third Ave., New York, N.Y., 10017. Mrs. Mimi Einstein, Juvenile Editor, buys fiction and nonfiction for early readers through the young teen-ager, from 5,000 to 60,000 words. Query.

Harper & Row, 10 E. 53d St., New York, N.Y., 10022. Publishes juvenile, elementary, secondary, and college level text books. Miss Ursula Nordstrom, editor of Junior Books, accepts manuscripts for picture and story books on up to fiction and nonfiction for teens. Payment by royalty contract.

Harvey House, Inc., Irvington-on-Hudson, N.Y., 10533. Editor Jeanne Gardner buys picture books and fiction and nonfiction for young readers. Especially interested in science and information books for readers in grades 2 to 5 and 5 to 8.

Hastings House Publishers, Inc., 10 E. 40th St., New York, N.Y., 10016. Miss Judy Donnelly, editor of juvenile books, prefers to receive query letter for nonfiction books only. Pays on royalty basis.

Hawthorne Books, Inc., 70 Fifth Ave., New York, N.Y., 10011. Publishes young adult nonfiction history, sports, biography, and current affairs. Send query to juvenile Editor Eunice Holsaert.

D. C. Heath, 125 Spring St., Lexington, Mass., 02173. Publishes textbooks for elementary, high school, and college level.

Holiday House, 18 E. 56th St., New York, N.Y., 10022. Publishes juvenile books, including science and nature books for kindergarten to teen-age. Query, with outline and sample chapter. Send science query to Edward Lindemann, Science Editor.

Holt, Rinehart, and Winston, Inc., 383 Madison Ave., New York, N.Y., 10017. Publishes juveniles. Send Query with outline and sample chapters.

Houghton Mifflin Co., 2 Park St., Boston, Mass., 02107. Publishes general juvenile and teen-age books. Send completed manuscript for fiction, query for nonfiction.

Jewish Publication Society, 222 N. 15th St., Philadelphia, Pa., 19102. Dr. Chaim Potok, editor. Publishes juvenile books with Jewish theme. Payment on royalty basis.

Alfred A. Knopf, Inc., 201 E. 50th St., New York, N.Y., 10022.

Juvenile Book Editor Virginie Fowler. Publishes all types of books for young readers including picture books, fiction and nonfiction for all ages. Query. Royalty payment.

Lantern Press, 354 Hussey Rd., Mt. Vernon, N.Y., 10552. Publishes juvenile fiction and nonfiction. Query.

Seymour Lawrence, Inc., 90 Beacon St., Boston, Mass., 12108. Publishes children's books. Query for nonfiction; send complete manuscript for fiction. Pays standard royalty rates.

Lerner Publications Co., 241 First Ave. N., Minneapolis, Minn., 55401. Publishes fiction and nonfiction for children.

J.B. Lippincott Company, 521 Fifth Ave., New York, N.Y., 10017. Dorothy Briley, Children's Book Editor, accepts manuscripts for juvenile fiction and nonfiction. Standard royalty payment.

Little, Brown & Co., 34 Beacon St., Boston, Mass., 02106. Juvenile Book Editor John G. Keller buys fiction and nonfiction.

Lothrop, Lee & Shepard, 105 Madison Ave., New York, N.Y., 10016. Publishes quality children's books, both fiction and nonfiction, including mysteries, westerns, biographies, adventure novels, hobby and craft books. Send outline and sample chapters for nonfiction.

McGraw-Hill Book Co., 330 W. 42d St., New York, N.Y., 10036. Junior Book Division publishes fiction and nonfiction books, especially history, biography, science and other subjects for younger readers.

David McKay Co., Inc., 750 Third Ave., New York, N.Y., 10017. Rose Dobbs, editor, juvenile department, buys juvenile fiction and nonfiction. Also publishes college text books.

The Macmillan Company, 866 Third Ave., New York, N.Y., 10022. Publishes children's books for all ages, fiction and nonfiction. Prefers query. Also text books.

Macrae Smith Co., 225 S. 15th St., Philadelphia, Pa., 19102. Publishes fiction and nonfiction for ages 8 to 10, 10 to 14, and 12 to 16. Editor Ruth Minor prefers to read complete manuscript for fiction, outline and chapters for nonfiction.

Merry Thoughts, Inc., Pelham, N.Y., 10803. Editor A. Kahn buys children's fiction and nonfiction from 1,000 to 4,000 words. Payment on acceptance.

Julian Messner, 1 W. 39th St., New York, N.Y. 10018. A Division of *Simon and Schuster.* Lee Hoffman, editor of Books for Boys and Girls, buys nonfiction for grades 4 to 6, especially social studies and biography, from 10,000 to 15,000 words. Gertrude Blumenthal, editor of Books for Young People, buys fiction and nonfiction for ages 12 to 17. Likes novels with strong themes showing personal adjustment.

Morehouse-Barlow Co., Inc., 14 E. 41st St., New York, N.Y.,

10017. Publishes children's religious nonfiction. Query with outline and sample chapter. Fee and royalty payment.

William Morrow and Company, Inc., 105 Madison Ave., New York, N.Y., 10016. Constance C. Epstein, editor of Morrow Junior Books, buys books for all ages except for pre-school children. Pays on royalty basis.

Thomas Nelson, Inc., 30 E. 42nd St., New York, N.Y., 10017. Mrs. Gloria Mosesson, editor of Junior Book Division, 250 Park Ave., New York, 10017, buys juvenile and young adult fiction and nonfiction. Prefers query on nonfiction.

W.W. Norton & Co., Inc., 55 Fifth Ave., New York, N.Y., 10003. Publishes juvenile books. Pays on royalty basis.

Oddo Publishing, Inc., Box 68, Beauregard Blvd., Fayetteville, Ga., 30214. Publishes juveniles for schools and libraries, kindergarten books to junior high books, on science, history, conservation, math, preferably in series form. Also remedial reading books. Query first. Royalty and outright purchase.

Pantheon Books, 201 E. 50th St., New York, N.Y. 10022. Fabio Coen, Juvenile book editor, accepts fiction and nonfiction manuscripts.

Parents' Magazine Press, 52 Vanderbilt Ave., New York, N.Y., 10017. Publishes picture books for children aged 4 to 8, with lengths running 500 to 1,500 words.

Parnassus Press, 2721 Parker St., Berkeley, Calif., 94704. Publishes children's books from pre-school to teen-age; picture books and teen-age novels. Pays by advance and royalties.

S.G. Phillips, Inc., 305 W. 86th St., New York, N.Y., 10024. Publishes fiction and nonfiction books for children and young adults. Prefers contemporary themes for today's youth. Especially interested in biographies, politics, history, archeology, anthropology, social sciences, architecture, city planning. Also quality fiction on all subjects for all age groups. Query for both fiction and nonfiction.

Platt & Munk, 1055 Bronx River Ave., Bronx, N.Y., 10472. Don Stern, editorial director, buys juvenile books for ages 1 to 14.

Prentice-Hall, Inc., Englewood Cliffs, N.J., 07632. Publishes juvenile books, both fiction and nonfiction. Also publishes college textbooks, educational textbooks. Query.

G.P. Putnam's Sons, 200 Madison Ave., New York, N.Y., 10016. Tom MacPherson, editor of Juvenile Department, buys fiction and nonfiction for children of all ages. Payment on royalty contract.

Rand McNally & Co., Box 7600, Chicago, Ill., 60680. Miss Roselyn Berman, editor of juvenile books, prefers a query letter for books to interest children of all ages. Publishes picture books, science, biography, history, nature, and a wide range of fiction. Payment on royalty basis.

Random House, Inc., 201 E. 50th St., New York, N.Y., 10022. Publishes juvenile fiction and nonfiction for all ages including picture books and easy-readers. Send juvenile manuscripts to Juvenile Department. Also school and college text book queries accepted; send to College Department.

Reilly & Lee Books, 114 W. Illinois St., Chicago, Ill. A division of *Henry Regnery Company.* Publishes nonfiction juvenile books for kindergarten through third grade. Query. Pays on royalty basis or flat fee.

The Ward Ritchie Press, 3044 Riverside Dr., Los Angeles, Calif., 90039. Publishes juvenile books. Standard royalty.

Richards Rosen Press, Inc., 29 E. 21st St., New York, N.Y., 10010. Publishes nonfiction books for teen-age guidance, to 40,000 words. Ruth C. Rosen, editor. Payment by arrangement.

Roy Publishers, Inc., 30 E. 74th St., New York, N.Y., 10021. Editor Hanna Kister prefers queries for juvenile books with emphasis on international interests.

Rutledge Books, Inc., 17 E. 45th St., New York, N.Y., 10017. Publishes juvenile fiction and nonfiction. Query with outline. Pays in advances and royalties.

St. Martin's Press, Inc., 175 Fifth Ave., New York, N.Y., 10010. Publishes juvenile books: history, political science, biography, the arts, and reference books and college text books. Pays on royalty contract.

Scholastic Books, 50 W. 44th St., New York, N.Y., 10036. Mrs. Norma Ainsworth, editor of Manuscript Department. Publishes fiction and nonfiction books for various school book clubs for pre-schoolers through young adults. Material used includes picture books, science, adventure, biography, mystery, how-to, and also fiction for slow readers. Payment by advance and royalties. Query for nonfiction.

Charles Scribner's Sons, 597 Fifth Ave., New York, N.Y., 10017. Publishes juvenile books. Submit query, not manuscript, to Miss Lee Anna Deadrick, Children's Book Department.

Seabury Press, 815 Second Ave., New York, N.Y., 10017. James C. Giblin, editor of Books for Young People, prefers contemporary fiction and nonfiction for books for young people, picture books for ages 5 and 8, and nonfiction for ages 8 to 12 and up. Subjects do not necessarily have to be religious. Payment on royalty basis.

Sherbourne Press, 1640 S. La Cienega, Los Angeles, Calif., 90035. Mrs. Shelly Lowenkophf, editor. Publishes juveniles for ages 12 to 16.

Simon and Schuster, 630 Fifth Ave., New York, N.Y., 10020.

Publishes juvenile books. Query only; returns all unsolicited manuscripts. Pays standard royalty rates.

Steck-Vaughn Company, Box 2028, Austin, Tex., 78767. Jane Moseley, editor of Children's Books. Publishes juveniles and textbooks.

Sterling Publishing Co., 419 Park Ave. S., New York, N.Y., 10016. Publishes sports, science, how-to books for young people. Query.

Franklin Watts, Inc., 845 Third Ave., New York, N.Y., 10022. Alice Dickinson, Juvenile Book Editor, buys picture books and fiction and nonfiction for children of all ages but especially of elementary school age. Query for nonfiction books.

Western Publishing Co., 1220 Mound Ave., Racine, Wisc., 53404. Publishes picture books under 800 words for young readers, and novels 35,000 words and up, for pre-teen and early-teen readers. Send query with short synopsis to William Larson for novels, and to Miss Betty Ren Wright for picture and story books. Payment by arrangement.

The Westminster Press, 900 Witherspoon Bldg., Philadelphia, Pa., 19107. Barbara Bates, Children's Book Editor. Publishes juvenile fiction and nonfiction for ages 8 and up. Payment on royalty basis.

World Publishing Company, 110 E. 59th St., New York, N.Y., 10022. Publishes juvenile books, both fiction and nonfiction. Archie Bennett, editor.

Young Scott Books (formerly *William R. Scott, Inc.*), 333 Avenue of the Americas, New York, N.Y., 10014. Carla Stevens, Editor. Publishes children's books for ages 2 to 14. Also books to supplement material in elementary school classrooms.

Zondervan Publishing House, 1415 Lake Dr. S.E., Grand Rapids, Mich., 49506. T. Alton Bryant, Editor. Publishes Protestant religious books for young people.

Paperback Publishers

Archway Paperbacks, 630 Fifth Ave., New York, N.Y., 10020. Published by *Pocket Books.* Publishes nonfiction for young readers aged 8 to 14. Interested mainly in biographies. Query.

Camelot Books, 959 Eighth Ave., New York, N.Y., 10019. A division of Avon Books. Nancy Coffey, Editor. Publishes fiction and nonfiction for ages 8 to 14. Payment is arranged. Query.

Fawcett World Library, 1 Astor Pl., New York, N.Y., 10003. Publishes reprints and original books for secondary schools and colleges. Pays on royalty basis.

The Natural History Press, The American Museum of Natural

History, 277 Park Ave., New York, N.Y., 10017. Publishes children's books on all areas of natural history including ecology, anthropology, and astronomy.

Tempo Books, 51 Madison Ave., New York, N.Y., 10010. Editor Ronald Buehl. Publishes fiction and nonfiction for young adults; mainly reprints, but some originals. Special need for contemporary nonfiction. Payment by royalty and advance. Query with outline.

10

HOW TO SELL TO BLACK PUBLICATIONS

Black magazine, newspaper, and book markets are among the fastest-growing in the publishing business, opening up good- to-top-paying opportunities for freelance writers and photographers.

Essentially, the needs of editors for this market are the same as for any other major market. Articles about problems and successes of contemporary life, with an emphasis on the black consumer market, are needed by all black publications, and also frequently are bought by editors of general magazines intended for all audiences.

New magazines are coming out so fast in the black publishing world that it is important for writers to check the daily business and financial pages of their newspapers, in order to keep abreast of new markets.

WHAT EDITORS DO NOT WANT

If there is any particular difference in writing for black publications, it is simply that the writer should not be overly concerned with racial differences. Editors of black publications generally reject articles and short stories that indulge in revolutionary ideology or emotional or sentimental rhetoric.

The editors of Johnson Publications in Chicago, one of the nation's leading publishers of black magazines, give a good general picture of the needs of editors in this market.

Herbert Nipson, executive editor of *Ebony*, which is primarily a picture magazine, says there is a continuing need for human interest articles about black people both famous and little-known, but the slant should be on some incident or viewpoint that has not yet hit the headlines.

Hoyt W. Fuller, managing editor of *Black World,* another Johnson publication, says he buys articles on all aspects of full and equal rights for all American racial minorities. Perceptive, purposeful articles and short stories are sought.

Johnson publications' newest magazine, *Black Stars,* is devoted to articles and photos about black entertainers of movies, television, recordings, and the stage. Mrs. Ariel Strong, editor, says most of her material will come from freelancers. Short text and good candid photos are wanted.

Another new magazine, *Black Enterprise,* published in New York by Earl Graves, a product of the Bedford-Stuyvesant ghetto in that city, is aimed at black men and women who want to get ahead.

In its first year, the magazine sold more than $900,000 in advertising, much of it in color. Thirty of its 51 advertisers are among the 100 largest corporations in the country. This gives an indication of the market both editors and advertisers are reaching, and writers and photographers should keep both in mind when submitting articles, stories, or queries.

Graves says the median income of his readers is $20,000, and the magazine is aimed at the 4 per cent of the black population that does 50 per cent of the black spending. He estimates the black consumer market to be 40 billion dollars annually.

Essence is another new magazine, aimed at young black women. Editor Marcia Gillespie says she is buying fiction and in-depth nonfiction for young black women both single and married. Subjects include careers, consumerism, raising families, and all the general topics that interest and appeal to women regardless of color.

OTHER MARKETS

Besides black magazines, there is a growing market for articles and photography for black newspapers and newspaper supplements. The leading supplement, *Tuesday at Home,* is issued monthly in many Sunday newspapers and is attracting an ever-widening audience. Material used covers the entire spectrum of general interest supplements: contemporary issues, politics, people in the news, sports, fashions, food, etc.

Books for and about blacks are also increasing in number. Publishers are aware of a vast audience in both adult and juvenile fiction and nonfiction readers among blacks, and are always interested in reading queries on book ideas.

Selling to black publications is by and large no different from selling to any other market. Quality writing and photography is essential, and a new slant on even a familiar subject can make you a sale. Study various magazines in this market and get to know what they are buying from reading them from cover to cover.

It also goes almost without saying that you do not need to be black to write for black publications, any more than you need be a child to write a children's book, or be a woman to write for a woman's magazine. What counts is the story and the pictures, as in any other market.

Black Magazines

Amistad, c/o Random House, 201 E. 50th St., New York, N.Y., 10022. A new literary journal for use in college courses, with essays and fiction providing basic material for Black Studies courses. Editors Charles F. Harris and John A. Williams want material from 2,500 to 3,000 words dealing in the interrelationships of blacks with Spanish-Americans, American Indians, Asians, and Africans. Payment varies, on acceptance.

Black Enterprise, 295 Madison Ave., New York, N.Y. Publisher Earl Graves buys articles for middle and upper income black readers, single and married. Primarily to serve the black business and professional community.

Black Sports, 386 Park Ave. S., New York, N.Y., 10016. Monthly sports magazine about black athletes, published by the Allan P. Barron Enterprises. Editor Joe Hemingway prefers short articles to 2,500 words on professional athletes on and off the playing field. Magazine is international in scope, with distribution to college campuses, military posts, and general markets. Also a need for articles on women athletes and black women married to athletes. Payment to $250. Query.

Black Stars, 820 S. Michigan Ave., Chicago, Ill., 60605. Editor Mrs. Ariel Strong pays up to $200 for articles about 2,000 words, about black movie, television, stage, and recording stars. Buys mainly from

HOW TO SELL TO BLACK PUBLICATIONS

freelancers, uses lots of pictures. Pays up to $250 for text-and-photo features. Query.

Black World, 820 S. Michigan Ave., Chicago, Ill., 60605. Hoyt W. Fuller, managing editor, pays from $35 to $150 for fiction and articles to 4,000 words on all aspects of full and equal rights for American racial minorities. Articles and fiction should deal with blacks or black life, humor and satire, little-known incident or crucial role in black history, essays on black literature and literary figures. Articles should be well-documented with quotes from authorities. Fiction should be perceptive and purposeful. Also buys short poetry for $10. Query on articles.

Ebony, 820 S. Michigan Ave., Chicago, Ill., 60605. Executive Editor Herbert Nipson buys articles and picture stories of general interest to black readers. Most material is staff-written, but freelancers can earn $150 and up for articles to 3,000 words and photo stories dealing with little-known human interest aspect of a famous or unknown black person. Query first.

Essence, 102 E. 30th St., New York, N.Y., 10016. Magazine of fiction and nonfiction aimed at young black women, married or single. Reader age range is from 18 to 34 years. Editor Marcia Gillespie buys in-depth articles on careers, consumerism, raising families, other aspects of life to interest black women. Pays $150, to $300 for short articles, about 1,500 words, and up to $350 for major articles to 3,000 words. Fiction Editor Sharyn Skeeter wants quality fiction for black women. Pays $300 for short-shorts to 1,000 words, $400 for stories about 3,000 words. Also pays $25 to $50 for poems. Query editors on articles.

Jet, 820 S. Michigan Ave., Chicago, Ill., 60605. Mostly staff-written. Query editors with article ideas.

New Lady, 24301 Southland Dr., P.O. Box 3577, Hayward, Calif., 94544. Editor Edward N. Evans, Jr., pays 2½ cents a word and up for articles 2,500 to 7,500 words for black women, teenagers and older. Fiction must have strong racial identification and be relevant to black women. Sample copy sent on request. Query not necessary for articles.

Sepia, 203 N. Wabash Ave., Chicago, Ill., 60601. Primarily a picture magazine, but also runs quality articles that reflect the interest and pride of blacks in what they are accomplishing in America, as well as their criticism of what is wrong with America. Query Editor Ben Burns with in-depth outlines. No fiction. Pays about $100 for articles about 2,000 words.

Stanita Designs, Inc., 461 Eighth Ave., New York, N.Y., 10001.

Publisher of black greeting cards. Pays $15 per caption or verse suitable for an artist to work into a greeting card for black buyers.

Tuesday at Home, 437 Madison Ave., New York, N.Y., 10022. W. Leonard Evans, Jr., president and editor, pays good rates for articles with strong appeal to black women. Monthly color feature supplement that appears in many leading Sunday newspapers throughout the country. Subjects include fashion, black women in the news, arts, stories for homemakers, child-rearing, etc.

11

HOW TO SELL TO FRATERNAL, RELIGIOUS, AND FOREIGN MARKETS

Fraternal, religious, and foreign markets are not necessarily similar markets. No attempt can or need be made to compare them. Each has its own particular editorial requirements and reader interests, and they are brought together here merely for reader convenience, placing them in a chapter of their own.

Fraternal Markets

Ted J. Rakstis, a versatile writer who has been freelancing for almost 15 years, knows the fraternal magazine market perhaps better than any other writer. An old college friend from Michigan State University, he kindly consented to share some of his knowledge of the fraternal field with other writers who might like to write for this growing and good-paying market.

"Since I began freelancing, I have written about 100 articles for consumer, or general interest magazines," Rakstis reports. "My heaviest output, however, has been in the fraternal field. I've written some 40 articles for *The Kiwanis Magazine*, about 20 for *The Lion*, half a dozen for *The Elks Magazine*, and several for *The Rotarian*.

"As a former Chicagoan who now lives in a Michigan community only 100 miles from Chicago, I began writing for the fraternal magazines mainly because the 'big four' are all located in the Chicago area. *Kiwanis* and *Elks* are in Chicago, *Lion* in Oak Brook, and *Rotarian* in Evanston. Their editors were accessible and, I found, responsive—much more so than their distant counterparts in New York. I began to get fairly frequent assignments and, since they liked my work, I developed close working relationships with these magazines.

"But mere geography soon became only a tangential reason for my tie-in with the fraternals. Within a short time, I began to closely identify with the readers of these magazines. I began to view them as 'my readers.'

"Surveys show fraternal organization members to be a fairly affluent business or professional man in a middle-sized community, and they are vitally concerned in community progress and civic life.

"My work on civic projects, both as a volunteer and a paid public relations professional, has brought me in contact with many service club members. I have developed a feeling of rapport with these people. In general, I understand their outlook and find myself in agreement with their goals.

"The interests of fraternal club members closely parallel the fields in which I am most interested and proficient in my writing: community service, business, health, and sports. Consequently, I have found that these magazines are receptive to article queries in the areas in which I have the greatest personal interest and can do the best job. Moreover, when I sit down to do a story for a service club magazine, I don't have to worry about using a scatter-shot technique. Knowing that I don't have to try to appeal to people of diverse tastes and economic backgrounds, I can zero in on my topic. I write the story as if I were preparing it for a group of my personal friends—which many of the fraternal members are.

"Yet even the service markets cannot be entirely viewed as homogeneous entities; each one is a little different from the other. Take the *Rotarian,* for example. The fact that I have only done a couple of articles for this attractive and informative magazine derives primarily from the fact that it tries to reach Rotarians in 149 nations, and has little interest in stories with a strictly American orientation. As a states-based writer, this limits me considerably.

"*Kiwanis,* on the other hand, is angled principally toward its members in the United States and Canada. This means the door is wide open for domestic stories, and *Kiwanis* also is very strong on general interest stories. In this respect, it resembles *Elks* to a considerable extent.

FRATERNAL NEEDS VARY

"*Lion*, in the past, has been interested mainly in stories on Lion service club projects, and I've done a good many of these. *Lion* also is tending to move more toward general interest stories. It's interesting to note that although Lions clubs are found in nearly as many countries as Rotary clubs—146 for Lions and 149 for Rotary—*Lion* is much more U.S. and Canadian oriented than *Rotarian*. The reason for this is that *Rotarian* is published only in English and Spanish, and these two editions must serve all its members. *Lion*, conversely, has official editions in 13 languages—English, Spanish, Japanese, French, Swedish, Italian, German, Finnish, Flemish-French, Farsi, Korean, Portuguese, and Dutch.

"As for the important question of money, the leading fraternal magazines generally pay about 10 cents a word. An article for these markets usually will fetch from $200 to $450, depending upon length and importance. The fraternals, in my view, are best characterized as good, reliable middle-range markets. In some cases, you can increase your article rate by supplying photos, but it's always best to check with the editor in advance, since photos for many stories are taken either by staff members or freelance professional photographers.

"I'm sold on the fraternal magazine markets. But don't assume that these editors are easy to sell to. Their standards generally are high, and you can expect to do a lot of library research and in-person or telephone or letter interviewing in the course of researching an article.

"I've known a couple of big-name New York writers who have tried to use the fraternals as dumping grounds for the articles they couldn't sell to the big New York slicks. Their efforts brought them only rejections slips, largely because they hadn't realized that the fraternals also insist on quality work. A fraternal editor is no different from any other editor—he wants articles that meet the needs of his readership. The article that might be perfect for another type of men's magazine, say *Playboy* or *True*, usually just won't make it with the fraternals. As with all magazines, I think the best bet is to send a query letter or outline rather than a finished manuscript.

"Aside from money and the pleasure of being able to write an article on a subject you're interested in, there is one other major side benefit in writing for the fraternals. If you're interested in community service, writing for the fraternals is one way to achieve this goal.

ARTICLES BRING ACTION

"About five years ago, I did a story for *Rotarian* on community foundations. Basically, these are non-profit foundations whose trustees are all respected local citizens. The foundation builds up a certain amount of capital through bequests and donations, invests it and then takes the interest and gives it to help needy community programs.

"As a result of my article, I'm told, numerous towns that did not have such organizations began to establish them, and I couldn't help but feel that I had played a role in an important philanthropic endeavor.

"When Kiwanis International began a major educational program in 1969 to combat drug abuse, I wrote a special 6,000-word section on drugs, which was reprinted and distributed across the nation as part of community drug education programs.

"As another example, early in 1971, *Lion* published a story I had written on a children's eye clinic sponsored by the Miami Beach Lions Club. I understand that the club had thousands of reprints made to try and get other communities to start similar clinics.

"One of the really great things about writing for fraternal magazines is that you know you're not writing something that will be merely scanned and tossed aside by the casual reader. You're writing for business leaders, lawyers, doctors, judges, Congressmen, city councilmen, and others who just might try to implement some of your ideas.

"I've talked here about the four major fraternal magazines, the ones I've worked with. However, the writer interested in getting to this field should not ignore the others. There are magazines published by such organizations as the American Legion, Eagles, Moose, Optimists, Veterans of Foreign Wars, Junior League, and others. Some of their editors may be ready and waiting for what you have to offer."

With that advice and inspiration from Ted Rakstis, here are the specific requirements of the leading magazines for fraternal and service organizations.

Fraternal and Service Organizations:

American Legion Magazine, 1345 Ave. of the Americas, New York, N.Y., 10019. Editor Robert B. Pitkin buys articles on national and international subjects of interest to former servicemen, including American history and military history. Query.

Eagle, 2401 W. Wisconsin Ave., Milwaukee, Wisc., 53233. Editor Arthur S. Ehrmann pays 5 cents a word, on acceptance, for articles on topics of general interest for male members of The Eagles. Subjects include sports, travel, hunting and fishing, safety, stories to improve the quality of life in the community. Pays $5 per photo. Query.

The Elks Magazine, 425 W. Diversey Pkwy., Chicago, Ill., 60614. Associate Editor D.J. Herda pays from 10 to 12 cents a word for articles bought on speculation. Pays higher for assigned articles. Particularly looking for ideas for major articles on important community issues to interest members. Query.

The Kiwanis Magazine, 101 E. Erie St., Chicago, Ill., 60611. Editor Dennis K. Moore pays from $200 to $400 for significant articles of interest to community leaders who are Kiwanis members. Moore says he has a considerable backlog of general interest articles including historical subjects and humor, and is mainly in need of articles of strong public interest. Recent subjects dealt with have included all aspects of drug abuse, new responsibilities of youth, the four-day work week, improved hospital care. Members are primarily business and professional men seeking to improve the quality of life in their community. Most articles are rejected because they are too short, superficial, or merely reflect the author's own viewpoint. Also buys articles on new applications of science in improving man's condition. Query The Editors.

The Lion, York and Cermak Rds., Oak Brook, Ill., 60025. Editor Dennis Brennan pays 10 cents a word and up, on acceptance, for topical articles related to the problems business and professional members of Lions clubs are trying to help solve in their community, North America, and elsewhere in the world. Also short humor, photo features, cartoons, stories on Lions club activities. In humor, prefers gentle treatment of human fallibilities. Query.

Optimist Magazine, 4494 Lindell Blvd., St. Louis, Mo., 63108. Managing Editor Gary Adamson pays up to $100, on acceptance, for articles 800 to 1,000 words, and photo stories, of interest to business and professional men in community service in the United States and Canada. Subjects include economics, industry, government, science, education, articles on community problems and success stories. Query. *The Rotarian,* 1600 Ridge Ave., Evanston, Ill., 60201. Editor Karl K. Krueger pays top rates, on acceptance, for articles 1,200 to 2,000 words to interest business and professional members of Rotary clubs throughout the world. Subjects include social and economic problems, business ethics, community and family improvement, travel, humor. Query.

Religious Magazines

When I was a reporter on *The Chicago Tribune,* I wrote a $100 prize article on a retired airline groundworker who put on operas in his living room. He changed costumes as the hero, heroine, and villain, moved his lips to recordings of the operas, and performed hilariously for friends and their guests.

He had done this for years, having gotten his love of opera one Easter Sunday in Munich when he saw *Parsifal.* Wagner's music had inspired him to become a priest, but a World War kept his ambition from becoming a reality. A German by birth, he came to this country, got a job, never became a priest, but turned his love of opera into a hobby that enriched the lives of many people.

There were not many religious tie-ins, but I queried the editor of *Catholic Digest* about the story and sold it—my first freelance sale to a magazine! As it turned out, they only ran it in their German language edition, but I was sent a copy of it and still enjoy looking at it, even though my German is too rusty for me to read it and I have long since spent the $200 they paid me.

Religious magazines are a good market for freelancers. While some pay only nominal rates, others pay among the best, and a not inconsiderable side benefit of writing for them is that they often take inspirational articles that other editors are too shy to run.

Editors of religious magazines have the same high standards as editors of general magazines. A zealous writer will not sell his work to this market unless it meets the regular requirements: factual reporting, smooth style, sustained interest, suitable subject matter, and no sermonizing. Articles and fiction should aim at

HOW TO SELL TO FRATERNAL, RELIGIOUS, AND FOREIGN MARKETS

encouraging readers to lead better lives and help them cope with and solve personal and social problems.

Many religious magazines run publications specifically for children and teen-agers, often used as Sunday School material. Other magazines include articles for and about children in their regular adult or family editions. Look through the juvenile markets in Chapter 9 for additional religious publications that are directed solely to children and teens.

Magazines published by the various denominations are numerous, and most pay less than 2 cents a word. Since this book is intended to include only the best-paying markets, only those magazines paying 2 cents a word or more will be listed here.

America, 106 W. 56th St., New York, N.Y., 10019. Editor Donald R. Campion, S.J., pays $50 to $75, on acceptance, for articles of political, social, and religious interest. Also articles on family life and humor. Lengths from 1,000 to 1,500 words.

The American Zionist, 145 E. 32d St., New York, N.Y., 10016. Editor Elias Cooper pays $50 to $100, on publication, for articles about 2,000 words, on Israel, the Middle East, Jewish issues in this country and abroad. Also buys poetry.

Baptist Leader, Valley Forge, Pa., 19481. Pays 2 cents a word and up, on acceptance, for articles about church school activities and social issues, 750 to 1,600 words. Buys photos with and without articles, and some poetry.

Brigade Leader, Christian Service Brigade, Box 150, Wheaton, Ill., 60187. Editor Daniel C. Jessen pays up to 3 cents a word for short stories and articles which men can use in boys' club meetings. Lengths run to 1,200 words, and material should have a definite Protestant emphasis. Pays $4 to $8 per photo. Send for free sample issue before submitting material.

Campus Life, Box 419, Wheaton, Ill., 60187. Editor Harold Myra pays 2 cents a word and up, on acceptance, for articles and fiction with evangelical slant for Christian teen-agers. Also nonreligious articles on unusual but wholesome activities of high school boys and girls. Query.

Catholic Digest, Box 3090, St. Paul, Minn., 55101. Pays $200 and up for original articles, $50 and up for reprints. Articles should be of general interest to Catholic readers, if possible with a Catholic angle. Also stories about leading Catholics, both famous and little-known. Uses mostly reprints but will accept manuscripts and query letters. Also pays $4 to $50 for fillers for various departments. No fiction.

Catholic Life, 9800 Oakland Ave., Detroit, Mich., 48211. Editor Robert C. Bayer pays 2 cents a word, on publication, for articles on Catholic missionary work in Hong Kong, East Pakistan, India, Burma, Japan, Latin America, and underdeveloped nations around the world. Lengths 600 to 1,200 words. Pays $2 for photos.

Catholic World, 304 W. 58th St., New York, N.Y., 10019. Rev. John B. Sheerin, editor, pays $75 and up, on publication, for articles and fiction to 2,800 words. Fiction should reflect a religious concern about contemporary problems. Articles should be on national and international events, politics, science, literature, etc. Uses poetry from 3 to 22 lines.

The Christian Century, 407 S. Dearborn St., Chicago, Ill., 60605. Editor Alan Geyer pays 2 cents a word, on publication, for articles on education, economics, social problems, current issues, the arts, etc., especially with a religious angle. Lengths 1,500 to 2,500 words. Poetry up to 20 lines; no payment.

Christian Herald, 27 E. 39th St., New York, N.Y., 10016. Editor Kenneth Wilson pays $100 and up for articles with moral or religious emphasis on contemporary social issues. Also personal experience articles dealing with application of Christian principles in solving problems of contemporary life. Pays $10 for short poems.

Christian Life Magazine, Gundersen Dr. and Schmale Rd., Wheaton, Ill., 60187. Editor Robert Walker pays up to $150, on publication, for fiction and articles. Fiction should be about problems faced by Christians today, solved by strong action by the characters rather than the writer as narrator. Lengths 3,000 to 4,000 words. Articles should be on evangelical Christian devotional subjects, mission work, spiritual development, inspirational articles on successful Christian living. Also buys photos. Query for nonfiction.

The Church Herald, 146 Division Ave., N., Grand Rapids, Mich., 49502. Magazine of the Reformed Church in America. Pays 2½ cents per word for articles on general interest subjects written from a Christian viewpoint. Lengths from 750 to 1,200 words. Also children's stories on contemporary themes with practical Christian moral. Lengths from 500 to 800 words.

Colloquy, 1505 Race St., Philadilphia, Pa., 19102. Editor John Westerhoff pays from $50 to $150, on acceptance, for articles and interviews on education. Lengths from 1,000 to 2,000 words.

Columbia, Box 1670, New Haven, Conn., 06507. Editor Elmer Von Feldt. Official magazine of the Knights of Columbus, Catholic fraternal order. Pays $100 to $300, on acceptance, for fiction and articles for the Catholic layman and his family. Subjects include topics of current interest to general readers, Catholic viewpoints on social, ecomonic, and educational subjects.

Commonweal, 232 Madison Ave., New York, N.Y., 10016. Catholic magazine on political, religious, social, and literary subjects. Editor James O'Gara pays 2 cents a word, on acceptance.

Event Magazine, American Lutheran Church Men, 422 S. 5th St., Minneapolis, Minn., 55415. Editor James Solheim pays 2 cents a word and up, on acceptance, for articles of interest to Lutheran men. Also fiction to 2,000 words and poetry, photography and artwork.

Face-to-Face, 201 Eighth Ave. S., Nashville, Tenn., 37203. Magazine of the United Methodist church. Editor Kenneth Winston pays 2 cents a word and up, on acceptance, for illustrated articles and fiction on problems and concerns of older teens. Query.

Franciscan Message, Franciscan Publishers, Pulaski, Wisc., 54162. Rev. Felician Tulko, editor, pays 2 to 3 cents a word for articles to 2,000 words dealing with Christian solutions to current problems.

Guideposts, 3 W. 29th St., New York, N.Y. Magazine published by Dr. Norman Vincent Peale which uses dramatic personal experience stories applying faith to solving everyday problems. Lengths run to 1,500 words. Pays $100. Send query or manuscript to Leonard LeSourd, executive editor.

Home Life, 127 Ninth Ave. N., Nashville, Tenn., 37203. Editor Joseph Burton. Magazine of the Southern Baptist church. Pays 2½ cents a word, on acceptance, for articles and fiction for parents, on rearing children, family interrelationships.

Jewish Frontier, 45 E. 17th St., New York, N.Y., 10003. Editor Marie Syrkin pays 2 cents a word, on publication, for articles and fiction dealing with Judaism, Zionism, Israel, in the U.S. or abroad. Lengths from 2,500 to 4,000 words.

Jewish Horizon, 55 Rudolph Terrace W., Yonkers, N.Y., 10701. Editor Rabbi William Herskowitz pays 2 cents a word, on publication, for fiction and articles concerning the Jewish American community and Israel. Length to 2,000 words. Poetry to 500 words.

The Living Light, Our Sunday Visitor Press, Noll Plaza, Huntington, Ind., 46750. Catholic publication. Editor Very Rev. Msgr. Russell J. Neighbor pays 5 cents a word, on acceptance, for articles 1,500 to 3,000 words, on Biblical theology, liturgy, teaching. Also pays 3 cents a word for book reviews. Query.

The Lutheran, 2900 Queen Lane, Philadelphia, Pa., 19129. Editor G. Elson Ruff pays 2 to 5 cents a word, on acceptance, for articles on Christian ideology, personal religious experience, church activities to interest wide audience.

Lutheran Standard, 426 S. 5th St., Minneapolis, Minn., 55415. Editor Dr. George Muedeking pays 2 cents a word and up, on acceptance, for articles on the Lutheran church and Christian application to solution of social, economic, political issues. Also personality articles. Lengths 500 to 1,300 words. Also fiction to 1,300 words.

Marriage, Abbey Press Publishing Div., St. Meinrad, Ind., 47577. Editor Brian Daly pays 5 cents a word, on acceptance, for articles dealing with the relationship between husband and wife. Query.

Maryknoll, Maryknoll Fathers, Maryknoll, N.Y., 10545. Publication of Maryknoll Catholic missions. Pays good rates for articles on mission people, social-economic studies of mission countries, etc. Pays $10 to $25 for photos; $100 to $150 for photo stories in black and white or color. Query.

Mature Years, 201 Eighth Ave. S., Nashville, Tenn., 37203. Editor Daisy Warren pays 3 cents a word, on acceptance, for articles to interest older adults of the United Methodist church. Also short stories and humor. Pays $1 per line for poetry to 12 lines.

Message, Southern Publishing Assn., Box 59, Nashville, Tenn., 37202. Editor W.R. Robinson pays up to 10 cents a word, on acceptance, for articles to interest the Negro family. Subjects include moral issues, mental health, temperance, nature, juvenile delinquency, the Bible, home and family. Lengths to 2,500 words.

Midstream: A Monthly Jewish Review, 515 Park Ave., New York, N.Y., 10022. Editor Shlomo Katz pays 3 cents a word, on acceptance, for articles and book reviews for general readers. Also fiction of Jewish or general social and political interest, to 8,000 words.

New Magazine, Unity School, Unity Village, Mo., 64063. Editor Charles Lelly pays 2 cents a word and up, on acceptance, for articles stressing the art of living for people of all faiths. Aim is for adult readers with liberal Christian views. Lengths to 2,000 words. Black and white photos should accompany manuscript. Sample sent on request.

The National Jewish Monthly, Published by B'nai B'rith, 1640 Rhode Island Ave. N.W., Washington, D.C., 20036. Editor Bernard Simon pays 5 to 10 cents a word, on acceptance, for articles 1,000 to 2,500 words of contemporary Jewish interest. Also short articles 200 to 800 words.

Our Sunday Visitor, Huntington, Ind., 46750. Pays 10 cents a word and up, on acceptance, for short articles to interest Catholic lay readers. Pays $15 to $30 for cartoons.

St. Anthony Messenger, 1615 Republic St., Cincinnati, Ohio, 45210. Editor Rev. Jeremy Harrington pays 5 cents a word and up for articles for the Catholic family. Subjects include Christian application to contemporary problems, major movements in the Church, education, the arts. Also humor and picture stories. Fiction should have Christian slant, but not preachy or sentimental. Query for nonfiction.

The Sign, Monastery Place, Union City, N.Y., 07087. Editor Rev. Augustine Hennessy pays $200 to $300, on acceptance, for articles and short stories of general or religious interest to Cathloics. Articles run to 4,000 words, fiction from 1,000 to 3,000 words.

Sunday Digest, 850 N. Grove Ave., Elgin, Ill., 60120. Editor L. Richard Burnap pays 3 cents a word and up, on acceptance, for articles to 1,800 words, on application of Christian faith to current problems, the Christian family, personalities, and Protestant church work. Black and white photos should be available. Also inspirational fillers to 300 words. Free samples and editorial fact booklet sent on request.

These Times, Southern Publishing Assn., Box 59, Nashville, Tenn., 37202. Editor K.J. Holland pays 10 cents a word, on acceptance, for articles to interest the Christian family. Lengths to 2,500 words.

Today's Family Digest, Noll Plaza, Huntington, Ind., 46750. Editor Mary Lou McGue pays 4 cents a word and up for articles for Catholic family reading, whether inspirational, educational, or entertaining. Lengths from 500 to 1,500 words.

Foreign Markets

It may at first seem far-fetched, but it is really not unrealistic to think of selling articles, fiction, and photography to foreign markets. Newspapers and magazines published throughout the world are curious about life in America, and quite often this curiosity is filled by publishing articles by American freelancers.

Some foreign publications accept articles by writers who visit their country on vacation or a work assignment, and who have something new and interesting to say about the quality of life in that foreign country. While you're in a foreign city, it would not hurt to ask for an interview with an editor and suggest an article idea to him.

And, of course, you don't have to be in the foreign country to sell to the foreign markets. Many European writers sell regularly to American publications; it is equally possible for American-based writers to sell to foreign markets.

When sending a manuscript or query letter, you will have to use international postage slips, available at your post office, for return of the manuscript. Sending the material to the foreign country requires American postage. Since postage will be higher for return of the manuscript, it is best to merely send a query letter, which will cost about 25 cents.

Canada and England are the easiest markets outside the United States, for obvious language reasons.

In addition to magazines and newspapers published outside the United States, the freelancer who lives near a major urban center in this country should consider submitting material to the foreign language press. Many cities with large ethnic populations have foreign-language newspapers which accept freelance feature articles and even fiction.

It can help, but is not necessary, that you write the article in the language of the foreign publication. But a good knowledge of the country and its people is important.

Payment varies greatly. In general, rates will be lower than for American publications.

To get a better idea of foreign magazines and what they publish, go to the periodical section of your local university. Most university libraries stock a variety of foreign magazines and newspapers. Reading them will help you determine whether you have an article or photos that they might buy.

The following are the best markets outside the United States:

British Markets

Building, The Builder House, 4 Catherine St., London, W.C. 2, England. Editor Ian M. Leslie buys articles on architecture and building. Payment is about $24 per 1,000 words.

Men Only, Mowbray House, 14 Norfolk St., London, W.C. 2, England. Editor Alfred Brockman buys articles to interest the intelligent male. Payment is good.

Motoring, The Nuffield Organization, Central Publicity, Box 41, G.P.O. Longbridge, Birmingham, England. Editor Peter Burdon buys articles for auto fans. Payment is about $24 for 1,000 words.

Parade, weekly general feature magazine with same address as *Men Only.* Also buys humor.

Town and Country Planning, The Planning Centre, 28 King St., London W.C. 2, England. Managing Editor Hazel Evans buys features on urban development, housing projects. Pays about $12 per 1,000 words.

Canadian Markets

B.C. Outdoors, 5543 129 St., Surrey, B.C., Canada. Editor Art Downs pays from $50 to $100 for articles, on acceptance, of current interest about people and places of British Columbia and the Yukon, including outdoors, hunting, fishing, travel, with black and white photos. Also historical subjects.

Canadian Audubon, 46 St. Clair Ave. E., Toronto 290, Ontario, Canada. Editor P.A. Hardy pays up to 3 cents a word for articles on natural science and conservation, to 2,500 words. Should have some significance to Canadian readers. Photos should accompany manuscript.

The Canadian Magazine, The Canadian Star Weekly, Simpson Tower, 401 Bay St., Toronto, 1, Ontario, Canada. Pays 10 cents a word and up, on acceptance, for controversial articles on timely subjects with Canadian interest. Lengths to 2,000 words. Buys sports, human interest, adventure, profiles of personalities. Query or send manuscript to Editor Michael Hanlon.

The Canadian Messenger, Box 100, Station G., Toronto 8, Ontario, Canada. Editor Rev. F.J. Power pays 2 cents a word, on acceptance, for articles and short stories on daily life of Catholic men and women in Canada. Especially wants humor. Send query or manuscript to Mrs. M. Pujolas.

Chatelaine, 481 University Ave., Toronto, Ontario, Canada. Editor Doris Anderson pays $300 and up, on acceptance, for articles to interest Canadian women. Subjects include contemporary and controversial issues, personalities, medicine, psychology, general woman interests.

Maclean's Magazine, 481 University Ave., Toronto, Ontario, Canada. Pays good rates for articles on Canadian business, politics, sports, entertainment. Lengths 2,000 to 3,000 words. Submit query with outline.

Our Family, Box 249, Dept. E. Battleford, Saskatchewan, Canada. Editor A.J. Materi pays to 2 cents a word, on acceptance, for articles for teen-agers concerning family life.

Saturday Night, 55 York St., Toronto 1, Ontario, Canada. Editor Robert Fulford pays up to $250, on publication, for articles of general interest to Canadians.

12

HOW TO SELL TO SCIENCE AND TECHNICAL MARKETS

There are, naturally, two distinct levels on which a freelancer can write for the science and technical markets. One is the professional level, writing for journals which are read by scientists and engineers. The other is the popular level, writing magazine articles, newspaper features, and books for general readers.

Either way, science and technical writing is a well-paying and growing market for freelancers. But there is a catch: you must be qualified to write on the subjects.

You need not be a scientist or an engineer to write on aspects of their work, but you should know enough about your subject so that you can write with accuracy and authority. Add to this the general skills of interviewing, research, and reporting, and you can develop into a writer who regularly sells to these specialized markets.

Men who write on science and technical subjects are usually more concerned with writing on the major topics which might be considered somewhat impersonal: space exploration, atomic energy, antibiotics, genetic engineering, computers and data processing.

Women are generally more interested in writing on the personal side of a scientific subject; something they can write that women would be interested in, perhaps directed to family and child health, sex, and psychiatry.

Ted Berland, one of the top science writers in the country, focuses his writing attention on books, magazine articles, and public relations writing for scientific organizations. But he recommends that the newcomer to the field try to sell to the popular magazines that often buy science-oriented articles with a more human-interest approach.

"The major national magazines rely mainly on science writers known to them," Berland cautions. "Also, many of their articles are staff-written.

"New writers would best devote their efforts to magazines such as *Today's Health*, *Family Health*, and local Sunday newspaper magazine markets.

"Yearbooks are another possible market," Berland suggests. "Many encyclopedias publish yearbooks in which new or revised articles are written on developments in science and technical fields. Query an encyclopedia publisher with an article idea, but of course be somewhat an authority on the subject. Perhaps it will be something you have written on extensively for newspapers and magazines.

"The major women's magazines are mostly interested in science or medical subjects with a strong interest to women, about how to improve the quality of their family and home life. On the other hand, *Popular Mechanics* and *Popular Science* are 'hardware-oriented.' Their editors want stories to interest men, especially if they have some practical application to a man's work or hobby.

"Even with a strong science or technical background, writing for the professional journals can be very tricky," Berland warns. "Most of their articles are written by scientists and engineers who go into much greater detail than the average freelance writer could be able to handle."

Following, in addition to those markets mentioned above and which will be found earlier in this book, are the leading scientific and technical markets.

Scientific and Technical Markets

Electronics Illustrated, One Astor Plaza, New York, N.Y., 10036. Editor Robert Beason pays up to $150 per published page for how-to articles on amateur and Citizens Band radio, hi-fi, and other electronic hobby interests. Also articles about new developments in electronics. Lengths to 1,500 words. Photos or drawings should accompany manuscript or be available. Query.

Environment, 438 N. Skinker Blvd., St. Louis, Mo., 63130. Editor Sheldon Novick pays $100 for factual articles with technical information on environment pollution effects of technology, told for the layman. Lengths 5,000 to 7,000 words. Query.

Mechanix Illustrated, One Astor Plaza, New York, N.Y., 10036. Editor Robert Beason pays $500 and up for feature articles on new inventions, discoveries in science, and recreational uses of science, such as improvements for mobile homes. Lengths from 1,500 to 2,500 words. Also pays $75 to $250 for short articles or picture stories, $400 for how-to projects, $10 to $20 for how-to tips with photos or drawings.

Oceanology International, Industrial Research, Inc., Beverly Shores, Ind., 46301. Editor Ken Edmiston pays good rates for articles on ocean science and technology. Writers should be qualified science writers, educators, scientists, etc., and should submit query.

Popular Mechanics, 224 W. 57th St., New York, N.Y., 10019. Editor Robert Crossley pays $300 to $500 for features on scientific, mechanical, and industrial subjects with a human interest action or adventure element for male readers. Also how-to articles on automotive subjects, housing, craft projects, shop work. Quality photos must be available.

Popular Science, 355 Lexington Ave., New York, N.Y., 10017. Editor Hubert Luckett pays $150 and up per printed page for articles on automobiles, television, hi-fi, electronics, boating, photography, hobbies, home workshop subjects, new products, space, aviation, invention, and new developments in science. Pays $20 per photo. Query.

Radio-Electronics, 200 Park Ave. S., New York, N.Y., 10003. Editor Larry Steckler pays good rates, on acceptance, for illustrated practical articles on radio and electronics, from 2,000 to 3,000 words. Style should be technical but easy-to-read and interesting. Good photos help sell the article.

Science and Mechanics, 229 Park Ave. S., New York, N.Y., 10003. Editor Tony Hogg pays $50 and up per printed page for how-to articles in layman's language on new and unusual developments in the physical sciences. Lengths from 1,000 to 1,500 words. Query.

Science Digest, 224 W. 57th St., New York, N.Y., 10019. Editor Richard Dempewolff pays from $50 to $350 for articles on the sciences that are accurate and timely, written for the average reader. Lengths to 1,500 words. Also picture stories, occasional cartoons. Query.

Science World, Scholastic Magazines, Inc., 50 W. 44th St., New York, N.Y., 10036. Editor Carl Proujan pays up to $125 for articles emphasizing the concepts and work of scientists presently engaged in specific research. Articles are aimed at science students in grades 7 through 12. Lengths from 1,000 to 1,800 words, with pictures. Sample copy sent on request. Query.

Scientific American, 415 Madison Ave., New York, N.Y., 10017. Editor Dennis Flannigan buys from professional scientists only.

Sea Frontiers, The International Oceanographic Foundation, 10 Rickenbacker Causeway, Virginia Key, Miami, Fla., 33149. Editor F.G. Walton Smith pays 5 cents a word and up, on acceptance, for articles to interest layman on recent scientific advances related to the sea. Also general articles on interesting life or phenomena of the sea and economic and industrial uses of marine sciences. Uses black and white and color photos and art work. Query.

13

HOW TO SELL TO LITERARY JOURNALS, POETRY AND GREETING CARD MARKETS

Those of us who write would naturally like to make some money at it. But the cold truth is, not everything we like to write is salable, at least not to the major markets and even to many minor ones. What we write, how we write it, or why we write it may limit its chances of getting published.

There are only so many magazines which run any kind of short story, articles, no matter how slightly outspoken they may be, or poetry of any kind—and also pay for it. The competition is extremely keen for sales to any paying market because hundreds of professionals are also submitting their manuscripts and, let's face it, a name helps.

Many writers turn to the literary magazines published by colleges, universities, and small independent publishers, resigned that even getting nothing for their work, but having it published, is better than not having it published and still getting nothing for it. Their hope is that editors who see these magazines may read their work and discover them.

That is a legitimate reason for submitting work to the literary magazines, but it is not quite accurate. The fact of the matter of who writes for the literary magazines is aptly put by Curt Johnson, editor and publisher of *December,* an independently published quarterly that has been around for some years.

"In general," says Johnson, "those who submit material to the literary magazines are teachers of English and creative writing, and 'creative' writers who cannot market elsewhere what they want to write about.

"It is commonly thought that the literary magazines are

where writers 'begin' to write, and then graduate to 'bonafide' markets. Not so. Literary magazines provide a major market for major writers and those of all ages and experience. This is due to the drying up of commercial markets for short stories, poetry, and taboo subjects or unconventional treatments."

WHAT DO EDITORS WANT?

"Editors of literary journals want 'good stuff,' " Johnson says. "That truism aside, editors of literary magazines look for material that, generally, has more life in it than that found in commercial magazines, is more unconventionally treated, and which deals with issues that are taboo in commercial publications.

"Fiction runs from 2,000 to 3,000 words, and seldom more than 5,000. Any subject and style is acceptable, but the conventional short story has to be very well done to find a sympathetic editor among those on literary journals. Of course, university-subsidized literary journals do publish more conventional short stories.

"In poetry, anything goes. The more feeling in it, the better. Narrative verse seldom is accepted, chiefly because of its usual length.

"As for nonfiction . . . critical articles go in academic journals, but you find these mainly being written and read by English professors. Most independent literary magazine editors accept articles on all contemporary themes, including recent pop Americana, music, movies, etc., and many even go back to historical subjects. Major factors are style and content. The popular style of Tom Wolfe is a good example of what is wanted. As for content, an article must be relevant to the readers of literary magazines."

Few literary journals pay anything at all to contributors. Payment is often in a few copies of the magazine. But the field is a good one for new writers because their work can be seen. Sometimes, editors of commercial magazines will contact a writer whose article or short story appeared in a non-paying literary journal, and assign him to do a piece. Writing for the literary magazines is a good way for many writers to improve their craft so they eventually do sell their work.

"The chief appealing aspect of writing for the literary

journals," says Johnson, "is that the writer can write what he wants to write, the way he wants to write, and he stands a good chance of finding a publisher for it. And the editor won't mess it up by turning it into commercially safe material."

Literary Magazines

Abyss, Box C, Somerville, Maine, 02143. Editor Gerard Dombrowski publishes poetry, fiction, articles, art, photos, cartoons, interviews, satire, criticism, reviews. Payment in copies.

The Antigonish Review, English Department, St. Francis Xavier University, Antigonish, Nova Scotia, Canada. Editor R.J. MacSween publishes short stories to 2,500 words.

The Antioch Review, Box 148, Yellow Springs, Ohio, 45387. Editor Lawrence Grauman, Jr., pays $8 per printed page for fiction, articles, satire, criticism, reviews, poetry.

The Arlington Quarterly, Box 366, University Station, Arlington, Tex., 76010. Editor Maurice Carlson offers token payment for fiction, poetry, articles, reviews. Literary journal of the University of Texas at Arlington.

Assembling, Box 1967, Brooklyn, N.Y., 11202. Editors Henry Korn and Richard Kostelanetz publish fiction, poetry, articles, art, photos, cartoons, interviews, satire, criticism, reviews. Payment in copies.

Beyond Baroque, 1639 W. Washington Blvd., Venice, Calif., 90291. Publishes fiction, articles, satire, art, photos, cartoons, poetry. Payment in copies. Strictly avant garde/experimental.

Boston University Journal, Box 357, B.U. Station, Boston, Mass., 02115. Publishes quality fiction to 6,000 words; poetry. Payment in copies.

Carleton Miscellany, Carleton College, Northfield, Minn., 55057. Editor Wayne Carver pays $8 per printed page for fiction, $10 per page for poetry. Prefers satire, casual approach. Payment on publication.

Carolina Quarterly, Box 1117, Chapel Hill, N.C., 27514. Editor Junius Grimes pays $5 per printed page for fiction to 7,000 words. Also publishes poetry, parts of novels, photos, pen and ink art, one-act dramas, satire.

The Chicago Review, University of Chicago, Chicago, Ill., 60637. Editor R.A. McKean publishes quality fiction, verse, verse translations, verse plays.

The Colorado Quarterly, Hellems 134, University of Colorado, Boulder, Colo., 80302. Editor Paul Carter pays up to $20, on acceptance, for quality fiction 2,000 to 4,000 words. Also nontechnical articles for general reader.

December, Box 274, Western Springs, Ill., 60558. Editor Curt Johnson publishes fiction, poetry, articles, art, photos, interviews, satire, reviews. Send poetry to Dave Etter, 416 S. First St., Geneva, Ill., 60134. Payment in copies.

DeKalb Literary Arts Journal, DeKalb College, Clarkston, Ga., 30021. Editor Mel McKee publishes fiction, articles, poetry, art, photos, cartoons, interviews, satire, criticism, reviews. Payment in copies.

Descant, English Department, Texas Christian University, Fort Worth, Tex., 76129. Editor Betsy Colquitt publishes fiction to 7,000 words, and short poetry. Payment in copies.

Dust, 5218 Scottwood Rd., Paradise, Calif., 95969. Editor Wally Depew publishes short fiction to 3,000 words, articles, poetry, art, photos, interviews, satire, criticism, reviews. Payment in copies.

Epoch, 251 Goldwin Smith Hall, Cornell University, Ithaca, N.Y., 14850. Publishes quality fiction, poetry, reviews, photos. Payment in copies.

Evergreen Review, 214 Mercer St., New York, N.Y., 10012. Editor Barney Rosset pays $45 a page, on publication, for quality fiction and articles. Query.

The Falcon, Belknap Hall, Mansfield State College, Mansfield, Pa., 16933. Editors Joe David Bellamy (fiction) and W.A. Blais publish short stories from 2,000 to 6,000 words (also parts of novels); poetry, interviews. Payment in copies.

Four Quarters, LaSalle College, Phila., Pa., 19141. Editor John Keenan pays $25 for short stories and articles; $5 for poetry; on acceptance.

Georgia Review, University of Georgia, Athens, Ga., 30601. Editor James Colvert pays nominal rates, on publication, for short fiction and serious poetry.

Hanging Loose, 301 Hicks St., Brooklyn, N.Y., 11201. Publishes fiction, poetry, drawings, songs including music. Also special "poets in high school" section, including drop-outs.

The Hudson Review, 65 E. 55th St., New York, N.Y., 10022. Editor Frederick Morgan pays 3 cents a word for fiction, $1 a line for poetry. Fiction lengths to 10,000 words. Also articles, interviews, satire, criticism, art, reviews, photos.

The Iowa Review, EPB 453, University of Iowa, Iowa City, Ia., 52240. Pays $10 per page for fiction, $1 a line for poetry, on publication.

Kansas Quarterly, University Press of Kansas, Denison Hall,

Kansas State University, Manhattan, Kan., 66502. Publishes fiction, poetry, articles, criticism, interviews, satire. Payment in copies.

The Little Magazine, Box 207, Cathedral Station, New York, N.Y., 10025. Publishes short stories under 5,000 words; poetry, interviews, satire, reviews. Payment in copies. Likes humor.

The Little Review, Box 2321, Huntington, W. Va., 25724. Publishes imaginative poetry, fiction, articles, satire, criticism, review. Payment in copies.

Mandala, Box 705, Iowa City, Ia., 52240. Publishes poetry, prose poems, fiction, articles, cartoons, interviews, satire, criticism, art, photos, collages, reviews. Payment in copies.

The Massachusetts Review, Memorial Hall, University of Massachusetts, Amherst, Mass., 01002. Publishes short fiction. Payment is modest.

Mediterranean Review, Browns Hills, Orient, N.Y., 11957. Publishes fiction, drama, poetry, interviews, articles, satire, criticism.

Michigan Quarterly Review, 3032 Rackham, University of Michigan, Ann Arbor, Mich., 48104. Editor Radcliffe Squires pays 2 cents a word, on acceptance, for fiction to 5,000 words; 50 cents per line for poetry.

Minnesota Review, Box 578, Cathedral Sta., New York, N.Y., 10025. Publishes poetry, fiction, articles, satire, criticism, reviews, art. Payment in copies.

North American Review, University of Northern Iowa, Cedar Falls, Iowa, 50613. Pays $10 and up, per published page, for fiction. Also articles, reviews, poetry.

Northwest Review, University of Oregon, Eugene, Ore., 97403. Editor John Haislip pays $10 and up for fiction, $5 and up for poetry. Also publishes articles, criticism, reviews.

The Ohio Review, A Journal of the Humanities, Ellis Hall, Ohio University, Athens, Ohio, 45701. Publishes short stories about 5,000 words, poetry, articles, interviews, criticism, reviews. Payment in copies.

Paris Review, 45-39 171 pl., Flushing, N.Y., 11358. Publishes quality fiction. Payment on publication.

Perspective, Washington University, St. Louis, Mo., 63130. Publishes serious fiction to 10,000 words. Payment in copies. Also gives annual awards.

Prairie Schooner, 201 Andrews Hall, University of Nebraska, Lincoln, Nebr., 68508. Editor Bernice Slote publishes fiction to 5,000 words, and poetry. Payment in copies.

Pyramid, 32 Waverly St., Belmont, Maine, 02178. Publishes

fiction, articles, poetry, art, interviews, satire, criticism, reviews, cartoons. Likes experimental prose and verse. Payment in copies.

Salt Lick, 721 St. Paul St., Baltimore, Md., 21202. Editor James Haining publishes poetry, fiction, articles, art. Also runs a graphic folio with each issue. Payment in copies.

The Seneca Review, Box 115, Hobart and William Smith Colleges, Geneva, N.Y., 14456. Pays $25 per short story; $5 per page for poetry, on publication. Translations welcomed.

Shenandoah, Box 722, Lexington, Va., 24450. Quarterly of Washington and Lee University. Publishes fiction, poetry, reviews, interviews, criticism, essays. Payment by arrangement.

The Smith, 5 Beekman St., New York, N.Y., 10038. Editor Harry Smith publishes quality fiction. Payment by arrangement.

South Dakota Review, Box 111, University Exchange, Vermillion, S.D., 57069. Editor John Milton publishes fiction with a western setting; also experimental fiction, poetry, criticism, reviews, interviews, art, photos. Payment in copies.

Southern Review, Drawer D, University Sta., Baton Rouge, La., 70803. Pays 3 cents a word and up, on acceptance, for fiction from 4,000 to 8,000 words.

Southwest Review, Southern Methodist University, Dallas, Tex., 75222. Editor Margaret Hartley pays nominal rates, on publication, for short stories from 3,000 to 5,000 words. Emphasis should be on characterization.

Sumac, Box 29, Fremont, Mich., 49412. Editors Dan Gerber and Jim Harrison publish fiction, poetry, photos, criticism, reviews. Payment in copies.

Transpacific, Antioch College, Yellow Springs, Ohio, 45387. Editor Nicholas Crome publishes fiction, poetry, art, photos. Payment in copies. Accepts translations.

Tri-Quarterly, University Hall, 101, Northwestern University, Evanston, Ill., 60201. Pays $10 per printed page for fiction; $1 per line for poetry. Also articles, satire, criticism, reviews, art, photos, cartoons.

University of Windsor Review, Sunset Ave., Windsor, 11, Ontario, Canada. Editor Dr. Eugene McNamara publishes fiction, poetry, articles, criticism, reviews, art. Payment in copies.

Vagabond, 66 Dorland, San Francisco, Calif., 94110. Editor John Bennett publishes fiction, poetry, interviews. Payment in copies.

Western Humanities Review, University of Utah, Salt Lake City, Utah, 84112. Editor Jack Garlington publishes fiction and poetry. Payment in copies.

Yale Review, 28 Hillhouse Ave., New Haven, Conn., 06520. Publishes quality short stories and poetry.

General Magazines Buying Poetry

American Legion Magazine, 1345 Ave. of the Americas, New York, N.Y., 10019. Pays $10 and up, on acceptance, for humorous poetry to 16 lines.

American Scholar, 1811 Q St., N.W., Washington, D.C., 20009. Editor Hiram Haydn pays from $35 to $75 for quality poetry.

The Atlantic, 8 Arlington St., Boston, Mass., 02116. Editor Robert Manning buys quality poetry. Good market for outstanding young poets.

Christian Science Monitor, One Norway St., Boston, Mass., 02115. Pays good rates, after publication, for quality poetry. Submit poems to Home Forum Page Editor.

Essence, 102 E. 30th St., New York, N.Y., 10016. Editor Sharyn Skeeter pays from $25 to $60, on publication, for poetry to 65 lines.

Family Weekly, 641 Lexington Ave., New York, N.Y., 10022. Pays $20 to $35, on acceptance, for humorous verse.

Good Housekeeping, 959 Eighth Ave., New York, N.Y., 10019. Pays $5 a line and up, on acceptance, for poetry to interest women. Assistant Editor Delores Hudson prefers short, light verse.

Harper's Bazaar, 717 Fifth Ave., New York, N.Y., 10022. Betsy Freund, literary editor, pays $1 a line, on acceptance, for quality poetry. Experimental poetry welcome.

Harper's Magazine, 2 Park Ave., New York, N.Y., 10016. Editor Willie Morris pays good rates, on acceptance, for poetry.

Humorama, Inc., 299 Madison Ave., New York, N.Y., 10017. Editor Ernest Devver pays 45 cents a line, before publication, for humorous verse from 4 to 48 lines. Same requirements and rates for *Jest, Laugh Riot, Laugh Digest, Comedy, Stare, Zip, Fun House, Romp, Joker, Gaze, Gee-Whiz, Breezy,* and *Quips.*

Mademoiselle, 420 Lexington Ave., New York, N.Y., 10017. Poetry editor Ellen Stoianoff pays $25 and up, for quality poems to 65 lines.

National Lampoon, 1790 Broadway, New York, N.Y., 10019. Pays good rates for poetry for sophisticated audience.

The New Yorker, 25 W. 43d St., New York, N.Y., 10036. Pays top rates, on acceptance, for both light and serious poetry.

Pen, 444 Sherman St., Denver, Colo., 80203. Editor Jean B. Ryan pays 50 cents a line, on acceptance, for humorous and serious poetry, for holiday issues. Lengths to 16 lines.

Quote Magazine, Box 4073, Station B, Anderson, S.C., 29621.

Pays $1 and up, on publication, for light verse to 4 lines, which can be used by public speakers.

The Saturday Review, 380 Madison Ave., New York, N.Y., 10017. Poetry Editor John Ciardi pays $2 a line for short poetry. No light verse.

Yankee, Dublin, New Hampshire, 03444. Editor Judson Hale pays $10 for serious poetry under 30 lines. Send to Jean Burden, poetry editor.

Greeting Card Markets

The greeting card market is a lucrative one for writers of serious and humorous verse, and an increasingly good one for photographers.

Basically, there are two types of greeting cards: "Studio" and "Conventional."

Studio cards are usually humorous, with one-liners or very short poetry. Most are rectangular in size, but some are printed in a square format. Most, also, are single-fold.

Studio cards are mainly for birthdays, get well wishes, friendship, I miss you, and Valentines. Usually the cover will have a one-liner such as in this birthday greeting: "I'm happy to pay you homage..." Inside, the line is completed with: "...it's cheaper!"

Puns, plays-on-words, switches in meaning are favorite forms of Studio card humor.

Ed Letwenko, creative director of United Card Company, which specializes in humorous contemporary Studio cards, says this market is growing about twice as fast as the rest of the greeting card market, although conventional cards are still big sellers.

Conventional cards are sentimental, sincere, serious, and generally contain short poetry or prose suitable for weddings, anniversaries, birthdays, sympathy, holidays, and religious occasions. Most are square-shaped in double-fold.

"From 200 to 300 writers sell to us regularly," Letwenko says. "But we are still a good market for newcomers. We get from 4,000 to 5,000 ideas a week, but read them all. We buy from 600 to 800 ideas a year. Payment, which is standard for the market, is from $25 to $50 per idea."

It is not necessary to send a drawing with your greeting card idea, unless you are a sufficiently accomplished artist. Most greeting card companies have staff artists to illustrate the cards. Some writers are skilled enough to submit sketches to help visualize their idea, but artists do the finished work.

Ideas or verse should be sent on individual index cards, one idea or verse per card. Each card should contain the sender's name and address. One return, stamped envelope is sufficient for return of rejected material.

The greeting card market is a growing one for photographers. Many companies use photos with a short message. Most are scenes of young couples in tastefully romantic situations, scenic photos, children, and pets. The photos of young couples are used primarily for friendship cards and contain a short line of sentimental prose.

Rarely is humorous photography used. Photos can be either black and white or color. If color, send transparencies, not prints. Transparencies may be 35mm, but larger formats of 2¼ x 2¼ and 4 x 5 are preferred.

Model releases are a must, if faces are showing or there is any chance of the subjects being recognized. Most photo cards of people are shot with models, but model releases are still required. Payment for photos ranges from $75 to $150.

"Most greeting card submissions fail for two reasons," Letwenko says. "They're either not funny enough or, if they are funny, they do not make a greeting card: they simply do not put across a thought or message."

Following are the major markets for greeting card material. For a more complete market list and additional information on this market, send for "Free Lance Market List" from The Greeting Card Association, 30 Rockefeller Plaza, New York, N.Y., 10020. Send 24 cents in stamps.

American Greetings Corporation, 1300 W. 78th St., Cleveland, Ohio, 44102. Pays top rates for Studio card ideas that are highly original. No Conventional verse. Send to Editorial Dept.

Barker Greeting Card Co., Box 9010, Cincinnati, Ohio, 45209. Editor George Wilson pays $20 and up, for Studio and novelty cards using attachments or mechanical action. Sends monthly market letter on request (enclose stamped, self-addressed envelope).

Buzza-Cardozo, 1500 S. Anaheim Blvd., Anaheim, Calif., 92803.

Editor Helen Farries pays $1.50 a line, on acceptance, for all types of greeting card material including Studio and Conventional cards.

Charm Craft Publishers, Inc., 33 35th St., Brooklyn, N.Y., 11232. Pays $1 per line for verse, $25 to $35 per idea for humor, $50 per idea for Studio cards. Send everyday and seasonal ideas to Verse Editor; humorous and Studio ideas to Humor Editor.

Curtis Contemporary Cards, Curtis Circulation Co., 641 Lexington Ave., New York, N.Y., 10022. Pays regular rates for humorous Studio cards only. Market letter sent on request.

D. Forer & Co., Inc., 18 W. 18th St., New York, N.Y., 10011. Pays $10 per idea for contemporary ideas for all types of cards.

Fran Mar Greeting Cards, Ltd., 160 E. 3d St., Mt. Vernon, N.Y., 10550. Pays $10 per idea, within a month after acceptance, for whimsical, short verse no longer than 4 lines. Appeal should be for teen-age and college market.

Fravessi-Lamont, Inc., 11 Edison Pl., Springfield, N.J., 07081. Pays good rates for Studio cards with humorous prose; some sentimental verse. No Christmas material.

Gibson Greeting Cards, Inc., 2100 Section Rd., Cincinnati, Ohio, 45237. Pays $25 for humorous Studio ideas, higher rates for unusual design or trick fold ideas, and $1.50 per line and up for Conventional verse. Payment on acceptance.

Hallmark Cards, Inc., Kansas City, Mo., 64141. Pays $25 to $50 per idea for all types of greeting card ideas, but requires a strong new idea.

Keep 'N Touch Greeting Cards, Inc., Box 912, Framingham, Mass., 01701. Pays $12 to $15 per idea for contemporary Studio card ideas. Likes sophisticated humor and general but not sentimental ideas. Accepts photography. Pays on publication. Newsletter sent on request (enclose self-addressed, stamped envelope).

Little Eve Editions, Blackberry Lane, Morristown, N.J., 07960. Pays $5 to $10 per idea for almost everything except seasonal material or verse. Prefers 1-to-2-liners that are whimsical, and humor.

Mister B Greeting Card Co., 3500 N.W. 52d St., Miami, Fla., 33142. Editor Alvin Barker pays good rates for humorous and novelty card ideas and Conventional and sentimental material.

Norcross, Inc., 244 Madison Ave., New York, N.Y., 10016. Pays $20 to $50 for Studio and humorous ideas; $1.50 to $3 a line for Conventional verse.

Novo Card Publishers, Inc., 3855 Lincoln Ave., Chicago, Ill., 60613. Pays good rates for Studio, humorous card ideas with a comic punch line or double meaning. No sentimental verse.

Onyx Enterprises, Inc., 115 W. Palisades Blvd., Palisades Park, N.J., 07650. Pays $15 each for Studio card ideas for all occasions. Pays higher rates for Giant dollar line.

The Paramount Line, Inc., Box 678, Pawtucket, R.I., 02862. Editor Dorothy Nelson pays good rates for humorous and Studio cards, 4-and-8-line verses, both everyday and seasonal. Likes casual, conversational material rather than sentimental.

Reed Sterling Card Co., 3331 Sunset Blvd., Los Angeles, Calif., 90026. Editor Reed Stevens pays $40 per idea, on acceptance, for humorous Studio card ideas. Likes copy to be conversational, for sophisticated adults. Everyday and holiday subjects. Also pays monthly cash prizes for top selling card ideas.

Roth Greeting Cards, Box 1455, 7900 Deering Ave., Canoga Park, Calif., 91304. Editor Charles Roth pays $20 for humorous Studio card ideas for all occasions. Also ideas for new line of whimsical cards. Payment on acceptance.

Rust Craft Greeting Cards, Inc., Rust Craft Park, Dedham, Mass., 02026. Dolores Anderson, editor-in-chief, pays $25 for Studio card ideas, $30 for humorous rhymes, $30 for juvenile novelty card ideas, and $1.25 per line for general and religious verse. Payment on acceptance. Market letter sent on request (enclose stamped, self-addressed envelope).

Stanita Designs, Inc., 461 Eighth Ave., New York, N.Y., 10001. Pays $15 per idea for Black greeting cards.

United Card Co., 1101 Carnegie, Rolling Meadows, Ill., 60008. Creative Director Ed Letwenko pays from $25 to $50 for humorous contemporary Studio card ideas, both everyday and seasonal.

Vagabond Creations, 2560 Lance Dr., Dayton, Ohio, 45409. Editor George F. Stanley Jr. pays $10, on acceptance, for Studio card ideas with inside punch line. Humor aimed at younger age group. Also double-meaning ideas in good taste for older market.

Vaughn Card Co., 6001 Canyonside, Crescenta, Calif., 91214. Pays good rates for contemporary Studio card ideas.

Warner Press Publishers, Anderson, Ind., 46011. Mrs. Dorothy Smith, Verse Editor, pays $1 a line for everyday and holiday card ideas, from 4 to 6 lines. Also religious greeting card verse.

14

HOW TO SELL HUMOR AND FILLER

Riding to work at the *Chicago Tribune* on a bus one morning, reading James Thurber to brighten my day, I suddenly realized that what he had to say about children taking over the world could be up-dated and made into a humorous article.

All I had to do was think about how my sister's and brother's four children each have played some prank on me or them, and I had more than enough material for an article. Without any trouble, I sold it to the paper's *Sunday Magazine* and got my start as a writer of humor. Soon I was turning out more humor for the magazine than anyone else.

In another article, I invented the 12 most ineligible bachelors of Chicago, writing a paragraph about each type of bachelor. Then I got into character for each of them and posed for the photographs! In still another, I wrote parodies on the typical foreign movies from six different countries, and teamed up with a secretary to pose in scenes from the movies I had made up.

Jack Sharkey, whom you met in Chapter 8 on science fiction, also is a very prolific writer of humor, and adds several thousand dollars a year to his income by selling humor and satire on the "nutsy" side. But make no mistake: the writing is the best, and so are his ideas.

Sharkey enjoys most having fun with words, and twisting old familiar themes into new ideas for humor. One recent sale to *Playboy* was an article of humorous satire on how the classic horror stories such as *Frankenstein* would read if they were written today, bringing in contemporary events, problems, and viewpoints.

"I read the markets when I started writing humor," Sharkey recalls. "I figured out what the editors must be sick unto death of reading about, and proceeded to send them material so utterly *different* from what had gone before, that I was sure they would at least read the manuscript start-to-finish—if only because it made such a pleasant change of pace for them."

Sharkey also is adding substantially to his income by writing humorous plays. He has written comedy sketches for top television and night club stars and two of his current plays, *Here Lies Jeremy Troy* and *M Is for the Million*, are regularly performed in dinner theaters and in summer stock. Often these plays are picked up for television and some become series shows.

Writing for the stage and for television is, however, primarily for the professionals who specialize in that type of writing. The competition is so keen, you should be firmly grounded in having sold novels or many short stories before you attempt playwriting or television.

Selling humorous short stories, articles, books, and filler, however, is within the scope of this book and within the realistic goals of the freelance writer.

Almost without exception, magazines and publishers of books are almost desperate for humor. Gladly will an editor run at least one good humorous article per issue of his magazine. The only catch is, it has to be *good*.

It has rightly been said that humor is the hardest of all forms of writing to write well. Humor, as a rule, requires some restraint. That is why Thurber and Robert Benchley and Dorothy Parker are at the top of the list when you think of great humorists. What they said was not insane; it was intelligent, perceptive, and witty.

While Jack Sharkey calls his humor "nutsy," it is really clever, intelligent, and inoffensive. Strongly worded social comment that is the writer's private vendetta against society may be written under the guise of humor, but it will turn most editors off. Humor, like all other writing, must be responsible and contain a reasonable amount of restraint.

Virtually every magazine editor listed in the previous chapters buys humor. Not only buys it, but yearns for it. Editors generally pay 2 to 10 cents a word or from $10 to $100 for humor, buying everything from one-and-two sentence filler items to longer humor of from 1,000 to 5,000 words. Longer humorous articles, of course, pay more. *Playboy* pays from $1,000 to $2,000 for humorous articles and fiction.

HOW TO SELL HUMOR AND FILLER

NOTE: When sending short humor or filler to any market, always keep the original, because many editors will not return filler items, especially those sent on cards or snips of paper.

Your local newspaper is another good source of market for humor. Direct your material to the various department editors.

Feature syndicates often buy humor and filler items. See Chapter 2 for a list of newspaper syndicates and their needs.

Humor and Fillers for Special Markets

Alive!, Christian Board of Publication, Box 179, St. Louis, Mo., 63116. Published for young teen-agers. Buys cartoons, puzzles, word games.

Check Magazine, Howard Swink Advertising, Inc., 372 East Center St., Marion, Ohio, 43302. Editor Ed Newton buys general interest and sports fillers for this house organ. Payment varies.

David C. Cook Publishing Co., 850 N. Grove Ave., Elgin, Ill., 60120. Pays 2 to 4 cents a word for games, puzzles, cartoons, short humor, creative projects, anecdotes about famous people, origins of words, for junior through adult members of Protestant Sunday schools.

Current Comedy, 1529 E. 19th St., Brooklyn, N.Y., 11230. Pays $2 per item for humorous one-liners and jokes on current subjects, fads, trends. Send material to Robert Orben, 67-00 192 St., Flushing, N.Y., 11365. Pays at end of month.

FM Guide, 1290 Ave. of the Americas, New York, N.Y., 10019. Pays good rates for brief articles, fillers, photos for FM radio listeners.

Human Events, 422 First St., S.E., Washington, D.C., 20003. Weekly political newspapers. Pays $5, on publication, for humorous one-paragraph shorts (to 50 words) on politics, or opinion to appeal to conservatives.

Humorama, Inc., 299 Madison Ave., New York, N.Y., 10017. Pays $1 for one-line fillers, 45 cents a line for verse, and 3 cents and up for prose, just before publication. Buys satire on contemporary issues, humorous fillers, to 1,000 words; Light verse to 48 lines. Same requirements and rates for *Breezy, Comedy Magazine, Fun House, Gee-Whiz, Jest, Joker, Laugh Digest, Laugh Riot, Quips, Romp,* and *Zip!*

Kanrom, Inc., 311 W. 43d St., New York, N.Y., 10036. Editor Alex Roman pays $5 per joke and $10 per cartoon, for adult humor books.

National Lampoon, 1790 Broadway, New York, N.Y., 10019.

Pays 10 cents a word for sophisticated humor and satire aimed primarily at college-educated men. Also buys poems to 8 lines that are outspoken on contemporary issues.

The New Yorker, 25 W. 43d St., New York, N.Y., 10036. Pays $5 and up, on acceptance, for light verse, humorous items published in newspapers, books, magazines, and also amusing anecdotes.

Pen, 444 Sherman St., Denver, Colo., 80203. Pays 3 cents a word for humor or informative filler to 350 words.

Playboy, 919 N. Michigan Ave., Chicago, Ill., 60611. Pays $50 for jokes and from $50 to $350 for humorous items on contemporary subjects for section called "After Hours." Submit material to Party Jokes Editor or After Hours Editor.

Quote, Box 4073, Station B, Anderson, S.C., 29621. Pays $1 and up, on publication, for short jokes, quips, 4-line light verse to be used by public speakers.

Reader's Digest, Pleasantville, N.Y., 10570. Pays $100, on publication, for humor and short items for a variety of regular monthly features: Life in These United States; Humor in Uniform; Laughter, the Best Medicine, etc. Submit material to individual department editor. Also pays $25 for items for "Toward More Picturesque Speech," and $10 per two-column line for original items for "Campus Comedy" and $25 for reprints. Fillers are not acknowledged or returned.

15

HOW TO SELL TO BOOK MARKETS

When I saw Howard James last, about six years ago, we were a couple of young reporters on *The Chicago Tribune*. A short time later, he became Chicago Bureau Chief of *The Christian Science Monitor*, and wrote two series of articles, one on the courts and another on juvenile delinquency, that later became books.

The first, *Crisis In the Courts*, won him the Pulitzer Prize for national reporting. The second, *Children in Trouble: A National Scandal*, attracted national attention to the need for reform in juvenile institutions.

He was awarded an honorary doctorate of laws degree from our alma mater, Michigan State University; has been making even more money from making speeches than he is making on the books, which is not inconsiderable; has publishers coming to him asking him to write books for them; and just returned from four months in Europe at the expense of a Swiss movie producer who asked him to write a screenplay which first will be put out as a book, then made into a movie.

"I've learned never to underestimate the exposure your writing can get from a newspaper," James told me. "*The Monitor* paid me a good salary and all expenses to do the two series, and from their front pages, publishers came to me after only two or three installments of the courts series, and asked to publish it in a book.

"I felt I owed a great deal to *The Monitor*, which of course I did, and so I suggested that the paper and I share in the profits from the book. When the second series started in the paper, five publishers came to me about making it into a book.

"I have four or five books in mind now, and several publishers say they'll take anything I write. Now it's just a question of finding the time to do them all.

"Meanwhile, I'm earning from $500 to $1,000 a speech, talking to government groups, universities, clubs, and other organizations, about the two subjects I became an authority on by writing the series. And the income from the books and the speeches will help me to finance more writing."

And I remember when Howard James used to spend his weekends ice-fishing!

BOOKS THAT SELL

This chapter is last in the book for a very good reason: everything else written in the preceding chapters about writing can be applied to writing books that sell. And books are, to most writers, the dream's end. Or a new dream's beginning.

How can you sell a book of fiction or nonfiction? The answer is a book in itself, but basically simple: write a good book. Your book must interest, challenge, and satisfy your reader. It must get him involved so that he cares, one way or another, about your characters or subject.

To give you the most practical advice on how to get a book published, I interviewed Howard James, several other authors, and a literary agent who does not advertise for clients. Their opinions and methods may vary slightly, but basically they all agree on important points and offer good insight into that big question of how to sell a book.

SHOULD YOU GET AN AGENT?

Roy Porter, a literary agent for many years and a man who has spent his life in the publishing business, sat down with me in his comfortable Evanston (suburban Chicago) home one evening and talked book publishing for four hours.

On first sight, I knew I was in the home of a man who lived with books, loved books, and knew a lot about them. While the autumn wind blew the leaves about outside, he had a good fire going in the fireplace, his living room was lined with shelves containing books, we each had a glass of bourbon and water, and his basset hound was curled up in a rocking chair, not absorbing any of the literary wisdom his master was dispelling.

"The secret in getting a book published," Porter began, "is in the talent and originality an author brings to a book. He must have an appealing or interesting subject and an ability to bring a fresh insight or treatment to the book."

From that beginning, we talked first about the fiction market.

"The fiction market is bad, and has been bad for several years, because publishers are in a bad economic slump," Porter said. "Very little federal money is going into books, especially to school libraries. For instance, 80 percent of juvenile books are sold to school markets. Without sufficient federal funds to school libraries, the buyers of books for the school market simply have to cut down.

"Besides the cut in federal money for books, publishers also must face the financial problem of high interest rates when they borrow money to run their company.

"Never has there been a better reading public for fiction than there is today. Especially 'escape' literature. It isn't for lack of reader interest that more novels aren't being published and more authors have been unable to sell their books. It is simply an economic situation. When the national economy improves, the publishing business, like all other businesses, will be on a stronger footing. This, of course, will be a major factor in getting a book published. Provided, you understand, that the book is worth publishing."

Porter was asked, while we were on fiction, what subjects have the best chance of getting published.

"Any good story has a good chance," he said. "Specifically, Gothic novels are always popular with publishers. Detective books come in cycles, but generally are a good market. So is historical fiction. Good biography is bought a lot and sells well, especially for the young adult market."

Next, Porter was asked what real chance an author of a novel has of getting a publisher if he does not have an agent. While he replied completely in favor of having an agent, his reasons sound logical and should be of interest to writers who wonder about the whole question of whether or not to be represented by an agent.

Agents get a 10 percent commission from an author's sales. If you pay him anything additional, he is not really an agent but an agent-editor who may ask a fee for editing or "polishing up" your manuscript. You may learn a lot from such editing, but it will cost you anything up to about $500, before a publisher has even seen your book, much less agreed to publish it.

Porter, who is an agent, not an agent-editor, although he will help his clients with editorial direction as part of his commission, described an agent's role in publishing:

"At most large publishing houses, unsolicited manuscripts are read by a lower echelon of the editorial staff. Most are men and women young to publishing. A reader knows what his particular publishing house buys. Therefore, he may be reluctant to recommend anything he isn't 100 percent sure of, or may hesitate to recommend anything new.

"An agent, on the other hand, will know what publisher is buying what kind of book. He will save the author time in getting rejects from publishers who simply do not buy his type of book. He also will get the book read by someone of higher authority, because the agent has, over the years, developed a relationship with the publisher in which the publisher knows that what an agent recommends is worth looking at.

"A writer's chances of getting a book published are infinitely better if he has an agent. An agent will often work with the writer to guide his book along to make it commercially salable, he may help the author polish up the book, and he will send the book to the best possible publisher. The publisher accepts this quality from an agent and is more likely to give the book a serious reading. Last, but not least, the agent will try to make the most money he can for the writer."

Of course it is an unfortunate fact of publishing life that most agents will not take on a writer who has not had at least some articles or fiction published. You can make a decision whether or not to try to get an agent after you have had some work published. Some publishers, especially in the trade book line, do publish books by writers who have had little or nothing published. But the author usually is an authority on a particular subject, or can do the research to become one.

ON THE SUBJECT OF MONEY

What can you expect to make on your novel or book of nonfiction? While it is true that it is generally easier to sell a nonfiction book than it is to sell a novel, it is also true that in most cases, you will make more money on a nonfiction book.

Payment for most books is on a royalty basis, with the author earning a percentage of the retail price of all copies of his book that are sold. Usually, a writer gets 10 percent of the book's purchase price.

An advance against future royalties is customarily paid before publication, the amount depending on the type of book, author's importance, potential of the book, etc. Royalty rates usually increase after a specified number of books are sold.

Also included in a book contract are provisions that cover subsidiary rights, book club sales, options, reprints, and other subsequent uses of the book.

When most publishers say they pay a "standard royalty," they mean they assume all cost of production, distribution, and promotion of a book, and pay the author a royalty usually beginning at 10 per cent of the list price cost of the book, with a possible escalation to 12 or 15 per cent after the first 15,000 books are sold. Foreign and other subsidiary rights are most generally equally split.

More lucrative arrangements often can be made if you have an agent. He will do his best to get you a bigger advance against expected sales, an escalation of percentage on books sold, and will work to get his client a better split on serialization, foreign and reprint rights, and any possible movie or television sales.

"A good first novel can bring a writer an advance of from $1,500 to $2,000," Roy Porter said. "Many novels do not even earn their advance, so on his first book, a new author will be lucky to have the advance and no more.

"An advance is usually better on nonfiction books. This is because more of it is published, more is read, and nonfiction simply sells better.

"*When* you get the advance depends on the caliber of the material, how much research is involved, and the professional status of the author. If you have sold previous books, or have made substantial magazine sales, you may get a higher advance and may get it earlier.

"Most advances on a book are paid to the author in two installments: half on signing a contract, and half on acceptance of what the publisher feels is an acceptable manuscript. Some publishers pay in three installments: upon signing a contract, when half the manuscript is finished, and on completion of the book.

"A nonfiction book can bring an author an advance of from $3,500 to $4,000, without an agent. With an agent, the author can usually do better. And a nonfiction book generally makes more than its advance."

WITHOUT AN AGENT

Porter was asked how an author can get a publisher interested in his book, if he does not have an agent.

"For fiction, you simply have to write the whole book," Porter said. "Send it off to a publisher with or without a short cover letter. But if you write, keep it brief.

"For nonfiction, write a short query letter. One or two pages is sufficient. Describe your proposed book in a few paragraphs, including reasons why the subject needs to be written, and why you are qualified to write on it.

"A chapter outline is always good to send along. Also include a brief narrative about each chapter. And, if you really want to give the publisher a good idea of what you would do with the book, send him one or two sample chapters."

Porter summarized: "What are publishers buying? Excellent books! Books that have something fresh to say, and which are written with a fresh style."

HOW TO SELL YOUR BOOK

Hal Higdon, former assistant editor of *Kiwanis Magazine,* is married, has three children, is 40 years old, and has been freelancing since 1959. He has written for many national magazines and has had nine books published, five of them for children. Here are some of his observations on how to get a book published:

"I sold my first book, *The Union vs. Dr. Mudd,* about the Civil War doctor who set John Wilkes Booth's broken leg after Booth assassinated Lincoln, to Follett, the standard way: I wrote an outline of what the book would be, and sent two chapters. I chose to write the first chapter and one from the middle of the book, because they were the easiest to write on a minimum of research. And the first chapter got the reader, or the publisher, interested in the subject.

"In nonfiction, it makes better sense to send an outline and a chapter or two, rather than to write the whole book. The writer simply saves himself a lot of time and effort, you get a quicker response if the publisher only has to read an outline and a chapter or two before making his decision, and also, the publisher may guide the direction of your book, which means you will have saved a lot of time in rewriting.

"I believe this is the route that most beginning authors have to follow. For one thing, you have to prove to the publisher that you can write, before he will offer a contract.

"On the other hand, if you have a reputation as a writer, you can sometimes get a contract on much less than that. This was the case with my third book, *Pro Football USA*, which also later came out in paperback. It began as a magazine article.

"Recently I sold another book, *On the Run from Dogs and People*, about my career as a long-distance runner, by showing Regnery a number of magazine articles I had written over the years on the subject of running.

"I got another contract for a book on the Indianapolis 500 race by simply telling the editor, Tom McPherson, of Putnam's, that I wanted to do a children's book on the subject. And I just signed a contract for another book for Putnam's on drag racing, on little more than my word that I will do something on the project. By now, they trust me.

"As for tips or shortcuts on researching or interviewing, that's a book in itself. My feeling is, the writer better know how to research and interview before he tackles a book. He should gain this experience from writing magazine or newspaper articles.

"I write books because they pay reasonably well and there is always the chance of striking it rich on a particular one.

"Part of the secret in having your books sell is in establishing yourself as a name among not only reviewers, but librarians and people who order books for schools and libraries. This assures your work a certain automatic sale. If the publisher knows this, he is more likely to offer you a contract than an unknown writer. This is particularly true in the case of children's books, which are like annuities, in that the royalties go on and on and on."

Which is a nice note on which to close an interview with a successful writer of books.

Higdon's method, you notice, was to submit the material by mail. Two friends, Jay Robert Nash and Ron Offen, who co-authored *Dillinger—Dead or Alive?*, worked much harder to get a publisher for that, their first book.

HOW A BOOK IS BORN

It all started when Nash, a feature magazine editor, was on a vacation in Wisconsin and stopped at a country tavern for some beer and pretzels. The proprietor exchanged pleasantries about the weather and the fishing, and this illogically led him to telling Nash that John Dillinger, one of Chicago's gangster czars back in the 1930s, had not been shot and killed by the F.B.I., as was commonly known. Instead, Federal agents had shot another man, claimed he was Dillinger, and thereby got him off the Most Wanted list. The real Dillinger was supposed to have spent some time in Wisconsin, then went off to California to live in peaceful retirement, and was still alive.

Nash was intrigued enough to do some research which lasted some months, with the help of Offen, his managing editor. When both were finally convinced they had a book, making a strong case in favor of the theory that Dillinger was indeed still alive, they wrote an outline and three chapters, contacted an agent in New York, and flew there with the material.

The agent went with them to four publishers, to whom they made individual presentations. Each publisher's response was: "It would make a great book, but it won't sell."

Regnery, back in Chicago, liked the book, but wanted the outline reworked and the chapters rewritten. Nash and Offen said they would do it, and Regnery gave them a contract and a considerable advance.

The publisher also paid for the authors' expenses on a coast-to-coast promotion of the book when it came out, including television talk-show appearances to plug the book. But the most fun for the authors was a special Chicago press party held for them and the book, at the Biograph movie theater, in front of which Dillinger was supposed to have been shot down 35 years earlier.

Nash and Offen, with cigars in their mouths, drove up to the theater in a canary yellow 1932 Phaeton, wearing white carnations in their lapels.

Their story did make a great book. What's more, it sold well, and both are working on other books.

The road to getting a book published often is circuitous. There certainly are easier ways to make a living. But the rewards, whether in money or satisfaction, or a little of both, are enough to keep writers writing, readers reading, agents agenting, and publishers publishing.

Book Publishers

Abbey Book Publishers, Box 32, Station J., Toronto, 275, Ont., Canada. Mrs. E. Lambert, fiction editor, wants well-written novels with strong plot, from 60,000 to 80,000 words. Accepts U.S. postage for return. Pays 10 percent royalty.

Abbey Press, Inc., St. Meinrad, Ind., 47577. Editor Brian F. Daly buys books on marriage and family life. Pays advance against royalties.

Abelard-Schuman Ltd., 257 Park Ave. S., New York, N.Y., 10010. Editor John Brimer buys fiction, nonfiction, science, biography, garden, and cookbooks. Mrs. Frances Schwartz buys children's books.

Abingdon Press, 201 Eighth Ave. S., Nashville, Tenn., 37203. Senior Editor Emory S. Bucke buys religious books, juveniles, college textbooks, biography, marriage and family, social subjects, recreation, and other contemporary subjects. Query with outline and sample chapters.

Addison-Wesley Publishing Co., Reading, Mass., 01867. Editor Ray Broekel buys picture books and fiction and nonfiction for readers aged 4 to 16. Standard royalty payment.

Alliance Press (London) *Ltd.,* 11 W. 42d St., New York, N.Y., 10036. Send fiction manuscripts to P.O. Box 604, Times Square Station, New York, N.Y., 10036. Prefers query. Pays 10 percent of published price.

Allyn and Bacon, Inc., (See Chapter 9.)

American Book Company. (See Chapter 9.)

American Heritage Press, 330 W. 42d St., New York, N.Y., 10036. Kenneth Leish, Editor-in-Chief of adult books, buys nonfiction only. Pays standard royalty rates. Query first. Kathleen N. Daly, editor of children's books, buys fiction and nonfiction for ages 12 and under.

American West Publishing Co., 599 College Ave., Palo Alto,

Calif., 94306. Editor Donald E. Bower buys nonfiction on the West, both natural and human history. Standard royalty rates. Query.

Amis Publishing Co., 38 W. 32d St., New York, N.Y., 10001. Harold Miller, president, buys nonfiction books on Jewish and Israeli subjects. Also juvenile nonfiction. Standard royalty rates. Query.

Arco Publishing Co., 219 Park Ave. S., New York, N.Y., 10003. Editor Fred Honig buys how-to books on passing tests, and books on business, sports, hobbies, as well as general nonfiction subjects. Send query or outline. Pays outright and by contract.

Arkham House, Sauk City, Wisc., 53583. Buys macabre fiction and poetry. Fiction lengths from 25,000 to 80,000. Standard royalty rates. Query.

Arlington House, Inc., 81 Centre Ave., New Rochelle, N.Y., 10801. Editor Malcolm Wright buys nonfiction self-help books, books for political conservatives, and nostalgia on the period 1920-1950. Mail order distribution. Query.

Association Press, 291 Broadway, New York, N.Y., 10007. Director Robert W. Hill buys nonfiction on sports, recreation, social and behavioral sciences, family life, marriage education, adult and sex education, religious and ethical subjects. Query.

Astor-Honor, Inc., 114 Manhattan St., Stamford, Conn., 06904. Publishes trade and nonfiction books. Also juveniles and quality paperbacks. Query.

Atheneum, 122 E. 42d St., New York, N.Y., 10017. Richard Kluger, editor-in-chief, buys quality nonfiction, particularly history and American social subjects. Also adult fiction and biography. Pays on royalty basis. For children's books, see Chapter 9.

Atlantic Monthly Press, 8 Arlington St., Boston, Mass., 02116. Editor Peter Davison buys fiction, biography, history, social science, poetry and juveniles (see Chapter 9 for children's books).

Auerbach Publishers, Inc., 1101 State Rd., Princeton, N.J., 08540. Publisher O.R. Petrocelli buys nonfiction subjects and technical, scientific, and business books. Pays by standard royalty.

Augsburg Publishing House, 426 S. 5th St., Minneapolis, Minn., 55415. Editor Roland Seboldt buys fiction and nonfiction on Christian themes, and juveniles. Buys outright or standard royalty rates.

Aurora Publishers, Inc., 619, 170 Fourth Ave. N., Nashville, Tenn., 37219. Publishes hardcover and paperback books; juveniles from read-to books through young adult. Standard royalty. Query.

Baker Book House, 1019 Wealthy St. S.E., Grand Rapids, Mich., 49506. Editor Cornelius Zylstra buys nonfiction from 30,000 to 60,000 words, including Bible study aids and Christian solutions to contemporary problems. Royalty payment.

A. S. Barnes, Box 421, Cranbury, N.J., 08512. Publishes books on sports, outdoors, art, cinema, horses, recreation, boating, electronics, aviation, automobiles, and subjects to interest women. Standard royalty rates. Query.

Barnes & Noble Books, A Division of Harper & Row, Publishers, 10 E. 53 St., New York 10022. Publishes educational paperback books for the college market. Query.

Richard W. Baron, 201 Park Ave. S., New York, N.Y., 10003. Publishes fiction and nonfiction.

Basic Books. (See Chapter 9.)

The Beacon Press, 25 Beacon St., Boston, Mass., 02108. Publishes general nonfiction: current events and problems of American life. Also scholarly works on contemporary affairs and liberal religious books. Standard royalty. Query.

Charles A. Bennett Co. (See Chapter 9.)

Better Homes and Gardens Books, See *Meredith Corporation.*

Binfords & Mort, 2505 S.E. 11th Ave., Portland, Ore., 97242. Editor L.K. Phillips buys books on the Pacific northwest (primarily nonfiction) about 70,000 words. Standard royalty.

Bloch Publishing Co., 31 W. 31st St., New York, N.Y., 10001. Editor Samuel Gross buys books on Jewish subjects.

Bobbs-Merrill Co., 4 W. 58th St., New York, N.Y., 10019. Robert M. Amussen, editor-in-chief, buys novels, biographies, autobiographies, travel, history, music, popular science, drama, religion. Query. Pays standard royalty. See Chapter 9 for juvenile books.

Thomas Bouregy & Co., 22 E. 60th St., New York, N.Y., 10022. Editor Reva Kindser buys romances and westerns. Prefers light, wholesome approach. Lengths from 45,000 to 55,000 words. Standard royalty rates.

Bradbury Press. (See Chapter 9.)

Charles T. Branford Co., 28 Union St., Newton Centre, Mass., 02159. Editor Ilse Jacobs buys nonfiction art books, natural history, how-to, hobby, and craft books. Standard royalty. Query.

George Braziller, Inc., One Park Ave., New York, N.Y., 10016. Edwin Seaver, editor-in-chief, buys history, literature, art, science, philosophy, social science books. Also quality fiction.

Broadman Press, 127 Ninth Ave. N., Nashville, Tenn., 37203. Publishes general religious nonfiction, inspirational nonfiction and fiction, and juvenile books. See Chapter 9 for children's books. Standard royalty. Query.

Bruce Publishing Co., 866 Third Ave., New York, N.Y., 10022. Publishes textbooks on religious education, vocational education, and industrial arts for elementary, high school, and college levels. Also craft and hobby books, Catholic trade books, theology and philosophy, and books on contemporary problems. Standard royalty. Query.

Caxton Printers, Ltd., Box 700, Caldwell, Idaho, 83605. Publishes authentic Americana, especially frontier and the West. No fiction. Standard royalty. Query.

Children's Press. (See Chapter 9.)

Chilton Book Co., 401 Walnut St., Philadelphia, Pa., 19106. Editor-in-Chief John F. Marion buys general nonfiction and books on arts and crafts; also young adult nonfiction. He accepts manuscripts and queries with outlines. Standard royalty.

Chronicle Books, 54 Mint St., San Francisco, Calif., 94103. Specializes in western nonfiction books up to 100,000 words, on history, travel, growth and development of the West. Query. Standard royalty payment.

Citadel Press, 222 Park Ave. S., New York, N.Y., 10003. Editor-in-Chief Allan J. Wilson buys mainly nonfiction but also publishes some fiction. Also publishes paperbacks.

Citation Press, Scholastic Books, 50 W. 44th St., New York, N.Y., 10036. Publishes professional paperback and hardcover books for teachers, administrators, and college students in teacher education. Books should focus on trends and new methods in education at all levels. Send query to Mrs. Norma Ainsworth, editor of Manuscript Department.

Arthur R. Clark Co., 1264 S. Central Ave., Glendale, Calif., 91204. Publishes research books, history, and biography related to Western North America. Send query with outline and sample chapter to Editorial Department. Catalog sent on request.

Cobble Hill Press, 271 Madison Ave., New York N.Y., 10016. Editors Sig Rosenblum and Charles Antin publish well-written books about the New Left, South America, nonviolence. Royalty payment.

Concordia Publishing House, 3558 S. Jefferson Ave., St. Louis, Mo., 63118. Publishes fiction and nonfiction with a moral or Christian tone. Also publishes juveniles and teen-age books. Standard royalty payment.

Cornell Maritime Press, Cambridge, Md., 21613. Editor Mrs. Mary Jane Cornell prefers query with outline on technical maritime books; also how-to books for boat owners. Royalty basis.

Coward, McCann & Geoghegan, 200 Madison Ave., New York, N.Y., 10016. Publishes quality fiction and general nonfiction except technical books. Also fiction and nonfiction for children, from read-to books to books for young adults. Prefers a query letter from unagented authors rather than seeing a manuscript. Standard royalty payment.

Cowles Book Co., 114 W. Illinois St., Chicago, Ill., 60610.

Publishes adult nonfiction on health, education, politics, international affairs, science, medicine, problems of contemporary life, sports, etc. Pays standard royalty. Query.

Thomas Y. Crowell Co., 666 Fifth Ave., New York, N.Y., 10019. Publishers adult nonfiction books, reference books, and children's books. Also college and secondary school texts. Regular royalty payment. Query.

Crown Publishers, Inc., 419 Park Ave. S., New York, N.Y., 10016. Publishes fiction and nonfiction for adults and children. Herbert Michelman, Editor-in-Chief, accepts queries for adult nonfiction; Morrell Gipson reads juvenile manuscripts.

Dartnell Corporation, 4660 Ravenswood Ave., Chicago, Ill., 60640. Publishes books on business. Standard royalty payment.

Jonathan David Publishers, Inc., 68-22 Eliot Ave., Middle Village, N.Y., 11379. Publishes nonfiction books to interest the Jewish book-buying market. Also juveniles and text books. Send query to Alfred J. Kolatch, Editor-in-Chief. Royalty payment or outright purchase.

The John Day Company, Inc., 257 Park Ave. S., New York, N.Y., 10010. Publishes fiction and nonfiction. Send query or fiction to Richard J. Walsh, Jr., president. Standard royalty.

John de Graff, Inc., 34 Oak Ave., Tuckahoe, N.Y., 10707. Publishes nonfiction, especially nautical books both technical and popular.

T. S. Denison & Co., 5100 W. 82d St., Minneapolis, Minn., 55431. Publishes nonfiction only: how-to books, inspirational books, game and party books, children's books, teachers' texts.

Devin-Adair Company, 1 Park Ave., Old Greenwich, Conn., 06870. Publishes nonfiction only: politically conservative books, books about nature and popular health subjects, and books about Ireland. Also books on ecology. Query. Standard royalty payment.

The Dial Press, 750 Third Ave., New York, N.Y., 10017. Publishes fiction and nonfiction (no mysteries, westerns, verse, romance, or technical books). Donald Hutter is editor-in-chief. Mrs. Phyllis Fogelman, children's book editor. Pays royalties and advances.

Dimension Books, Inc., P.O. Box 811, Denville, N.J., 07834. Thomas Coffey, editor prefers query for nonfiction books, Catholic books, children's books, and travel.

Diplomatic Press, Inc., P.O. Box 604, Times Square Station, New York, N.Y., 10036. Editor Nigel Sefton Paneth accepts queries and manuscripts on nonfiction of current interest to general readers. Standard royalty payment.

Dodd, Mead, & Company, Inc., 79 Madison Ave., New York, N.Y., 10016. Publishes general nonfiction, some fiction, and all types of juvenile books. Thomas H. Lipscomb prefers query. Standard royalty.

Doubleday & Co., Inc., 277 Park Ave., New York, N.Y., 10017. Publishes all types of nonfiction, fiction, juveniles, history, travel, religious subjects, science. Also western and science fiction novels and detective, mystery, and crime books for The Crime Club. Pays by standard royalty.

Dow Jones-Irwin, Inc., 1818 Ridge Rd., Homewood, Ill., 60430. Publishes business books. Norman F. Guess, editor. Pays by standard royalty.

E.P. Dutton & Co., Inc., 201 Park Ave. S., New York, N.Y., 10003. Publishes nonfiction, fiction, mysteries, children's books, quality paperback books. Standard royalty.

William Eerdmans Publishing Co., 255 Jefferson Ave. S.E., Grand Rapids, Mich., 49503. Publishes nonfiction on Christian religious subjects. Calvin Bulthuis, editor. Standard royalty.

Elk Grove Press. (See Chapter 9.)

Emerson Books, Inc., 251 W. 19th St., New York, N.Y., 10011. Publishes how-to books, puzzle, math books with popular appeal, self-help books, collecting books, books on gems and jewelry, and reference books. Royalty payment.

Paul S. Eriksson, Inc., 119 W. 57th St., New York, N.Y., 10019. Publishes adult fiction, nonfiction, biography, etc. Standard royalty payment. Query.

Farrar, Straus and Giroux, 19 Union Sq. W., New York, N.Y., 10003. Publishes fiction and nonfiction. Also *Noonday Press* paperbacks and *Octagon Books,* scholarly reprints.

Frederick Fell, Inc., 386 Park Ave. S., New York, N.Y., 10016. Publishes *Fell's Guide Series* of craft and hobby books (query Roger Blair, editor); *Fell's Business and Financial Book Shelf,* business and financial books (query Frederick Fell); and *Fell's Better Health Series*, books on physical and mental health (query Mr. Blair as health editor). Also nonfiction on current social subjects, mysticism, the occult, biography, autobiography (query Margaret Brilant with outline and sample chapters). Royalty payment.

Fides Publishers, Inc., Notre Dame, Ind., 46556. Publishes religious books and books on modern education, Montessori applications. Standard royalty payment.

Finney Company, 3350 Gorman Ave., Minneapolis, Minn., 55426. Publishes occupational guidance workbooks for high school graduates, special education classes, and rehabilitation classes. Query first with outline and bibliography. Pays by outright purchase or standard royalty.

Fleet Press Corp., 156 Fifth Ave., New York, N.Y., 10010. Publishes nonfiction except science and technical subjects. No fiction. Query. Also *Fleet Academic Editions, Inc.,* books on the humanities and social sciences. Query.

Follett Publishing Co., 1010 W. Washington Blvd., Chicago, Ill., 60607. Publishes adult reference books, general nonfiction, and sports, poetry, and criticism. Also quality juvenile fiction and nonfiction (See Chapter 9).

Fortress Press, 2900 Queen Lane, Philadelphia, Pa., 19129. Publishes books on theology for the layman, the student, and the minister and scholar. Standard royalty.

Fountainhead Publishers, Inc., 475 Fifth Ave., New York, N.Y., 10017. Publishes some adult fiction, minimum length 65,000 words. Send query with complete manuscript to Frances Robotti, editor-in-chief. Standard royalty payment.

Four Winds Press, Scholastic Magazines, Inc., 50 W. 44th St., New York, N.Y., 10036. Publishes adult nonfiction and juvenile and young adult fiction and nonfiction. Send complete manuscript for fiction, outline and sample chapters for nonfiction. Standard royalty payment.

The Free Press (division of *The Macmillan Company*), 866 Third Ave., New York, N.Y., 10022. Publishes nonfiction books in the social sciences and humanities; college texts. Royalty payment.

Funk & Wagnalls (division of *Reader's Digest Books*), 666 Fifth Ave., New York, N.Y., 10019. Publishes Adult nonfiction, English usage books, reference books, current affairs, science, biography, how-to, and handbooks. Query Gordon Carruth, editor. Royalty payment.

Gambit, Inc., 437 Boylston St., Boston, Mass., 02116. Publishes general fiction and nonfiction.

Bernard Geis Associates, 128 E. 56th St., New York, N.Y., 10022. Publishes general fiction, nonfiction, and biographies. Query.

Ginn and Company, Statler Bldg., Park Square, Boston, Mass. 02117. Publishes textbooks for elementary schools, high schools, and colleges. Query. Send queries for college level books to College Division, Xerox College Publishing, 275 Wyman St., Waltham, Mass., 02154.

Golden Gate Junior Books. (See Chapter 9.)

Golden Press, 850 Third Ave., New York, N.Y., 10022. Publishes adult nonfiction and fiction and nonfiction for children. Also reference books.

The Stephen Greene Press, Box 1000, Brattleboro, Vt., 05301. Publishes quality nonfiction and New England regional books. Query with table of contents and one or two chapters. Pays by royalty contract.

Grosset & Dunlap, Inc., 51 Madison Ave., New York, N.Y., 10010. Publishes general nonfiction for adults including history, biography, literature, science, fine arts; also practical and self-help books such as cookbooks, reference books. Complete line of children's books (see Chapter 9).

Grossman Publishers, Inc., 44 W. 56th St., New York, N.Y., 10019. Publishes general fiction and nonfiction. Query.

Grove Press, Inc., 53 E. 11th St., New York, N.Y., 10003. Publishes fiction and nonfiction; also *Evergreen Books,* paperback series. Query Barney Rosset, editor and publisher. Standard royalty payment.

Harcourt Brace Jovanovich, Inc., 757 Third Ave., New York, N.Y., 10017. Publishes general fiction and nonfiction for adults. Query Edwin Barber, Editor-in-Chief. Also children's books (See Chapter 9).

Harper & Row, 10 E. 53rd St., New York, N.Y., 10022. Publishes general fiction and nonfiction for adults. Also children's books and textbooks (See Chapter 9).

Harvey House, Inc., (See Chapter 9).

Hastings House, Publishers Inc., 10 E. 40th St., New York, N.Y., 10016. Publishes general nonfiction including Americana, biography, travel, guide and photographic picture books, books on cooking and wines. Query Walter Frese, editor. Also juvenile books (query Miss Judy Donnelly, editor). For books on communication arts including movies, television, and radio; graphic and visual arts, query Russell F. Neale. Royalty payment.

Hawthorn Books, 70 Fifth Ave., New York, N.Y., 10011. Publishes how-to, business, gardening, history, cooking, self-help books. Query with outline and sample chapter. Paul Fargis, editorial director. Royalty payment.

Hearthside Press, Inc., 445 Northern Blvd., Great Neck, N.Y., 11021. Publishes home, needlecraft, antiques, and gardening books. Editor Nedda C. Anders.

D. C. Heath. (See Chapter 9).

Hill and Wang, Inc., 19 Union Sq. W., New York, N.Y., 10003. Publishes fiction and nonfiction including science, history, social history, and drama. Query Editor Arthur W. Wang. Standard royalty payment.

Hobbs, Dorman & Co., 441 Lexington Ave., New York, N.Y., 10017. Publishes educational textbooks, supplementary reading books, how-to books. Query.

Holiday House. (See Chapter 9).

Holt, Rinehart and Winston, Inc., 383 Madison Ave., New York, N.Y., 10017. Publishes general fiction and nonfiction. Query with outline and sample chapters. Address query to General Book Division. Also publishes juveniles. Pays royalties twice annually.

Horizon Press, 156 Fifth Ave., New York, N.Y., 10010. Publishes general trade books, nonfiction, art, architecture, science, and reference books. Also some fiction. Query Ben Raeburn, editor. Standard royalty payment.

Houghton Mifflin Co., 2 Park St., Boston, Mass., 02107. Publishes contemporary, historic, and general fiction; nonfiction history, natural history, biography, social-political books, humor; general juvenile and teen-age books. Also awards literary fellowships to finance work in progress.

Howell Book House, Inc., 845 Third Ave., New York, N.Y., 10022. Publishes nonfiction books on care, training, breeding of pure-bred dogs; also how-to books, histories, behavior and other aspects of dog knowledge. Standard royalty rates.

Howell-North Books, 1050 Parker St., Berkeley, Calif., 94710. Publishes books on railroad history, Western Americana (mostly well-illustrated). Editor F.D. North. Pays royalties. Query.

International Marine Publishing Co., 21 Elm St., Camden, Maine, 04843. Publishes books on oceanography, maritime history, sea ecology, sailing, motorboating and other marine subjects. Send query or manuscript to Roger C. Taylor, editor and president. Standard royalty payment.

Jewish Publication Society, 222 N. 15th St., Philadelphia, Pa., 19102. Publishes nonfiction, fiction, and juveniles bearing on Jewish life, literature, history, biography, etc. Query Dr. Chaim Potok, editor. Standard royalty payment.

Judson Press, Valley Forge, Pa., 19481. Publishes religious books with contemporary themes; inspirational, and devotional books. Standard royalty.

P.J. Kenedy & Sons, 866 Third Ave., New York, N.Y., 10022. Publishes liturgical books, books on religious and moral issues, Bibles and related books. Standard royalty. Query.

Robert R. Knapp, Publisher, Box 7234, San Diego, Calif., 92107. Publishes reference and textbooks on the humanities and social sciences, especially psychology, psychiatry, and statistics. Query. Pays standard royalty.

Alfred A. Knopf, Inc., 201 E. 50th St., New York, N.Y., 10022. Publishes quality fiction and nonfiction, college texts in humanities and social sciences, and juveniles (see Chapter 9). Royalty payment.

John Knox, Box 1176, Richmond, Va., 23209. Publishes books on social, ethical, or cultural aspects of religion. Query H. Davis Yeuell, editor. Royalty payment.

Lantern Press, 354 Hussey Rd., Mt. Vernon, N.Y., 10552. Publishes adult nonfiction and juvenile fiction and nonfiction. Query.

Lawrence Publishing Co., 617 S. Olive St., Los Angeles, Calif., 90014. Publishes adult fiction, biography, autobiography, history, religion, travel, politics, and juvenile books. Also textbooks (See Chapter 9). Send query with outline and sample chapters to Editor Joseph Lawrence. Royalty payment. Catalog on request.

Seymour Lawrence, Inc., 90 Beacon St., Boston, Mass., 02108. Publishes fiction, books on child care and development, and children's books. Royalty payment. Query about nonfiction.

Lenox Hill Press, 419 Park Ave. S., New York, N.Y., 10016. Publishes science fiction, westerns, light romances, from 55,000 to 60,000 words. No sex or violence emphasized. Pays $250 for romances, $150 for westerns, $200 for science fiction.

Lerner Publications Co. (See Chapter 9).

Lion Press, 52 Park Ave., New York, N.Y., 10016. Publishes adult books and juvenile and young adult books (See Chapter 9).

J.P. Lippincott Co., 521 Fifth Ave., New York, N.Y., 10017. Publishes adult and juvenile fiction and nonfiction. Special interests include biography, social history, nature, contemporary affairs, sports, and humor. Query Editor-in-Chief Edward L. Burlingame for adult books, Dorothy Briley for juveniles. Royalty payment.

Little, Brown & Co., 34 Beacon St., Boston, Mass., 02106. Publishes adult fiction and nonfiction and juvenile books. Query Eliot Fremont-Smith for adult books, Ralph C. Woodward for juveniles.

Liveright Publishing Corp., 386 Park Ave. S., New York, N.Y., 10016. Publishes quality fiction and nonfiction, especially psychology, sociology, politics, current affairs. Send query and synopsis with biographical sketch. Royalty payment.

Longman Canada Ltd., 55 Barber Greene Rd., Don Mills, Ontario, Canada. Publishes adult fiction 80,000 words and up. Managing Editor Alistair Hunter prefers to see completed manuscripts and does not require return postage for return of manuscripts.

Lothrop, Lee & Shepard Co. (See Chapter 9).

Robert B. Luce, Inc., 2000 N St., N.W., Washington, D.C., 20036. Robert D. Van Roijen, president, prefers nonfiction, public affairs books, but also accepts fiction. Payment by advance and royalty.

McGraw-Hill Book Co., Trade Dept., 330 W. 42d St., New York, N.Y., 10036. Publishes fiction and nonfiction including biography, history, humor, popular science, religion, business, reference, how-to books, art books. Robert Sussman Steward, editor. Also juveniles (See Chapter 9).

David McKay Co., Inc., 750 Third Ave., New York, N.Y., 10017. Publishes adult fiction including Gothics, suspense, fast-paced novels; nonfiction including history, cookbooks, contemporary interests, human behavior, science, medicine, and health; juvenile fiction and nonfiction; and college textbooks. Query Jane Axt, managing editor, for nonfiction adult books, with outline and sample chapters. Rose Dobbs, editor of juvenile books.

The Macmillan Company, 866 Third Ave., New York, N.Y., 10022. Publishes fiction and general nonfiction including religion, medical and health books, business technical; textbooks on all levels; and juveniles. Query.

Macrae Smith Co., 225 S. 15th St., Philadelphia, Pa., 19102. Publishes adult nonfiction, trade and reference books, and fiction. Also juvenile and young adult fiction, nonfiction, and reference books. For adult books, query Donald B. Macrae, president.

Meredith Corporation, Consumer Book Division, 1716 Locust St., Des Moines, Ia., 50303. Published by *Better Homes and Gardens Books and Creative Home Library.* Editorial Director Don Dooley prefers outlines on sewing, health, decorating, gardening, money affairs, home entertainment, cars, building. Query. Pays flat fees or royalties.

Merry Thoughts, Inc. (See Chapter 9).

Julian Messner. (See Chapter 9).

Moody Press, 820 N. LaSalle St., Chicago, Ill., 60610. Publishers of Evangelical books for the Moody Bible Institute, including fiction and nonfiction with conservative doctrine. Looking for contemporary fiction reflecting faith in God.

Morehouse-Barlow Co., Inc., 14 E. 41st St., New York, N.Y., 10017. Publishes nonfiction, especially textbooks, and adult and children's religious books. No fiction. Pays by fee and royalty. Query with outline and sample chapter.

William Morrow & Co., 105 Madison Ave., New York, N.Y., 10016. Publishes fiction and nonfiction. Query Editor-in-Chief John C. Willey for adult nonfiction. Also juveniles (See Chapter 9).

Nash Publishing Co., 9255 Sunset Blvd., Los Angeles, Calif., 90069. Publishes controversial nonfiction, how-to, self-improvement, psychological books. Query Editor Cynthia Swan. Pays by flat fee or royalty.

Nelson-Hall Publishers, 325 W. Jackson Blvd., Chicago, Ill., 60606. Publishes nonfiction about the family, employment, the community, contemporary problems, educational and informative books on health and the behavioral sciences for the layman. Query Editor V. Peter Ferrara. Royalty payment.

Thomas Nelson, Inc., 30 E. 42nd St., New York, N.Y., 10017. Publishes adult nonfiction, biographies, the arts, history, religion. No adult fiction. Query Editor William Gentz. Also juvenile and young adult fiction and nonfiction. Query Mrs. Gloria Mosesson, Junior Book Editor, at 250 Park Ave., New York, N.Y., 10017.

Nitty Gritty Productions, P.O. Box 457, Concord, Calif., 94522. Publishes cookbooks. Send manuscript or query to Miss Peggy Treadwell, editor.

W.W. Norton & Co., Inc., 55 Fifth Ave., New York, N.Y., 10003. Publishes fiction and nonfiction. Royalty payment.

Oceana Publications, Inc., 75 Main St., Dobbs Ferry, N.Y., 10522. Publishes books on law. Query Managing Editor W.W. Cowan. Pays flat fee or royalty.

Oddo Publishing, Inc. (See Chapter 9).

Ohara Publications, 5650 W. Washington Blvd., Los Angeles, Calif., 90016. Publishes books on Oriental philosophy. Query with synopsis and resume. Royalty payment.

Outerbridge And Lazard, 200 W. 72nd St., New York, New York, 10023. Books on American culture and traditions. Query Editor Harris Dienstfrey. Standard royalty.

Oxford University Press, 200 Madison Ave., New York, N.Y., 10016. Nonfiction on literature, history, religion, philosophy, biography, government, economics, art, science, music, and college textbooks and medical books. Query.

Pantheon Books, 201 E. 50th St., New York, N.Y., 10022. Fiction and nonfiction, art, history, and juveniles.

Parents' Magazine Press. (See Chapter 9).

Parker Publishing Co., West Nyack, N.Y., 10994. Publishes general nonfiction self-help, how-to-do-it, and reference books on a variety of professional and general subjects. Pays on a royalty schedule. Sample catalog on request. Query.

Parnassus Press, 2721 Parker St., Berkeley, Calif., 94707. Query for adult fiction and nonfiction. Also children's books (See Chapter 9). Advance and royalties.

Paulist/Newman Press, 304 W. 58th St., New York, N.Y., 10019. Catholic books on religious education, theology, philosophy, etc.

George A. Pflaumn, Publisher, 38 W. 5th St., Dayton, Ohio, 45402. Publishes books on mental health, religious education, film study, teacher training. Royalty payment. Query Editor John M. Heher.

S.G. Phillips, Inc. (See Chapter 9).

Pitman Publishing Corp., 6 E. 43d St., New York, N.Y., 10017. Publishes nonfiction on business, the arts, arts and crafts, college economics, education, history, psychology, general nonfiction. Royalty payment.

Platt & Munk. (See Chapter 9).

Clarkson N. Potter, Inc., 419 Park Ave. S., New York, N.Y., 10016. General trade books and nonfiction, especially Americana, science, arts, antiques, folk art, current affairs. Query.

Praeger Publishers, Inc., 111 Fourth Ave., New York, N.Y., 10003. Publishes nonfiction current affairs, international relations, history, military affairs, political and social science, urban affairs, education, art, architecture, archaeology, design. Query. Royalty payment. Arnold Dolin, Editor-in-Chief.

Prentice-Hall, Inc., Englewood Cliffs, N.J., 07632. Adult fiction and nonfiction, especially biography, history, politics. No westerns, mysteries, drama, poetry, or popular romances. Query. See Chapter 9 for juvenile books.

Price/Stern/Sloan Publishers, Inc., 410 N. La Cienega Blvd., Los Angeles, Calif., 90048. Publishes hardcover and paperback books of original humor. Query.

Pruett Publishing Co., P.O. Box 1560, Boulder, Colo., 80302. History and development of the West; railroads; outdoor books on the Rocky Mountain states; hiking, camping, mountain climbing. No adult fiction. Query Editor Gerald Keenan. Also textbooks and fiction for slow readers. Query Editor Elizabeth Opal.

Public Affairs Press, 419 New Jersey Ave. S.E., Washington, D.C., 20003. Nonfiction, especially current affairs and social sciences. Payment varies.

G.P. Putnam's Sons, 200 Madison Ave., New York, N.Y., 10016. Fiction and nonfiction for adults and children of all ages. Query William Targ for adult books, Tom MacPherson for juveniles. Payment on royalty basis.

Quadrangle Books, 12 E. Delaware Pl., Chicago, Ill., 60611. A subsidiary of the *New York Times.* Publishes nonfiction of general interest. Query Managing Editor Ivan R. Dee. Standard royalty payment.

Rand McNally & Co., Box 7600, Chicago, Ill., 60680. Adult nonfiction on travel, history, adventure, exploration, world environmental problems, nature, etc. Also juvenile fiction and nonfiction.

Random House, Inc., 201 E. 50th St., New York, N.Y., 10022. Quality fiction and nonfiction including reference and college textbooks. Also juvenile books (See Chapter 9). Catalog on request. Also publishes *Vintage Books,* paperbacks.

Red Dust, Inc., 218 E. 81st St., New York, N.Y., 10028.

Publishes adult fiction. Catalog on request. Send query and sample chapter.

Henry Regnery Co., 114 W. Illinois St., Chicago, Ill., 60610. General nonfiction, some fiction. Query Dominick Abel, Editor-in-Chief.

Reilly & Lee Books. (See Chapter 9).

Fleming H. Revell Co., Old Tappan, N.J., 07675. Publishes inspirational and devotional religious books, self-help, biographies. Query Editor Richard Baltzell. Royalty payment.

Ward Ritchie Press, 3044 Riverside Dr., Los Angeles, Calif., 90039. Cookbooks, Western Americana, Western travel, juveniles. Royalty payment.

Ronald Press Co., 79 Madison Ave., New York, N.Y., 10016. Professional reference books, general information books, handbooks, encyclopedias, and college texts.

Richards Rosen Press, Inc., 29 E. 21st St., New York, N.Y., 10010. Nonfiction teen-age guidance books to 40,000 words. Query Editor Ruth C. Rosen. Payment by arrangement.

Roy Publishers, Inc., 30 E. 74th St., New York, N.Y., 10021. General fiction and nonfiction with emphasis on international subjects. Query first. Also juveniles.

Rutledge Books, Inc., 17 E. 45th St., New York, N.Y., 10017. Quality fiction, cookbooks, juvenile fiction and nonfiction. Query with outline. Advance and royalty.

Sage Books, 1139 S. Wabash Ave., Chicago, Ill., 60605. Nonfiction books about the American West. Royalty. Published by *Swallow Press.*

St. Martin's Press, Inc., 175 Fifth Ave., New York, N.Y., 10010. Fiction, general nonfiction, juveniles, history, political science, biography, music, reference books, college textbooks. Royalty payment.

Scholastic Books. (See Chapter 9).

Charles Scribner's Sons, 597 Fifth Ave., New York, N.Y., 10017. Adult and children's fiction and nonfiction of all types. Queries only.

Seabury Press, 815 Second Ave., New York, N.Y., 10017. Publishers of books for the Episcopal Church. Mainly interested in sociological and religious adult nonfiction and juvenile books (See Chapter 9). Royalty contract.

Sheed & Ward, Inc., 64 University Pl., New York, N.Y., 10003. Philosophy, theology, psychology, sociology, and history with religious slant.

Sherbourne Press, 1640 S. La Cienega, Los Angeles, Calif., 90035. Modern fiction, science fiction, mystery and suspense (no spy or western novels). Also general nonfiction, self-help, expose, consumer protection. Catalog on request. Also juveniles for ages 12-16. Royalty payment.

Sierra Club Books, 597 Fifth Avenue, New York, N.Y., 10017. Books on conservation, natural history, outdoor guidebooks, recreation. Query.

Simon and Schuster, 630 Fifth Ave., New York, N.Y., 10020. General fiction, nonfiction, and mysteries. Queries only. Standard royalty payment.

Stackpole Books, Cameron and Kelker Sts., Harrisburg, Pa., 17105. Books on camping guns, sports, outdoors, military services, recreation, general nonfiction. Royalty payment. Query.

Steck-Vaughn Co. (See Chapter 9).

Stein and Day, 7 E. 48th St., New York, N.Y., 10017. Fiction including mysteries and general nonfiction except technical books. Send outline and sample chapter for nonfiction, first chapter only for novels. Royalty payment.

Sterling Publishing Co., 419 Park Ave. S., New York, N.Y., 10016. Information books, how-to, science and sports for adults and young readers. Payment by outright purchase or royalty. Query first. David A. Boehm, president.

Straight Arrow Books, 625 Third St., San Francisco, Calif., 94107. Hardcover and paperback books on history, politics, how-to, music religion, spiritualism. Also fiction and reference books. Standard royalty rates. Query Editor Alan Rinzler.

Sunset Books, Lane Magazine & Book Co., Menlo Park, Calif., 94025. Nonfiction books on crafts, hobbies, building, gardening. Query Editor David E. Clark.

Swallow Press, 1139 S. Wabash Ave., Chicago, Ill., 60605. General nonfiction. Publishers of *Sage Books,* nonfiction about the American West. Query Editor Durrett Wagner. Pays regular royalties.

Templegate Publishers, 719 E. Adams St., Springfield, Ill., 62705. Publishes religious books, general fiction, and nonfiction. Query.

Trident Press, 630 Fifth Ave., New York, N.Y., 10020. A division of *Simon & Schuster.* Publishes hardcover original fiction and nonfiction. Query.

Tudor Publishing Co., 572 Fifth Ave., New York, N.Y., 10036. General nonfiction, how-to, and books on the fine arts. Query Norman Blaustein. Pays by royalty contract.

Tupper and Love, Inc., Suite 3226, First National Bank, 2 Peachtree St. N.W., Atlanta, Ga., 30303. General nonfiction, fiction, and juveniles. Query.

Twayne Publishers, Inc., 31 Union Sq. W., New York, N.Y.,

10003. General fiction and nonfiction. Query Editor Jacob Steinberg. Royalty payment.

Union of American Hebrew Congregations, 838 Fifth Ave., New York, N.Y., 10021. Publishes books on Jewish religious education, history, biography, literature, current problems affecting Jews, and application of Reform Judaism to everyday living. Also children's books. Query Rabbi Jack D. Spiro, editor.

United Church Press, 1505 Race St., Philadelphia, Pa., 19102. Nonfiction, especially for college and university readers, on subjects including politics, humanities, social sciences, etc. Royalty rates. Query Editor David F. Marshall with sample chapter and detailed outline.

The Vanguard Press, Inc., 424 Madison Ave., New York, N.Y., 10017. Fiction and nonfiction of all kinds, especially politics, biography, history, economics, humor, how-to, personal experiences, adventure. Also juvenile fiction and nonfiction.

Van Nostrand Reinhold Co., 450 W. 33d St., New York, N.Y., 10001. A division of *Litton Educational Publishing, Inc.* Publishes adult trade books, informative nonfiction on the arts, crafts, design; juvenile books; reference, technical, scientific, business; college textbooks. Query.

The Viking Press, Inc., 625 Madison Ave., New York, N.Y., 10022. Quality fiction, biography, history, science, sociology, art, travel. Also juveniles. Royalty payment.

Walker and Co., 720 Fifth Ave., New York, N.Y., 10019. General adult fiction and nonfiction, juvenile fiction and nonfiction, business biomedical, technical, and reference books. Query.

Ward Ritchie Press, 3044 Riverside Dr., Los Angeles, Calif., 90039. Publishes Western Americana, travel guidebooks, general nonfiction, cookbooks, and juveniles. Query Editor Dorothy Bellesiles with outline and sample chapters. Royalty payment.

Frederick Warne & Co., Inc. (See Chapter 9).

Ives Washburn, Inc. (See Chapter 9).

Watson-Guptill Publications, 165 W. 46th St., New York, N.Y., 10036. How-to books for artists, art teachers, art students and hobbyists.

Franklin Watts, Inc. (See Chapter 9).

Western Publishing Co., Inc. (See Chapter 9).

The Westminster Press. (See Chapter 9).

Weybright and Talley, 750 Third Ave., New York, N.Y., 10017. Quality fiction and nonfiction. Query with outline or table of contents and sample chapter.

Whitehall Co., 601 Skokie Blvd., Northbrook, Ill., 60062. Pub-

lishes college textbooks. Send complete manuscript. Royalty payment.
John Wiley & Sons, Inc., 605 Third Ave., New York, N.Y., 10016. Technical, scientific, business books. Query Editorial Director Robert Polhemus. Royalty contract.
Wilshire Book Co., 12015 Sherman Rd., North Hollywood, Calif., 91605. Publishes self-help books, technical, inspirational and psychological books. Query Editor Melvin Powers. Royalty contract. Catalog sent on request.
Winter House, 1123 Broadway, New York, N.Y., 10010. Publishes fiction and nonfiction including Gothics, westerns, sex. Query. Managing Editor Sarah Nichols.
World Publishing Co., 110 E. 59th St., New York, N.Y., 10022. General fiction and nonfiction, juveniles, reference, religion.
Thomas Yoseloff, Inc., Box 421, Cranbury, N.J., 08512. General nonfiction, occasional fiction.
Young Scott Books. (See Chapter 9).
Zondervan Publishing House, 1415 Lake Drive S.E., Grand Rapids, Mich., 49506. Inspirational books on Protestant subjects for adults and young readers. Also textbooks and handbooks for schools and clergymen.

Paperback Book Publishers

Ace Books, Charter Communications, Inc., 1120 Avenue of the Americas, New York, N.Y., 10036. Original science fiction and western novels up to 75,000 words; nurse romance, suspense novels for women readers, women Gothic suspense romances, some general fiction. Also general nonfiction. Pays up to $2,500 advance against standard royalties.
Archway Paperbacks (published by *Pocket Books*), 630 Fifth Ave., New York, N.Y., 10020. Fiction, mysteries, animal stories, adventure, young romance, humor, sports, etc. Also nonfiction for readers 8 to 14, especially biographies. Query.
Arco Books, Inc., 219 Park Ave. S., New York, N.Y., 10003. Nonfiction originals and reprints, 50,000 words and up. Outright purchase or royalty payment. Query Editor Fred Honig.
Avon Books, 959 Eighth Ave., New York, N.Y., 10019. Modern nonfiction for the popular market; also educational nonfiction. Query Peter M. Mayer, Editor-in-Chief. Pays good royalties against advance on signing of contract.
Ballantine Books, Inc., 101 Fifth Ave., New York, N.Y., 10003. Contemporary fiction, historical fiction, mystery and suspense reprints.

Also publishes original science fiction, westerns, and subjects of wide audience interest. Query. Royalty payment.

Bantam Books, Inc., 666 Fifth Ave., New York, N.Y. Accepts manuscripts only from agents and publishers.

Belmont Productions, Inc., 185 Madison Ave., New York, N.Y., 10016. Publishes mysteries, Gothics, westerns, science fiction, general modern novels, novels with strong sex emphasis, 50,000 to 60,000 words. Query with outline and sample chapter. Pays standard royalties.

Berkley Publishing Corp., 200 Madison Ave., New York, N.Y., 10016. Science fiction, mysteries, suspense, spy novels, but no adventure novels. Query Thomas A. Dardid, vice-president. Query. Payment varies.

Camelot Books. (See Chapter 9).

Collier Books, 866 Third Ave., New York, N.Y., 10022. General nonfiction. Query Robert Markel, Editor-in-Chief, trade books. Royalty payment.

Cornerstone Library, Inc., 630 Fifth Ave., New York, N.Y., 10020. Books on chess, bridge, tennis, golf, other leisure-time subjects; also guide books and how-to-books. Originals and reprints. No fiction. Query. Royalty payment.

Curtis Books, 770 Lexington Ave., New York, N.Y., 10021. Westerns, mysteries, suspense, science fiction, historical novels, war novels, humor, general nonfiction, crossword puzzle books. Query Miss Anne Holden, editor. Royalty rates.

Dell Books, 750 Third Ave., New York, N.Y., 10017. General fiction and nonfiction, 60,000 words and up. Query. Mrs. Peggy Roth, executive editor.

Lyle Engel, Canaan, N.Y., 12029. Publishes sex-adventure novels including the Nick Carter-Killmaster and Richard Blade series. Will pay $1,250 to writers to produce novels to fit needs of new series he is creating. Writers must send a copy of a book they have had published.

Fawcett World Library, 1 Astor Pl., New York, N.Y., 10003. Fiction and nonfiction reprints. Also original and reprints of college and secondary books. Query. Royalty payment.

Gold Medal Books (a division of *Fawcett World Library*), 1 Astor Pl., New York, N.Y., 10003. Quality suspense, western, humor Gothic novels, science fiction, occult, cartoon books. Query Editor Walter Fultz. Royalty payment.

Grosset "Specials" (a division of *Grosset & Dunlap, Inc.*), 51 Madison Ave., New York, N.Y., 10010. Original and reprints, nonfiction, for popular reading market.

Lancer Books, 1560 Broadway, New York, N.Y., 10036. Original fiction and nonfiction. Query Editors. Royalty payment.

Laurel Editions, Dell Publishing Co., 750 Third Ave., New York, N.Y., 10017. Nonfiction for general and academic readers. Original books on history, psychology, science, literature, philosophy, etc. Query Richard Huett, Editor-in-Chief.

Leisure Books, Inc., 6340 Coldwater Canyon, North Hollywood, Calif., 91606. Fiction and nonfiction from 40,000 to 60,000 words. Query Miss Yvonne MacManus with sample chapters. Advance paid against royalties.

Macfadden Books, Macfadden-Bartell Corp., 205 E. 42d St., New York, N.Y., 10017. Fiction and nonfiction reprints and originals. Query George A. Glay, Editor-in-Chief.

The Natural History Press, (a division of *Doubleday*), Publisher for The American Museum of Natural History, 277 Park Ave., New York, N.Y., 10017. Adult trade books, illustrated books on natural history, anthropology, ecology, astronomy. Also children's books.

New American Library, 1301 Avenue of the Americas, New York, N.Y., 10019. Publishes *Signet Books,* novels with strong contemporary themes, and popular nonfiction, both original and reprints. Query Edward T. Chase, editorial vice-president. Standard royalty contract.

Paperback Library, 315 Park Ave. S., New York, N.Y., 10010. Romantic historical novels and biographies, war humor, general humor, Gothic novels, mystery novels with a continuing hero, and novels with backgrounds that describe the inner workings of an industry, profession, career, life-style, etc. Lengths run from 50,000 to 90,000 words. Query with outline and two sample chapters. Pays advance and royalties. Jerry Gross, editorial director.

Penguin Books, Inc, 72 Fifth Avenue, New York, N.Y., 10011. Publishes quality fiction, mysteries, science fiction. Also general nonfiction, social, political subjects. Query Editor Richard Rose with outline, summary, and sample chapter. Pays advance and royalties.

Pocket Books (division of *Simon & Schuster*), 630 Fifth Ave., New York, N.Y., 10020. Some originals, mainly reprints. Query.

Popular Library, Inc., 355 Lexington Ave., New York, N.Y. Publishes mainly reprints, some originals, especially if topical. Publishes reprints of mysteries, suspense, adventure, spy novels, historical fiction, westerns, some humor and science fiction. Lengths 40,000 words and up. Pays on royalty basis. Send query to David L. Williams, executive editor.

Powell Publications, Inc., 18554 Sherman Way, Reseda, Calif., 91335. Fast-paced fiction: mystery, Gothic mystery, western, fantasy, war, science fiction, adventure. Also some fiction for teen-age market. President William P. Trotter prefers completed manuscripts for fiction;

outline and sample chapter for nonfiction. Primarily original works, but also publishes reprints.

Pyramid Books, 919 Third Ave., New York, N.Y., 10022. Fiction and nonfiction, originals and reprints. Query.

Tempo Books, 51 Madison Ave., New York, N.Y., 10010. Fiction and nonfiction for young adults; primarily reprints, but publishes some originals, especially timely nonfiction. Advance and royalties. Query with outline.

Tower Publications, Inc., 185 Madison Ave., New York, N.Y., 10016. Contemporary nonfiction, consumer books, true adventure, occult, camping, outdoors, handbooks, cookbooks. Query. Royalty rates.

Universal Library (division of *Grosset & Dunlap*), 51 Madison Ave., New York, N.Y., 10010. Reprints and originals in fields of literature, criticism, social and political sciences, humanities, for intellectual readers.

Washington Square Press, (published by *Pocket Books*), 630 Fifth Ave., New York, N.Y., 10020. Educational and scholarly books and also general nonfiction. Standard royalties.

Wilshire Book Co., Inspirational, psychological, self-help, astrology. Standard royalty rates. Query.

INDEX

INDEX

A

Abbey Book Publishers, 191
Abbey Press, 191
Abelard Schuman Ltd., 136, 191
Abingdon Press, 136, 191
Accent on Living, 60
Accent on Youth, 129
Ace Books, 207
Action Time, 52
Active Handicapped, 60
Adam, 92
Addison-Wesley Publishing Co., 136, 191
Advance, 187
Adventure, 92, 122
Adventure Magazine, 123
Advertising agencies, 34
Aero Magazine, 83
After Dark, 64
Agents, 184
Agricultural markets, 67
Agway Cooperator, 52
Air Line Pilot, 52
Akron Sunday Beacon, 24
Alabama Review, 29
Alaska, 29
Alfred Hitchcock's Mystery Magazine, 114
Alive!, 181
Alliance Press, 191
Allied Publications, 100
Allis-Chalmers Reporter, 52
Allyn & Bacon, 136

Aloft, 77
Ambassador Life, 123
Ambassador, TWA, 78
America, 157
American Agriculturalist, 67
American Art Enterprises, 92
American Artist, 64
American Baby, 60, 105
American Book Co., 137
American Family Physician, 60
American Field, 83
American Forests, 62, 78
American Fruit Grower, 67
American Girl, 129
American Greetings Corp., 176
American Heritage, 42
American Heritage Press, 137, 191
American Home, 100
American Journal of Nursing, 61
American Legion Magazine, 155, 174
American Newspaper Boy, 129
American Red Cross Journal, 129
American Red Cross Youth News, 123
American Scholar, 42, 174
American School and University, 66
American School Board Journal, 66
American Way, 52
American West, 42
American West Publishing Co., 191
American Youth, 52
American Zionist, 157
Amis Publishing Co., 137, 192

Amistad, 148
Analog, 116
Animal Kingdom, 62
Annals of the Holy Childhood, 123
Antigonish Review, 170
Antioch Review, 170
Antiques Journal, 100
Apartment Ideas, 100
AP Newsfeatures, 45
Archery World, 78
Archway Paperbacks, 144, 207
Arco Books, 207
Arco Publishing Co., 192
ARCO Spark, 52
Area Development, 52
Argosy, 78
Arizona, 29
Arizona Highways, 29, 79
Arizona Wildlife Sportsman, 79
Arkham House, 192
Arlington House, 192
Arlington Quarterly, 170
Armchair Detective, 114
Army Times, 25
Art markets, 63
Arts Magazine, 64
Assembling, 170
Association Press, 192
Astor-Honor, 137, 192
Astrojet News, 52
Atheneum Publishers, 137, 192
Athletic Journal, 66
Atlanta, 29
Atlanta Journal, 24
Atlantic Monthly, 40, 174
Atlantic Monthly Press, 137, 192
Auction, 64
Auerback Publishers, 192
Augsburg Publishing House, 137, 192
Aurora Publishers, 137, 192
Austin, 29
Auto and Flat Glass Journal, 53
Automobile magazines, 76, 86
Avon Books, 137, 207
Ayer's Directory of Newspapers and Periodicals, 24

B

Baby Care, 100
Baby Talk, 101
Baker Book House, 192
Baker Greeting Card Co., 176
Ballantine Books, 207
Baltimore Magazine, 29
Bantam Books, 208
Baptist Leader, 157
Barnes, A.S., 193
Barnes and Noble, 137, 193
Baron, Richard W., 193
Barrett, Charles A., 137
Basic Books, 137
Baush & Lomb Focus, 53
B.C. Outdoors, 163
Beacon Press, 193
Bell-McClure Syndicate, 45
Belmont Productions, 208
Berkley Publishing Corp., 208
Best for Men, 92
Best Western Way, 81
Better Camping, 79
Better Homes and Gardens, 101
Better Homes and Gardens Books, 193, 201
Beyond Baroque, 170
Big Farmer, 68
Binfords and Mort, 193
Birmingham Magazine, 29
Black Enterprise, 147, 148
Black publications, 146
Black Sports, 148
Black Stars, 147, 148
Black World, 147, 149
Blast, 129
Bloch Publishing Co., 193
Bluebook, 92
Boating, 88
Boating markets, 88
Bobbs-Merrill Co., 137, 193
Bolex Reporter, 53
Bon Voyage, 79
Boston Magazine, 29
Boston University Journal, 170
Bostonian Magazine, 29
Bouregey, Thomas, 137, 193
Bow and Arrow, 83
Bowling, 83
Boys' Life, 130
Bradbury Press, 138
Branford, Charles T., 193
Braniff International Magazine, 77

INDEX

Braziller, George, 193
Brides Magazine, 101
Brigade Leader, 157
British markets, 162
Broadcasting Yearbook, 34
Broadman Press, 138, 193
Broadside, 92
Bruce Publishing Co., 138, 193
Buffalo, 30
Building, 162
Business Farming, 68
Business West, 53
Buzza-Cardozo, 176

C

California Today, 24
Camelot Books, 144
Camera, 35, 64
Camper Coachman, 79
Camping Guide, 79
Camping Journal, 79
Camping Yearbook and Hunting Guide, 79
Campus Life, 130, 157
Canadian Audubon, 163
Canadian Magazine, 163
Canadian markets, 163
Canadian Messenger, 163
Canadian Motorist, 76
Canadian, The, 24
Canner/Packer, 53
Caravanner, 53
Car Craft, 87
Carleton Miscellany, 170
Carolina Quarterly, 170
Cars, 87
Carte Blanche, 42
Cat Fancy, 84
Catalyst, 130
Catholic Digest, 157
Catholic Life, 158
Catholic School Journal, 66
Catholic World, 158
Cattleman, The, 68
Cavalier, 91, 93
Caxton Printers Ltd., 194
Central Press Assn., 46
Channels of Business Communications, 53
Charger, 96

Charm Craft Publishers, 177
Chatelaine, 163
Check Magazine, 181
Chicago Daily News, 26
Chicago Magazine, 30
Chicago Review, 170
Chicago Sun-Times, 26
Chicago Sun-Times Showcase, 24
Chicago Today, 24
Chicago Tribune-New York News Syndicate, 46
Chicago Tribune Sunday Magazine, 24
Chicago Tribune Travel Section, 75
Child Life, 123
Children's Friend, 123
Children's House, 66
Children's Playmate, 123
Children's Press, 138
Chilton Book Company, 138, 194
Christian Century, 158
Christian Herald, 158
Christian Home, 101
Christian Life, 158
Christian Science Monitor, 24, 101, 123, 174
Christian's Friend, 124
Chronicle Books, 194
Church Herald, 158
Cincinnati Magazine, 30
Cincinnati Pictorial Enquirer, 25
Citadel Press, 194
Citation Press, 194
City Desk Features, 46
Clark, Arthur B., 194
Climb, 123
Cobble Hill Press, 194
College Management, 66
College Store Executive, 53
Collier Books, 208
Colorado Magazine, 30
Colorado Quarterly, 170
Columbus Dispatch Sunday Magazine, 25
Co-Ed, 130
Colloquy, 158
Columbia, 158
Compass, 53
Commonweal, 159
Commonwealth, 30

INDEX

Community service organizations, 34
Computer Decisions, 54
Concordia Publishing House, 138, 194
Confidential, 42
Confidential Confessions, 109
Confidential Detective Cases, 114
Conquest, 130
Conservation markets, 61
Consultant work, 50
Contact, 130
Contemporary, 25
Continental Magazine, 43, 54, 76
Cook, David C., 181
Cooking for Profit, 54
Cornell Maritime Press, 194
Cornerstone Library, 208
Coronet, 40
Cosmopolitan, 76, 101
Counselor, 54
Country Club News, 84
Coward-McCann, 138
Cowles Book Co., 194
Craft Horizons, 64
Creative Crafts Magazine, 64
Creative Home Library, 201
Crime Detective, 144
Crowell, Thomas A., 138, 195
Crown Publishers, 138, 195
Crusader, 123
Cue, 30
Current Comedy, 181
Curtis Books, 208
Curtis Contemporary Cards, 177
Cushman Dealer, 54
Cycle, 87
Cycle World, 87

D

Dallas Magazine, 30
Dallas Times Herald Sunday Magazine, 25
Dance Magazine, 64
Dance Perspectives, 64
Daring, 96
Daring Romances, 110
Dartnell Corp., 195
David, Jonathan, 138, 195
Day, John, 138, 195
December, 168, 171
de Graff, John, 195
DeKalb Literary Arts Journal, 171
Dell Books, 208
Denison, T.S., 139, 195
Dental Economics, 61
Denver Post, 25
Descant, 171
Desert Magazine, 79
Design, 54
Design and Environment, 54
Des Moines Sunday Register Picture, 25
Detective markets, 113
Detroit News Sunday Magazine, 25
Devin-Adair Co., 195
Dial Press, 139
Dimension Books, 139, 195
Diners Club Magazine, 44, 76
Diplomatic Press, 195
Discovery (children's), 123
Discovery (travel), 76
Dixie-Roto, 25
Dodd-Mead & Co., 139, 195
Dodge News, 55, 77
Dog Fancy, 84
Doubleday & Co., 139, 196
Dow Jones-Irwin, 196
Dust, 171
Dust Topics, 55
Dutton, E.P., 139, 196

E

Eagle Magazine, 80, 155
Earth, 130
Ebony, 149
Ecology markets, 61
Editor & Publisher Annual Directory of Syndicated Features, 45
Editor & Publisher Yearbook, 24
Educate, 66
Education markets, 65
Eerdmans, William, 196
Electronics Illustrated, 165
Elk Grove Press, 139
Elks Magazine, 151, 152, 155
Ellery Queen's Mystery Magazine, 114

INDEX

Emerson Books, 196
Empire, 25
Encounter, 130
Enthusiast, 87
Environment, 165
Environmental Quality, 62
Epoch, 171
Eriksson, Paul S., 196
Essence, 147, 149, 174
European's Guide to Camping North America, 80
Event (adult), 159
Event (children), 110
Evergreen Review, 171
Exciting Confessions, 110
Expecting, 101
Expecting Parents, 61
Explore, 124
Exploring, 131

F

Face-to-Face, 131, 159
Falcon, 171
Family Circle, 102
Family Handyman, 102
Family Health, 61, 165
Family Houseboating, 88, 102
Family Magazine, 25
Family Weekly, 102, 174
Fantasy & Science Fiction, 116
Farm Quarterly, 68
Farm Supplier, 68
Farrar, Straus & Giroux, 196
Fawcett World Library, 144, 208
Federated Feature Syndicate, 46
Fell, Frederick, 196
Fides Publishers, 196
Field & Stream, 80
Filler markets, 179
Finney Co., 196
Fish & Game Sportsman, 80
Fishing World, 80
Fitness for Living, 61
Five/Six, 124
Fleet Press, 197
Flightime, 78
Fling, 93
Floor & Wall Covering News, 55
Florida & Tropic Sportsman, 80

Florida Trend, 30
Floridian, The, 25
Florist & Nursery Exchange, 55
Flower & Garden Magazine, 102
Flying A, 55
FM Guide, 181
Focus-Midwest, 30
Follett Publishing Co., 139, 197
For Men Only, 93
For Teens Only, 131
Ford Times, 77
Ford Truck Times, 55
Forecast for Home Economics, 66, 102
Foreign Car Guide, 88
Foreign markets, 151, 161
Forer, D., 177
Fort Worth Magazine, 30
Fortress Press, 197
Founders Express, 55
Fountainhead Publishers, 197
Four Quarters, 171
Four Winds Press, 139, 197
Fran Mar Greeting Cards, 177
Franciscan Message, 159
Franessi-Lamont, 177
Fraternal markets, 151
Free Press, 139, 197
Freeman, The, 43
Friend, The, 124
Friends, 43, 76
Front Page Detective, 115
Frontier Times, 96
Frontiers, 62
Fun for Middlers, 124
Funk & Wagnalls, 197
Furrow, The, 55, 68

G

Galaxy, 117
Gallery, 93
Gambit, Inc., 197
Gateway Magazine, 78
Gator, The, 100
Gebbie House Magazine Directory, 51
Geis, Bernard, and Associates, 197
Gem, 93
General Features Corp., 46

218 INDEX

Gentleman's Quarterly, 93
Georgia Farmer, 68
Georgia Magazine, 30
Georgia Review, 171
Gibson Greeting Cards, 177
Ginn & Co., 139, 197
Girl Talk, 102
Glamour, 102
Going Places, 55
Gold Medal Books, 208
Golden Gate Junior Books, 140
Golden Press, 140, 197
Golf Digest, 84
Golf Magazine, 84
Good Housekeeping, 103, 174
Gourmet, 93, 103
Grace Log, 55
Greater Indianapolis, 30
Greene, Stephen, Press, 197
Greeting card market, 168, 175
Grit, 25
Grosset & Dunlap, 140, 198, 208
Grossman Publishers, 198
Grove Press, 198
Guideposts, 159
Gun Digest, 84
Guns, 84
Guns & Ammo, 84
Gunsport, 84

H

Hair Do & Beauty, 103
Hallmark Cards, 177
Handloader's Digest, 84
Hanging Loose, 171
Harcourt Brace Jovanovich, 140, 198
Harper & Row, 140, 198
Harper's Bazaar, 40, 103, 174
Harper's Magazine, 40, 174
Harvest, 56
Harvest Years, 43
Harvey House, 140
Hastings House Publishers, 140, 198
Hawthorne Books, 140, 198
Health, 61
Hearthside Press, 198
Heath, D.C., 140

Hers, 110
HiCall, 131
High, 131
High Fidelity, 64
Highlights for Children, 124
Hill & Wang, 198
Hobbs, Dorman & Co., 198
Hockey Times, 84
Holiday, 74
Holiday House, 140
Hollywood Informer Syndicate, 46
Holt, Rinehart, & Winston, 140, 198
Home Garden Magazine: Flower Grower, 103
Home Life, 159
Home Modernizing Guide, 104
Horizon, 43
Horizon Press, 199
Horseman, 84
Horticulture, 103
Hot Rod, 87
Houghton Mifflin Co., 140, 199
House & Garden, 103
House Beautiful, 103
Houston Chronicle Texas Magazine, 26
Houston Chronicle Zest Magazine, 27
Howell Book House, 199
Howell-North Books, 199
Hudson Review, 171
Hughes Rigway, 94
Human Events, 181
Humor markets, 179
Humorama, 174, 181
Humpty Dumpty's Magazine, 124

I

If Science Fiction, 117
Impact, 131
Indianapolis, Greater, 30
Industrial Arts & Vocational Education, 66
Industrial Ecology, 56
Industrial Photography, 65
Ingenue, 132
Inland, 56
Inside Detective, 115

INDEX

International Marine Publishing Co., 199
International Railway Journal, 56
International Wildlife, 81
Interplay, 43
Intimate Confessions, 110
Intimate Story, 110
Iowa Review, 171
Iron Worker, 56
Island Monthly Reader, 26

J

Jack & Jill, 124
Jet, 149
Jet Cadet, 125
Jewish Frontier, 159
Jewish Horizon, 159
Jewish Publication Society, 140, 199
Judson Press, 199
Junior Discoveries, 125
Junior Hi Challenge, 132
Junior Life, 125
Junior Scholastic, 132
Junior Trails, 125
Juvenile markets, 125

K

Kanrom, Inc., 181
Kansas Quarterly, 171
Keep 'N Touch Greeting Cards, 177
Kenedy, P.J., & Sons, 199
Kentucky Farmer, 68
King Features Syndicate, 46
Kindergartner, The, 125
Kids, 125
Kiwanis Magazine, 76, 151, 152, 155
Knapp, Robert R., 199
Knight, 94
Knopf, Alfred A., 140, 199
Knox, John, 199

L

Ladies' Home Journal, 104
Ladycom, 104
Lady's Circle, 104
Lancer Books, 208
Lantern Press, 141, 200
Laurel Editions, 209
Lawrence Publishing Co., 200
Lawrence, Seymour, 200
Leatherneck, 43
Ledger Syndicate, 46
Leica Photography, 65
Leisure Books, 209
Lenox Hill Press, 200
Lerner Publications Co., 141
Life, 41
Lincoln Business, 31
Lincoln Review Preview, 31
Lion, The, 151-155
Lion Press, 200
Lippincott, J.B., 141, 200
Literary Cavalcade, 132
Literary Journal, 168
Little, Brown & Co., 141, 200
Little Eve Editions, 177
Little Magazine, 172
Little Review, 172
Litton Educational Publishing, 206
Liveright Publishing Co., 200
Living Light, 159
Living Now, 104
Living Wilderness, 62
Longman Canada Ltd., 200
Lookout, The, 56
Los Angeles Magazine, 31
Los Angeles Times, 27
Lothrop, Lee, Shepard, 141
Louisville Courier-Journal & Times, 26
Louisville Magazine, 31
Luce, Robert B., 200
Lutheran Standard, 160
Lutheran, The, 159

M

Macfadden Books, 209
Maclean's Magazine, 163
Macmillan Co., 141, 201
Macrae Smith Co., 141, 201
Mademoiselle, 104, 174
Magazine of Horror, 117
Mainliner, 78
Male, 94

Mandala, 172
Man's Conquest, 92
Man's Illustrated, 92
Man's Magazine, 94
Man's World, 94
Marriage, 160
Maryknoll, 150
Massachusettes Review, 171
Master Detective, 115
Mature Years, 160
McCall's, 104
McGraw-Hill Book Co., 141, 200
McKay, David, 141, 201
McNaught Syndicate, 46
Men Only, 162
Men's markets, 90
Meredith Corp., 201
Merry-go-Round, 125
Message, 160
Messner, Julian, 141
Miami Herald, 27
Michigan Quarterly Review, 172
Midstream, 160
Midwest, 26
Mike Shayne Mystery Magazine, 115
Military Life, 43
Milwaukee Magazine, 31
Minnesota AAA Motorist, 77
Minnesota Review, 172
Minutes, 56
Mister B Greeting Cards, 177
Modern Bride, 104
Modern Cycle, 87
Modern Girl, 104
Modern Love, 111
Modern Man, 94
Modern Maturity, 43, 105
Modern Romances, 110
Modern Screen, 105
Mohawk Airlines Gateway Magazine, 78
Moody Press, 201
More, 125
Morehouse-Barlow Co., 141, 201
Morrow, William, 141, 201
Mother Earth News, 132
Mothers-to-Be, 105
Mothers' Manual, 105
Motor, 87

Motor Boating, 88
Motor Club magazines, 76
Motor Coach Travel, 80
Motor Home Life, 80
Motor News, 77
Motor Trend, 87
Motorcycle markets, 86
Motoring, 162
Movie Mirror Yearbook, 105
Ms., 105
Music markets, 63
My Confession, 110
My Love Secret Confession, 110
My Romance, 110
Mystery markets, 113

N

Nash Publishing Co., 201
Nashville Magazine, 31
Nation, The, 41
Nation's Agriculture, 68
Nation's Schools, 66
National Enquirer, 43
National Future Farmer, 68, 132
National Geographic, 74
National Insider, 44
National Jewish Monthly, 160
National Lampoon, 133, 174, 181
National Mobile Home Journal, 80
National Motorist, 44, 77, 87
National Newspaper Syndicate, 46
National Police Gazette, 81, 94
National Sportsman's Digest, 85
National Wildlife, 62, 81
Natural History, 62, 81
Natural History Press, 144, 209
Nelson-Hall Publishers, 201
Nelson, Thomas, 142, 202
Nevada Highways & Parks, 31
Nevada Magazine, 31
New American Library, 209
New England Galaxy, 31
New Englander, 31
New Hampshire Profiles, 31
New Lady, 149
New Magazine, 160
New Mexico Magazine, 31
New Republic, 41
New Woman, 105

INDEX

New York Magazine, 31
New York Times Magazine, 41
New York Times Travel Section, 74
New Yorker Magazine, 41, 174, 182
News Explorer, 125
News/time, 126
News Trails, 126
Newspaper Enterprise Assn., 46
Newspapers, 23-27
Nitty Gritty Productions, 202
Norcross, Inc., 177
North American Newspaper Alliance, 46
North American Review, 172
Northeast Outdoors, 81
Northliner, 81
Northeast Review, 172
Norton, W.W., 142, 202
Novo Cards, 177
Nursery Days, 126

O

Oceana Publishers, 202
Oceanology International, 166
Oceans, 62
Oddo Publishing, Inc., 142
Office Economist, 56
Office Products Magazine, 56
Official Detective Stories, 115
Ohara Publishers, 202
Ohio Review, 172
Oklahoma Today, 32
Old West, 96
On the Line, 133
One/Two, 126
Onyx Enterprises, 178
Opera News, 65
Optimist Magazine, 155
Oral Hygiene, 61
Organic Gardening & Farming, 63, 68
Oui, 94
Our Family, 163
Our Little Friend, 126
Our Sunday Visitor, 160
Our World, 57
Outdoor Life, 81
Outdoor markets, 71, 78
Outdoor World, 81

Outdoors, 81
Outerbridge & Lazard, 202
Oxford University Press, 202

P

Pacific Discovery, 63, 81
Pageant, 41
Panorama, 26
Pantheon Books, 142, 202
Paperback Library, 209
Parade, 47
Parade (British), 162
Paramount Line, 178
Parents' Magazine, 105
Parents' Magazine Press, 142
Paris Review, 172
Parker Publishing Co., 202
Parnassus Press, 142, 202
Paulist-Newman Press, 202
Pen Magazine, 44, 174, 182
Penguin Books, 209
Penthouse, 94
Perfect Home, 106
Personal Romances, 111
Perspective, 172
Pflaumn, George, 202
Philadelphia Inquirer Today Magazine, 26
Philadelphia Magazine, 32
Phillips, S.G., 142
Photography markets, 63
Pitman Publishing Corp., 202
Platt & Munk, 142
Playbill, 65
Playboy, 90, 95, 182
Playthings, 57
Pocket Books, 207, 209
Poetry Markets, 168, 174
Points, 57, 82
Popular Ceramics, 65
Popular Hot Rodding, 88
Popular Library, 209
Popular Mechanics, 165, 166
Popular Photography, 65
Popular Science, 82, 106, 165, 166
Posh, 76
Potomac, 26
Potter, Clarkson N., 203
Poultry Meat, 69

Poultry Tribune, 69
Powell Publishers, 209
Praeger Publishers, 203
Prairie Schooner, 22
Prentice-Hall, 142, 203
Presbyterian Life, 126
Prevention, 63
Price/Stern/Sloan Publishers, 203
Primary Treasure, 126
Printing Salesman's Herald, 57
Private Pilot, 85
Pro Football Guide, 85
Probe, 133
Profitable Hobby Merchandising, 57
Progressive, The, 44
Progressive Woman, 106
Providence Journal & Evening Bulletin, 26
Pruett Publishing Co., 203
Psychic, 44
PTA Magazine, 105
Public Affairs Press, 203
Public relations, 34
Publications Management Newsletter, 82
Publishers-Hall Syndicate, 47
Putnam's, G.P., Sons, 142, 203
Pyramid, 172, 210

Q

Quadrangle Books, 203
Query letters, 20
Quest, 82
Quest (children's), 126
Quote Magazine, 174, 182

R

Radio Electronics, 166
Railroad Magazine, 44, 85
Rand McNally Co., 142, 203
Random House, 143, 203
Ranger Rick's Nature Magazine, 126
Reachout, 133
Reader's Digest, 41, 182
Reader's Digest Books, 197
Reader's Guide to Periodical Literature, 39
Real Confessions, 111
Real Frontier, 44
Real Romances, 111
Real Story, 111
Real West, 44
Record, The, 57
Recreation markets, 83
Red Dust, 203
Redbook, 106
Reed Sterling Cards, 178
Reflection, 133
Register & Tribune Syndicate, 47
Regnery, Henry, 204
Reilly & Lee Books, 143
Religious markets, 151
Religious News Service, 47
Researching, 39
Revealing Romances, 111
Revell, Fleming H., 204
Revue des Beaux Arts, 65
Rhode Islander, 26
Ritchie, Ward, Press, 143, 204, 206
RN, 61
Roadrunner, 127
Rogue, 94
Roland Press, 204
Roll Call, 32
Rolling Stone, 133
Romance magazines, 108
Romantic Confessions, 110
Rosen, Richards Press, 143, 204
Rotarian, 151-155
Roth Greeting Cards, 178
Roy Publishers, 143, 204
Royalty payment, 187
Rudder, 88
Rust Craft Greeting Cards, 178
Rutledge Books, 143, 204
RxSports & Travel, 85

S

Saga, 82
Sage Books, 204
St. Anthony Messenger, 160
St. Martin's Press, 143, 204
St. Petersburg Times, 25
Salt Lick, 173
San Antonio Magazine, 32
San Francisco Magazine, 32

INDEX

Saturday Evening Post, 41
Saturday Night, 163
Saturday Review, 41, 175
Scholastic Books, 143
Scholastic Scope, 133
Scholastic Teacher, 67
Scholastic Voice, 133
School Management, 67
School markets, 36
Science & Mechanics, 166
Science Digest, 166
Science fiction markets, 113, 115
Science markets, 164
Science World, 134, 166
Scientific American, 166
Scouting Magazine, 82
Scribners, Charles, Sons, 143, 204
Sea Classics, 85
Sea Frontiers, 166
Seabury Press, 143, 204
Search, 127
Seattle Times Sunday Magazine, 26
Secret Romances, 111
Secret Story, 110
Secretary, The, 106
Secrets, 111
Seneca Review, 173
Senior Hi Challenge, 134
Sepia, 149
Seventeen, 134
Seventy-Six Magazine, 57
Sheed & Ward, 204
Shenendoah, 173
Sherbourne Press, 143, 204
Shoe—The Coast Shoe Reporter, 57
Shooting Times, 85
Sierra Club Books, 205
Sign, The, 161
Signature, 44, 76
Singer Features, 45
Sir!, 95
Ski Magazine, 85
Skiing Magazine, 85
Skipper, 89
Small World, 44
Smith, The, 173
Smithsonian Magazine, 44
South Dakota Review, 173
Southern Review, 173
Southland Sunday Magazine, 26

Southwest Review, 173
Spadea Syndicate, 47
Spectrum, 32
Spectrum/International Journal of Religious Education, 67
Speech writing, 50
Spirit, 134
Sport, 85
Sportfishing, 85
Sports Afield, 82
Sports Car Graphic, 88
Sports Digest, 85
Sports Illustrated, 86
Sports markets, 83
Stackpole Books, 205
Stag, 95
Standard royalty, 187
Stanita Designs, 149, 178
Star Weekly, 26
Startling Detective, 115
State, The, 32
Steck-Vaughn, 144
Stein & Day, 205
Stereo Quarterly, 65
Sterling Publishing Co., 144, 205
Story Friends, 127
Story Trails, 124
Straight, 134
Straight Arrow Books, 205
Strength & Health, 61
Success Unlimited, 45
Successful Farming, 69
Sumac, 173
Summer Time, 127
Sunday Digest, 161
Sunday supplements, 23-27
Sunset Books, 205
Sunset Magazine, 32, 106
Swallow Press, 205
Swinger, 95
Syndicates, 45

T

Technical markets, 164
Teen Magazine, 134
Teen Time, 133
Teen-Age markets, 118, 129
Teens Today, 135
Television markets, 33

Templegate Publishers, 205
Tempo Books, 145, 210
Texaco Tempo, 57
Texas Magazine, Houston Chronicle, 26
Texas Parade, 32
Theatre markets, 63
These Times, 161
Think, 57
Three/Four, 127
Thrilling Love Stories, 110
Times-Picayune, 25
Today's Catholic Teacher, 67
Today's Family Digest, 161
Today's Health, 60, 71, 76, 165
Today's Secretary, 106
Toledo Blade Sunday Magazine, 27
Toledo Star Syndicate, 47
Tower Publishers, 210
Town & Country Planning, 162
Trade journals, 48
Trailer Life, 83
Trails, 127
Trained Men, 58
Transpacific, 173
Transworld Feature Syndicate, 47
Travel, 75
Travel & Leisure, 75
Travel markets, 71
Treasure Chest, 127
Trenton Magazine, 32
Trident Press, 205
Tri-Quarterly, 173
Tropic, 27
True, 86
True (British), 111
True Adventures, 95
True Confessions, 111
True Detective, 115
True Experience, 111
True Love, 111
True Police Cases, 115
True Romances, 112
True Secrets, 110
True Story, 112
True West, 95
Tudor Publishing Co., 205
Tuesday at Home, 147, 150
Tulsa Magazine, 32
Tupper & Love, Inc., 205

TV & Movie Screen, 106
TV Guide, 107
TV Picture Life, 101
TV Radio Talk, 107
TWA Ambassador, 78
Twayne Publishers, Inc., 205
Twelve/Fifteen, 129

U

Uncensored Confessions, 112
Union Gospel Press, 135
Union of American Hebrew Congregations, 206
United Card Co., 175, 178
United Church Press, 206
United Feature Syndicate, 47
Universal Library, 210
Universal Trade Press Syndicate, 47
University markets, 36
University of Windsor Review, 173

V

Vacation Fun, 127
Vacations Unlimited, 83
Vagabond, 173
Vagabond Creations, 178
Valleys of History, 32
Vanguard Press, 206
Van Nostrand Reinhold Co., 206
Vaughn Card Co., 178
Venture, 135
Vermont Life, 33
Viking Press, 206
Vogue, 45, 107

W

Walker & Co., 206
Wallaces Farmer, 69
Ward Ritchie Press, 143, 204, 206
Warner Press, 178
Washington, 27
Washington Post, 26
Washington Square Press, 210
Washington Sunday Star, 27
Washingtonian, 33
Water Land & Life, 63
Water Skier, 58

INDEX

Watson-Guptill Publishers, 206
Watts, Franklin, 144
Wee Wisdom, 128
Weight Watchers Magazine, 107
Weirdbook, 117
West, 27
Western Fiction Magazine, 96
Western Gateways, 83
Western Humanities Review, 173
Western Publishing Co., 144
Westminster Press, 144
Westways, 33, 83
Weybright & Talley, 206
Wheels Afield, 88
Whenever Whatever, 128
Whisper, 96
Whitehall Co., 206
Wildcat, 96
Wilshire Book Co., 207, 210
Wiley, John, & Sons, 207
Win Magazine, 135
Winter House, 207
Wisconsin Tales & Trails, 33
Witness, 128
Woman/Golfer, 86, 107
Woman, The, 107
Woman's Day, 107
Woman's World, 108
Women's markets, 98
Wonder Time, 128
Woodmen of the World, 128
Words of Cheer, 133
Workbasket, 108
Workbench, 108
World Book Encyclopedia Science Service, 47
World Car Guide, 88
World Over, 135
World Publishing Co., 144, 207
World Wildlife Illustrated, 63
Wyoming Stockman Farmer, 69
Wyoming Wildlife, 63

Y

Yachting, 89
Yale Review, 173
Yankee, 33, 175
Yoseloff, Thomas, 207
You, 108
Young adult markets, 129
Young Ambassador, 135
Young Crusader, 128
Young Judean, 135
Young Miss, 135
Young Scott Books, 144
Young World, 128
Your New Baby, 108
Youth Alive, 135
Youth in Action, 136

Z

Zest, 27
Zondervan Publishing House, 144, 207